Shakespeare, the Bible, and the Form of the Book

Routledge Studies in Shakespeare

Shakespeare, the Bible, and the Form of the Book
Contested Scriptures

Edited by Travis DeCook and Alan Galey

*For Mom & Dad
with love & thanks,
Alan*

Routledge
Taylor & Francis Group
NEW YORK   LONDON

First published 2012
by Routledge
711 Third Avenue, New York, NY 10017

Simultaneously published in the UK
by Routledge
2 Park Square, Milton Park, Abingdon, Oxfordshire OX14 4RN

First issued in paperback 2014

*Routledge is an imprint of the Taylor & Francis Group,
an informa business*

© 2012 Taylor & Francis

The right of Travis DeCook and Alan Galey to be identified as the authors
of the editorial material, and of the authors for their individual chapters,
has been asserted by them in accordance with sections 77 and 78 of the
Copyright, Designs and Patents Act 1988.

Typeset in Sabon by IBT Global.

Library of Congress Cataloging-in-Publication Data

    Shakespeare, the Bible, and the form of the book : contested scriptures /
edited by Travis DeCook and Alan Galey.
        p. cm. — (Routledge studies in Shakespeare ; 5)
Includes bibliographical references and index.
  1. Shakespeare, William, 1564–1616—Religion.   2. Religion
and literature—England—History—16th century.   3. Religion
and literature—England—History—17th century.   4. Religion
in literature.   5. Bible—In literature.   I. DeCook, Travis,
1976– II. Galey, Alan, 1975–
    PR3012.S55 2011
    822.3'3—dc22
    2011003849

ISBN13: 978-0-415-88350-4 (hbk)
ISBN13: 978-1-138-79375-0 (pbk)

For Sarah, Ben, and Jenny

Contents

Figures

Acknowledgements

The genesis of this collection began when we found ourselves both holding postdoctoral fellowships in the Department of English and Film Studies at the University of Alberta in 2006–7. With one of us specializing in early modern Biblical studies (DeCook), and the other specializing in Shakespeare (Galey), we realized that our respective specializations could be having a more interesting conversation than the one we were finding in the well-trodden ground of allusion-hunting and biographical speculation. In search of collaborators, we led a seminar on "Shakespearean Scripture: Biblical Contexts for Reception and Transmission" at the 2008 meeting of the Shakespeare Association of America in Dallas. This volume developed out of these conversations, and grew to include some old and new colleagues along the way.

Our first thanks, then, go to the funding agencies that supported our postdoctoral fellowships, The Killam Trust (DeCook) and the Social Sciences and Humanities Research Council of Canada (Galey), as well as to the Department of English and Film Studies at the University of Alberta for hosting us, and the Shakespeare Association of America (and especially Lena Orlin) for a place to discuss the project with others. We are also grateful for the support of our current institutional homes, the Department of English Language and Literature at Carleton University, Ottawa (DeCook), and the Faculty of Information at the University of Toronto (Galey). For advice, encouragement, material support, and informative conversations along the way, we would like to thank M.J. Kidnie, Grant Williams, Andrew Barnaby, Michele Osherow, the University of Toronto Libraries (especially the staff of the Thomas Fisher Rare Book Library), who provided several images, and students in our 2008–10 graduate seminars as this volume took shape. Our research assistants, Andrew Connolly, Peter Gorman, Rebecca Niles, and Emily Monks-Leeson improved the volume in more ways than we can count. We would also like to thank Liz Levine and Erica Wetter at Routledge, the two anonymous reviewers for the press and Michael Watters at Integrated Book Technology.

Our warmest thanks, as always, go to Sarah Brouillette and Jenny Kerber for rising and shining when the world seems dark, and to Ben, who was born while this book was coming together.

1   Introduction

Scriptural Negotiations and Textual Afterlives

Travis DeCook and Alan Galey

I   CONTESTING SCRIPTURES

Shakespeare and the Bible seem unable to escape each other. Since not long after the canonization of Shakespeare, countless generalizations about the tradition of so-called great books have yoked the Biblical and Shakespearean corpora together as mutually reinforcing sources of cultural authority. George Bernard Shaw, for example, voices a literary commonplace: "That I can write as I do [. . .] is due to my having been as a child steeped in the Bible, *The Pilgrim's Progress*, and Cassell's *Illustrated Shakespeare*"; similarly, a favorite quotation among Victorian bardolators, attributed to John Sharp (1645–1714), casts the same idea in blunter political terms: "The Bible and Shakspeare have made me Archbishop of York."[1] The linkage is a familiar trope, especially for Shakespeare scholars, who have benefited from Shakespeare's quasi-divine canonical status while sometimes also resisting the purposes to which that authority has been put. John Drakakis describes the ideological stakes: the "acknowledgement of Shakespeare as universal, transcendent, and eternal confers upon a quintessentially English writer—whose 'works' are regarded as a miraculous contingency of his being and detached supreme consciousness—a divine status. Shakespeare, removed thus from human history, becomes for us the 'Absolute Subject' whose all-embracing 'Word' takes its place alongside the Bible as our guarantee of civilisation and humanity."[2]

The cultural work of the Shakespeare–Bible link is reinforced by specific cultural assumptions about the book, particularly its associations with unity and monumentality. This is evident in Charles Wordsworth's dedication to his 1864 book *On Shakespeare's Knowledge and Use of the Bible*, offering the dyad of Shakespeare as "THE BOOK OF MAN" and the Bible as "THE WORD OF GOD" (and carefully emphasizing that the Bible is the more important of the two).[3] Stephen Greenblatt comments on the bibliographic nature of the link at the end of *Shakespearean Negotiations*, when he relates a story about how the Victorian journalist and explorer H.M. Stanley, upon being asked by African villagers to burn his field notebook before departing, substituted his Chandos edition of Shakespeare for the fire. In telling his story—whose facts may have been exaggerated for his readers—Stanley "could have achieved his narrative effect with only two books: Shakespeare and the Bible."[4] In considering Shakespeare and the Bible, it is all too easy to forget that, as books, they are simultaneously metaphor and material. A perspective informed by book history and textual theory reminds us of the material, historical, and institutional contexts that shore up these supposedly stable monuments—questioning the nature of the shelf, so to speak, upon which Wordsworth's two metaphorical books sit, and the imprimatur that authorizes them.

This collection of articles seeks to resist the transcendentalizing tendency Drakakis describes, by historicizing the two monumental traditions of Shakespeare and the Bible and understanding their cultural formation in terms of the history of the book. In doing so, the essays gathered here attempt to illuminate aspects of the twinned histories of Shakespeare and the Bible that have been overlooked in previous approaches. Critics talk about the Bible and Shakespeare all the time, of course. Even though the quasi-religious bardolatry of the late Victorians has been unfashionable for decades, more focused critical projects have persisted in two main forms: source study, the identification and analysis of Biblical references and themes in Shakespeare's works; and biography, especially the kind that speculates about Shakespeare's own religious beliefs. These two critical projects are mutually reinforcing, as evidenced most influentially in recent years by Greenblatt's *Hamlet in Purgatory* and its more mainstream follow-up, *Will in the World*—both of which resuscitated the notion that Shakespeare was a crypto-Catholic.[5] (A related biographical project, more marginal but still persistent, seeks to prove Shakespeare's involvement in the production of the King James Bible.)

More recently, the spiritual turn in recent critical theory has motivated studies that inquire into Shakespeare's negotiation of the complex religious currents of his time.[6] In a similar spirit of departure from conventional source study and biography, this volume brings together leading scholars of Shakespeare, book history, and the Bible's role in culture, who question the often naturalized links between the Shakespearean and Biblical corpora, and examine the historically contingent ways these links have been forged. Granting the ideological nature of the link between Shakespeare and the Bible—in other words, the conditions that motivate scholars in the first place to trace Shakespeare's Biblical references or muse about his doctrinal leanings—the essays that follow explore the less familiar parts of the story, especially those that have been neglected by more traditional approaches. Rather than amassing data to reveal some doctrinal *truth* about Shakespeare—an unfinishable project, which may explain critical investment in it—we seek to uncover the cultural *work* performed by the links between Shakespeare and the English Bible.

Books and reading practices serve as specific sites of that cultural work. Indeed, as Wordsworth's grandiose dedication attests, for Shakespeare and the Bible *the book* is a term that slides between the material and metaphorical with disarming ease. We can see that dynamic at play in Rudyard Kipling's late short story "Proofs of Holy Writ" (1934), in which readers are treated to a wish-fulfillment scenario as two of Western literature's most idealized scenes of writing converge.[7] Characters named "Ben" and "Will," relaxing in the latter's back garden, discuss theatre, originality, authorship, style, and translation, all in terms recognizable to readers who infer the characters' last names to be "Jonson" and "Shakespeare." Following an exchange about their theatrical careers, full of in-jokes in the style of *Shakespeare in Love*, the conversation is interrupted by the arrival of a messenger bearing the proof-pages mentioned punningly in the story's title.[8] Will reveals to an envious Ben that he has been approached by Miles Smith, an Oxford scholar, "'for a tricking out of his words or the turn of some figure.'"[9] The two then work through a revision of Isaiah 60, with Will's literary genius on display as he feels his way toward the right language. Eventually settling upon phrasing very close to what was printed in 1611, the two send the revised proofs back to Smith with the messenger, with Ben asking in passing, "'Who will know we had part in it?'"[10] (Will's answer is "God.")

Kipling's story gives narrative shape to one of Shakespeare studies' persistent urban legends, and the text of the King James Bible thus makes its fictional transit through Shakespeare's back garden. There is no real evidence that such collaboration between Shakespeare and the King James Bible scholars ever took place; the question is only pursued seriously as pseudo-history, like anti-Stratfordian conspiracy theories. Nonetheless, as fiction, "Proofs of Holy Writ" helpfully formalizes aspects of the cultural narratives it deploys. Indeed, Ben and Will's scene of textual work on an imaginary Stratford afternoon could serve as a thematic hub for this collection, with the individual chapters following different lines of inquiry outward from the symbolic intersection Kipling shows us in Will's garden.

Many of the chapters that follow converge on the question of Scripture as *source* versus Scripture as *process*, whether that scripture is Biblical or Shakespearean. Kipling's interest in the story is clearly in the compositional process over the literary product, and the King James Bible itself is present as a book only implicitly, as an artifact known to the story's readers but not to its characters—at least not known to them yet as a unified body of writing. The Bible is anything but *the* Bible here, instead taking composite form in Ben's description of the revisers' synoptic project: "'The learning of Oxford and Cambridge [...] and Westminster, to sit upon a clutch of Bibles. Those 'ud be Geneva (my mother read to me out of it at her knee), Douai, Rheims, Coverdale, Matthews, the Bishops', the Great, and so forth.'"[11] Will's reply emphasizes the weaving of fragments rather than original creation or divine inspiration: "'They are all set down on the page there—text against text. And you call me a botcher of old clothes?'"[12]; later, he freely stitches fragments of other translations together to submit as his own version of a line from Isaiah: "Lay the tail of Geneva to the head of

Coverdale and the last is without flaw."[13] Scripture here is decidedly not the unified product it sometimes appears to be in traditional source study; rather, Kipling shows us the Biblical text as it was in English through most of the sixteenth century—not just a single book like the Geneva version, for Shakespeare to pick up and cite, but a contestable and ever-changing network of fragments. Kipling shows us only friendly, essentially aesthetic debates between Ben and Will, but, of course, doctrinal contestation of Scripture pulled the Biblical text (and its interpretive apparatus) in different directions with deadly force.

However, there is also a certain tension, even incommensurability between the scriptural processes and products depicted, both Biblical and Shakespearean. As Peter France notes, "Perhaps Kipling is cheating, taking as his point of arrival a translation which has acquired sacred status in the English-speaking world and putting the comments into the mouth of the author of our other 'holy writ.'"[14] The proleptic structure of the story is highlighted by the paratextual inclusion of the opening and closing lines of Isaiah 60 which Will revises, printed in one place so that readers can appreciate, in advance, the unity of effect toward which Will works in bits and pieces. Reprintings of "Proofs of Holy Writ" position this item of paratext as an epigraph before the story proper, but the layout of the story's first publication in *Strand Magazine* is more complex. Placed four pages into the story (p. 353) as an insert balanced between the *Strand*'s typical two-column page layout, and surrounded by a solid rectangular border to set it off from the surrounding text, the Isaiah text in the *Strand* version is anything but a polite epigraph that says its piece and then exits the stage. Rather, it makes an entrance visually, in terms of the layout that elbows the story columns to the side, and temporally, in that it appears not at the beginning of the story but on the page where Will first begins to discuss the Isaiah translation in detail. Epigraphs are to be read in sequence, leaving it to the reader to notice implicit connections between fragments, but the story's first readers in 1934 experienced the Isaiah quotation as an interruption, part of the same visual rhythm that advertisements create. In this way, the paratextual effect of the *Strand* layout is more akin to early modern Bibles themselves, with glosses, cross-references, and other annotations that produce the "text against text" effect that Will mentions with regard to his own synoptic reading tools.

But even as the magazine's layout hints at the kind of reading environment that early modern Bible readers would have known, the text also simplifies the King James Version of Isaiah by leaving out the apparatus that readers of the 1611 book would have seen (Figure 1.1). Ironically, the first line that Will wrestles with—"Arise, shine, for thy light is come, and the glory of the LORD is risen upon thee"—is not finalized even on the published 1611 page: a marginal gloss offers the alternative, "Or, be enlightened: for thy light commeth."[15] It is worth recalling that for early modern readers of the Bible, the important differences between Bibles—the differences worth fighting over—often were not the translations themselves but the glosses that surrounded them. Nonetheless, sharp-eyed readers may also notice that some of the word-choices Will settles upon do not match the 1611 text as printed.[16] Indeed, the numerous differences in phrasing, spelling, and punctuation between the Isaiah that Will composes orally, the Isaiah printed in 1611, and the Isaiah printed in 1934 add up to exactly the kind of complexity in transmission that prompted W.W. Greg's theory of substantives and accidentals.[17] Shakespeare himself cannot settle the text of the Bible, it would seem.

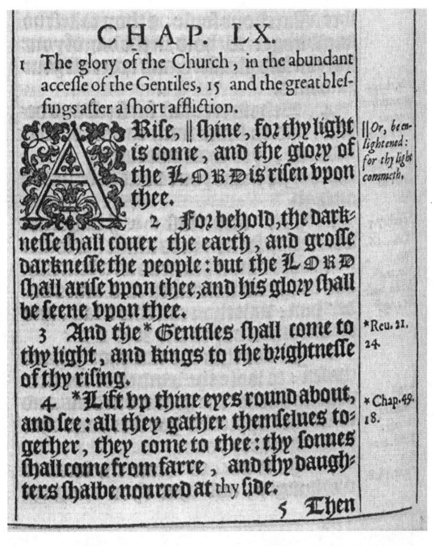

Figure 1.1 The beginning of Isaiah, verse 60, as printed in the 1611 King James Bible. Image courtesy of the Thomas Fisher Rare Book Library, University of Toronto.

Even at the heart of this authorship fantasy, then, writing is not self-identical: versions proliferate, and small differences add up to question the transmissibility of pure language. Will quotes from memory his own lines from *Macbeth*, yet for readers (and for Kipling the author) this is an iteration of a print artifact—though not a perfect iteration, since the 1934 text modernizes the spelling and punctuation of *Macbeth*'s only authoritative printed version, from the 1623 First Folio.[18] Very likely, at this moment in the story the character Will is unknowingly quoting whichever modernized edition of Shakespeare it was that Kipling had on hand.[19] For Will's Biblical contributions, Kipling gives us a composition scenario close to the Shakespearean ideal that has been advanced ever since the famous claim that Shakespeare's "mind and hand went together: And what he thought, he vttered with that easinesse, that wee haue scarse receiued from him a blot in his papers," made in John Heminges and Henry Condell's prefatory note "To the great Variety of Readers" of the 1623 Folio.[20] Kipling writes, "He [Will] walked to the table and wrote rapidly on the proof margin all three verses as he had spoken them. 'If they hold by this,' said he [...], 'they'll not go far astray.'"[21] However, as we have seen, the text does go astray, at least in small degrees, in the interval between this fictional moment of writing and our reception of the texts—Shakespearean and Biblical—through history.

What intervenes here between mind and hand is materiality: the embodiment of texts in physical documents, subject to the same vicissitudes of time as all human artifacts, as opposed to idealized patterns of language or expressions of divine truth. Will's primarily oral composition is nonetheless aided by printed documents whose materiality is a matter of note from their first appearance: "Ben caressed lovingly the hand-pressed proofs on their lavish linen paper."[22] With materiality comes vulnerability, as the story emphasizes when Will entrusts the secret packet of documents to an evidently unreliable messenger:

> "He'll lose it by the way." Ben pointed to the sleeper beneath the tree.
> "He's owl-drunk."
> "But not his horse," said Will. He crossed the orchard, roused the man; slid the packet into an holster which he carefully rebuckled [...].[23]

As the probable writer of at least one lost play (*Cardenio*), Will's trust in the communications channel may well seem ironic to those who know that the messenger (or his horse) sometimes failed. A similar appreciation may be gained by looking on the fragmentary and fragile text of the Book of Isaiah that appears among the Dead Sea Scrolls. Mutability, vulnerability, and loss: the story exposes the inescapable anxiety that such is the way of all text, even holy writ.

These are just some of the threads of inquiry which could be followed outward from this fictional intersection between Shakespearean and Biblical textuality, though they all lead back to questions about cultural authority that unite both traditions. As Douglas Brooks puts it in his insightful reading of Kipling's story:

> Compelled to speak from beyond the grave more than three centuries after his death by an author shortly before his own death, Will could very well be describing the production of another sacred text that would subsequently command the attention of most—if not all—English scholars.[24]

There are other directions one could take from this intersection; Brooks, for example, focuses on the nature of collaborations and the power of James's kingship as a mediating force. The essays in this collection follow several other paths outward from Will's imaginary scene of (re)writing the Bible, exploring the Shakespeare–Bible link from the perspective of cultural authority, pedagogy, secularism, textual scholarship, and the materiality of texts. Covering an historical span from Shakespeare's post-Reformation era to present-day Northern Ireland, the volume uncovers how Shakespeare and the Bible's intertwined histories illuminate the enduring tensions between materiality and transcendence in the history of the book. Although many studies of Shakespeare and Scripture hold to a strict distinction between the Bible as an influence *upon* Shakespeare, and others assume but do not investigate the mechanisms behind Shakespeare's and the Bible's combined influences on culture, we argue for the value of considering those two phenomena within the same scope. We will therefore turn next to ways we might rethink the connection between Shakespeare and Scripture in his own time.

II SCRIPTURAL NEGOTIATIONS

In "Hamlet's Tables and the Technologies of Writing in Renaissance England," Peter Stallybrass, Roger Chartier, J. Franklin Mowery, and Heather Wolfe identify an evocation of the Tablets of the Law given to Moses in Hamlet's textual metaphors expressing his commitment to his father's memory.[25] What Hamlet calls the "Table of my Memory" containing "triuiall fond Records," an allusion to erasable wax tablets widely used during the Renaissance, is contrasted with the father's "Commandment" which "all alone shall liue / Within the Booke and Volume of my Braine / Vnmixt with baser matter."[26] These contrasting ways of remembering are articulated through the difference between the quotidian, practical technology of the erasable wax tablet and the monumentalizing book, representing opposite poles of early modern inscription. The word "tables" is also the word used in the Geneva and King James Bibles to refer to the Mosaic Tablets of the Law, and, as Stallybrass et al. note, the Tablets of the Law themselves point to the ephemerality as well as indelibility of writing: the first tablets, given by God, were destroyed by Moses in his wrath, and the second tablets, inscribed by Moses, were the ones that endured and "came to signify the permanence of the Father's 'command.'"[27]

This article thus exemplifies how *Hamlet*, noteworthy for its extensive representation of books and reading, registers Shakespeare's engagement with the most foundational form of Biblical textuality, the originary act of divine inscription.[28] That this play resonates in this fashion is not surprising, given that Shakespeare's was an age when the material substrate through which the Word of God was accessed and transmitted was visible and contentious in new and pressing ways, owing to the textual scholarship of Renaissance humanism, the advent of printing, and the Protestant Reformation. These upheavals made apparent the tension between the transcendent nature of the Word of God and the vulnerability of the material substrates through which it is accessed, as well as the fraught theological and political contexts and conflicting institutions mediating its material form, transmission, and reception.

A little over a generation before Shakespeare's birth, William Tyndale was executed for his unauthorized translation of Scripture, driven by the reformers' privileging of Scripture reading and the resulting imperative to make the Word available to all people in the vernacular. Throughout the sixteenth century, different versions of the Bible were used as weapons by battling confessional groups. Once Henry VIII severed the English church's link with Rome, he authorized a vernacular version to be read aloud in every church, ironically largely dependent on Tyndale's translation. In the last years of Henry's reign this version, called the Great Bible because of its large size, became the only one that could be lawfully read, other versions with marginal annotations having been deemed subversive. During the Catholic Queen Mary's reign, Calvinist exiles produced the Geneva Bible, first published in 1560, which was the most popular English Bible until well after its eventual replacement, the King James Version, first appeared in 1611. The Geneva Bible was smaller and cheaper than the Great Bible and therefore highly popular, and was notable for its extensive marginal glosses, maps, and other tools designed to assist (or manage) the reader. Additionally, it was the first English Bible to break the text into numbered verses. This vehemently Protestant Bible was met with the Counter-Reformation Rheims translation of the New Testament in 1582 and Douay translation of the Old Testament in 1609–10; this English translation of the Latin Vulgate included polemical annotations to combat the Geneva's.

Despite the popularity of the Geneva version, it was never officially authorized by the established church. The Great Bible was replaced with the Bishops' Bible in 1568, spearheaded by the moderate Archbishop Matthew Parker, and appears to have represented a conservative reaction to the strongly reformist Geneva Bible. In 1611, the King James Version was produced; while the impetus for this version originated with puritan calls for a new translation, James seems to have viewed this as an opportunity to undermine the Geneva version. Some glosses in the Geneva had a politically subversive potential, including the statement that it was at times right to disobey the monarch if the secular and sacred laws were at odds.[29]

During Shakespeare's lifetime, then, a number of competing Bibles were in circulation. In contrast to nineteenth- and early twentieth-century Christian scholarship aiming to demonstrate Shakespeare's grounding in and reinforcing of Biblical morality,[30] increasingly over the twentieth century a welter of studies took a more objective approach to the relationship between Shakespeare and Scripture, concentrating on identifying allusions and quotations in Shakespeare to his era's various Bible versions.[31] This tradition of scholarship is most notably exemplified by Naseeb Shaheen's magisterial *Biblical References in Shakespeare's Plays*, which represents the culmination of many years' work identifying such references.[32] Given the period when Shakespeare was writing, at those moments when his Biblical references can be identified with a particular version it is usually with the Geneva Bible, although the Bishops' is also represented. While the Bishops' would have been encountered through oral delivery in church, Shakespeare's extensive quotations from the Geneva, including its marginal glosses, indicates his intensive reading of this text. In addition, some of Shakespeare's allusions to Biblical passages derive from the Book of Common Prayer.[33] The diversity of versions reflected in Shakespeare's writing indicates how "Shakespeare's Bible" cannot be taken for granted as unitary, since it consists of a network of different translations, accessed in varying contexts (private reading, church) and through varying media (printed text, gloss, oral sermon, liturgy).

Not all scholarship on Shakespeare and the Bible has been focused on reference hunting and enumeration. In recent years there have been more sustained and systematic studies of Shakespeare's engagement with Scripture. Steven Marx's *Shakespeare and the Bible* is one of the few developed treatments of Shakespeare's engagement with the Bible, going beyond pointing out the presence of Biblical allusions.[34] By contrast, Marx employs the traditional Biblical interpretive modes of typology and *midrash* to examine Shakespeare's complex refractions of Biblical themes, narratives, and images over the course of several plays. However, Marx exemplifies the tendency, found in most treatments of Shakespeare's Biblical references, to present Shakespeare and the Bible as a binary in which stable, unproblematic Scriptural texts await the playwright's aesthetic transformation. As a result, there has been a marked lack of sustained attention to the theological, social, and political meanings undergirding the period's conflicting Bible versions and the effect of Scripture's contested status as a material and historical artifact on Shakespeare's literary production.

Beatrice Groves's *Texts and Traditions: Religion in Shakespeare 1592–1604* approaches these concerns only to a point.[35] Groves's book responds directly to the explosion of interest in Shakespeare's personal religious beliefs, ignited by evidence suggesting a Catholic background. She usefully gets beyond such biographical preoccupations by considering how both the Protestant and Catholic traditions influenced Shakespeare, thereby acknowledging the Bible's role in sectarian conflict. However, neither Marx nor Groves provides substantial focus on the material and historical embeddedness of the Bible, which was given dramatic visibility by the era's politically and theologically fraught Bible versions.

By contrast, *Shakespeare, the Bible, and the Form of the Book* gives sustained attention to the Bible's multiple forms and contested status, to the fraught tension between the Bible as transcendent Word of God and politically and historically mediated material text, and to how these interlinked phenomena were taken up by Shakespeare.

A small number of individual articles have confronted such issues. Groves's essay "Shakespeare's Sonnets and the Genevan Marginalia" is one of the few studies to examine how Shakespeare addressed the cultural status of a particular Bible version.[36] This article suggests a relationship between the Sonnets' status as a text designed for private reading and their prevalent quoting of the Geneva Bible glosses, glosses which were not typically read aloud but were used for private study. She also picks up on an earlier analysis of reference to the Geneva glosses in *Hamlet*, found in James Black's *Edified by the Margent: Shakespeare and the Bible*, which takes its title from Horatio's sarcastic remarks about Osric's elaborate language.[37] Developing Black's work by pointing out that this reference is only found in the second quarto version of the play, a version possibly designed for reading rather than performance on stage, Groves furthers her argument that Shakespeare most alludes to and quotes from the Geneva glosses in texts closely aligned with a reading public.[38]

In addition to Shakespeare's registering of the cultural associations of the Geneva version, he also may have taken up the politically charged nature of Bible translation. This issue is addressed by Andrew Barnaby and Joan Wry in "Authorized Versions: *Measure for Measure* and the Politics of Biblical Translation." This essay suggests ways *Measure for Measure* engages the issues at the heart of James's project to produce a new version of the Bible, a project that began in 1604, the same year the play was written and first performed. Particularly, Barnaby and Wry examine the King James Version as an attempt to assert the authority of the crown by extending interpretive authority over the Word of God. *Measure for Measure*'s depiction of those with political power deploying divine authority, in often highly Machiavellian ways, might be considered a reflection of what the King James Version at some level embodies.

While the work of Groves, Barnaby, and Wry indicates how the cultural and political embeddedness of the Bible was reflected upon in Shakespeare's writings, surprisingly little scholarship confronts such issues. This is surprising because the recent critical turn to material culture and the sociology of texts prompts new questions about the nature of allusion and intertextuality. If the Biblical tradition from which

Shakespeare drew was neither monolithic nor unified, how might that productive instability inform the study of his plays and poems? How do Shakespeare's writings negotiate the increasingly diverse material forms through which Scripture was mediated and accessed in his era, not just in multiple versions of the Bible, but in the form of sermons, liturgy, and devotional texts? While such questions are clearly relevant to the religious and political conflicts shaping the production, circulation, and reception of early modern Biblical culture, the textual scholarship and translation work underwriting the new Bible versions opened up new ways of thinking about the Bible as a historical artifact as well as the transcendent Word of God. By increasingly understanding the Bible as a text—a historical and material entity—such habits of thought presented the Christian Bible as having in some respects always been a contested collection of books. Its canonization was a disputed process, it was frequently translated and therefore reinterpreted, and it was vulnerable to the corruptions of transmission and other vagaries of history. Given Shakespeare's immersion in post-Reformation Biblical culture, in what ways does his writing respond to and engage with such emergent understandings of Scripture? To take up such questions is one of the aims of *Shakespeare, the Bible, and the Form of the Book.*

III TEXTUAL AFTERLIVES

If approaching Shakespeare's use of Scripture with an understanding of the unstable and contested nature of the Bible complicates past assumptions about the Shakespeare–Bible relationship, so too does an exploration of the parallel histories of their textual afterlives. As noted above, we have inherited a cultural predisposition in which the link between Shakespeare and the Bible is seen as inevitable. It is the kind of link that presents itself in the present as fully formed and naturalized through connections to institutions like family and nation. "Shakespeare was our family Bible," claims Karl Marx's daughter Eleanor, invoking a domestic space of reading not that far removed from the colonial counterpart imagined by Matthew Arnold in his defense of Thomas Babington Macaulay: "It is said that the traveller in Australia, visiting one settler's hut after another, finds again and again that the settler's third book, after the Bible and Shakespeare, is some work by Macaulay. Nothing can be more natural."[39] Noteworthy in both examples are the connections to further bodies of writing, those of Marx and Macaulay respectively. Both examples underscore the generative function of such linkages, in which certain culturally invested texts serve as coordinating principles for future history. As George Saintsbury claims in his 1887 *History of Elizabethan Literature*, inveighing against the recent Revised Version of the King James Bible:

> The plays of Shakespeare and the English Bible are, and will ever be, the twin monuments not merely of their own period, but of the perfection of English, the complete expressions of the literary capacities of the language, at the time when it had lost none of its pristine vigour, and had put on enough but not too much of the adornments and the limitations of what may be called literary civilisation.[40]

David Norton offers the apt term *AVolatry* (i.e. bibliolatry of the Authorized Version) for positions like Saintsbury's, which ostensibly stabilize the past and future of cultural history while at the same time forestalling any possibility of critical reevaluation in the present: Shakespeare and the Bible are foundational, but also incontestable.[41] Norton's point, moreover, is that AVolatry and bardolatry are linked: "it is instructive to see bardolatry and AVolatry coming together in what we may call an imaginative truth."[42] By the time of Charles Wordsworth, quoted above, speculative literary history could entertain Kipling-esque scenarios in which the Bible is a source for Shakespeare, who in turn becomes a source for the KJV; by the late Victorian period, Norton argues, "Bardolatry and AVolatry have almost merged into one: Shakespeare is biblical, and the Bible is Shakespearean."[43] Indeed, in Norton's analysis of emergent treatments of the Bible according to literary criteria, the frequency of Shakespeare as a reference point prompts the question of whether we can categorize anything as literature *without* recourse to Shakespearean criteria, whether acknowledged or not.

The utopian gesture of drawing a circle around Shakespeare and the Bible, or any other texts, for the sake of "literary civilisation" may seem distinctly Victorian—it is no coincidence that the examples from Marx (1858), Arnold (1877), and Saintsbury (1887) coincide with the rise of the British Empire—but the Victorian period is only the most visible phase of the intertwined Shakespearean and Biblical afterlives which have long and varied histories. Linda Rozmovits's argument about Victorian bardolatry can be applied to the Shakespeare–Bible relationship: "it is best understood not as a phenomenon that has been fundamentally continuous over the last three hundred years but as one that has been remarkable for the strikingly different inflections it has assumed at different times."[44] This sort of broadly comprehensive concern with the afterlife (*Nachleben*) of a given cultural work is central to book history's perspective, and this kind of study can reveal the forces at work behind claims, like Arnold's, that "Nothing can be more natural" in the received state of cultural institutions.[45]

Walter Benjamin, who developed the notion of *Nachleben* within his own historiography, suggests in a note in his *Arcades Project* that "Historical 'understanding' is to be grasped, in principle, as an afterlife of that which is understood; and what has been recognized in the analysis of the 'afterlife of works' [. . .] is therefore to be considered the foundation of history in general."[46] Graeme Gilloch describes the Benjaminian approach to afterlife or after-history (*Nachgeschichte*) as not simply a recovery project, but a generative process: the study of afterlives contends that "the meaning and significance of a text are not determined by the author at the moment of writing, but are contested and conceptualized anew as [. . .] [the text] is subject to reading and criticism through time"[47]; in temporal terms, afterlife "is the time in which the object is subject to transformations and interventions which re-cognize its significance and 'actualize' its potential: translation, transcription, imitation, criticism, appropriation, (re)construction, reproduction, remembrance, redemption."[48] Book historians, bibliographers, and textual scholars of all kinds should recognize in this description their discipline's turn toward the sociology of texts, following D.F. McKenzie, Jerome McGann, and others. Indeed, Gilloch's list could easily include terms like *editing*, *publishing*, *commentary*, and *philology*, all of which are no less sites for the contestation and reconceptualization that he identifies at the core of Benjamin's conception of the afterlives of works.

However, the monumental status of some texts demands particular attention to the critical apparatus that governs how we talk about them, since these authoritative meanings represent highly politicized sites of culture. As Gary Taylor puts it, "The Bible, the *Aeneid*, Homer, Shakespeare, the US Constitution, the Communist Manifesto—once a society enshrines a text, that text accumulates all the meanings of the clerisy of its interpreters."[49] For this reason, contestation is an essential point of focus for the study of afterlives, as Gilloch recognizes. The linked afterlives of Shakespeare and the Bible have become fraught, especially following Shakespeare's own enshrinement via what David Scott Kastan describes as his "full cultural theogony": "The plays, rescued from their Restoration appropriations, increasingly became a kind of secular scripture—not, of course, the divine Word but the words of the 'divine *Shakespeare*,' as Dryden seems to be the first to call him."[50] Kastan locates this elevation of Shakespeare in the mid-eighteenth century, but is careful to note that even in years prior, "the language of religious engagement had already begun to surround the texts of the plays, and [. . .] knowledge of debates in biblical criticism affected the approach to Shakespeare's text."[51] Kastan, like Louis Marder before him, provides a sampling of divine metaphors from eighteenth-century commentators in support of the point that "Studying [Shakespeare] was almost equivalent to studying Holy Writ."[52] This elevation of Shakespeare, also fuelled by David Garrick's 1769 jubilee celebrations, would become nonetheless difficult to reconcile with the textual problems that editors such as Edward Capell, Samuel Johnson, and Edmund Malone were recognizing in the Shakespearean corpus around the same time.[53]

Another example from 1870 shows the incommensurability between Scripture and "divine Shakespeare" in a debate over reading practices that erupted when the Cincinnati Board of Education enacted a rule against the reading of the Bible (actually of all religious books) in public schools. In the resulting court challenge against the Board, a member of its defense team, Stanley Matthews (later an Associate Justice of the US Supreme Court and,

according to Norton, a "Presbyterian elder"[54]), used Shakespeare to argue
in favor of the prohibition on the grounds of a distinction between devotional reading and literary analysis. According to Matthews, in devotional
exercises "the necessary implication is that you are listening to the inspired
and revealed word of God," but in literary exercises the Bible is read merely
"as a beautiful specimen of English composition [. . .] and stands, so far as
that exercise is concerned, on the same footing precisely as a soliloquy from
Hamlet, or the address of Macbeth to the air drawn dagger."[55] Matthews
would have none of the equivalency Marder describes; he saw bardolatry's
potential influence on the Bible as a battle to be fought (though his team
lost the case). Yet even today, in the shadows cast by these monuments one
still finds what Drakakis describes as "resistance to viewing Shakespearean
texts as sites of struggle, and as repositories of ideology."[56] The more monumental the text, the greater the need for awareness of, in Drakakis's phrase,
"the power of ideology to efface contradiction."[57]

In Marder's phrase, "almost equivalent to studying Holy Writ," the
word "almost" is telling: it is symptomatic of a way of thinking about
Shakespeare and the Bible that structures their textual afterlives as parallel trajectories for English culture and language, each an analogy for the
other's value and authority. There is an undeniable value in using Shakespeare and the Bible as mutually illuminating examples, as we can see, for
example, throughout Norton's landmark volumes on the Bible as literature.
But can we understand the relationship in terms not limited to analogy
or to parallel lines of tradition that never intersect? Essays in this volume
probe points of intersection where the textual afterlives of Shakespeare and
the Bible have each affected the construction of the other, and, in so doing,
illuminate the cultural and political motives at work in these intersections.
For example, when the Puritan William Prynne condemned the material
similarities between Shakespeare and the Bible in folio, his point was not
simply that Shakespeare and the Bible were functioning as stable parallels
to each other—as they would by the height of Victorian bardolatry—but
rather that publishers had crossed the line. As he claims in his prefatory
epistle "To the Christian Reader," "Shackspeers Plaies are printed in the
best Crowne paper, far better than most Bibles."[58] Notably, Prynne's objection reverses the polarities of source study: his preoccupation is not, so to
speak, with the Bible in Shakespeare, but with Shakespeare in the Bible—or
at least in the Bible's place. Prynne hints at the specter of substitution,
which the Victorian Charles Wordsworth was so careful to avoid at a time
when the Bible was in danger of displacement. Readers looking to the most
magisterial books, in terms of format and paper stock, find Shakespeare
where they should find Bibles.

Looking ahead in the afterlives of these texts, we can see that Prynne's
fears of convergence would come true. To return to George Bernard Shaw's
description of himself as a "a child steeped in the Bible, *The Pilgrim's
Progress*, and Cassell's *Illustrated Shakespeare*," it is worth noting that

in addition to the two texts of which Prynne might have approved, Shaw invokes Shakespeare in the form of a specific book. The Cassell edition Shaw mentions was likely the 1877 illustrated volume better known as *The Leopold Shakespeare* for its dedication to the Belgian Prince Leopold, patron of Frederick Furnivall's New Shakespeare Society (Furnivall provided an introductory essay).[59] In a contemporary review that deals with this edition and Bible study texts in the same paragraph, Henry Morley metaphorically closes the circuit: "In *The Leopold Shakespeare* (price 6s.) Messrs. Cassell & Company have produced the lay-Bible of England for the English people."[60] Yet at almost the same time, nearly identical claims about Shakespeare as secular scripture, and his works as a "Bible of Humanity," were made by the circle that published the *Oracle of Reason*, the first openly atheist periodical to be published in English.[61] Shaw's seemingly offhand comment about his literary development thus reflects a certain amount of ideological contestation over the precise position of these books in the scheme of things, a conflict frequently expressed and reproduced by the material forms of books.

The traditional understanding of the dynamic between Shakespeare and the Bible, when it is not restricted to uni-directional source study (or the more convoluted imaginings of Wordsworth and Kipling), has been that of the parallel. Some recent critics, however, have shown how these afterlives can intersect. Among scholars of the Bible as literature, Norton has most productively considered the Shakespearean influence on AVolatry; his account includes substantial discussions of the connection throughout.[62] On the Shakespearean side, there have been relatively few critical studies which have approached the relationship in these terms, especially with an eye to ideological contexts or material artifacts; fewer still discuss both.[63] A notable exception is Graham Holderness, Stanley E. Porter, and Carol Banks's article, simply titled "Biblebable," in which the authors challenge the idea that "this apparently to some degree fortuitous, perhaps even arbitrary, contingency owes more to subsequent appropriations of Shakespeare for quasi-religious ideologies, than to any substantive cultural and historical connection."[64] The authors instead examine the 1611 KJV and the 1623 Shakespeare First Folio both as books and as publication events, demonstrating a remarkable number of shared bibliographic circumstances between them, especially having to do with canonicity and authenticity of texts: "The *KJV* and the *Complete Works of Shakespeare* are both cultural Towers of Babel. Though based in a variety and multiplicity of texts, [. . .] the editors sought to establish a common discourse, a uniformity of contents and a particular significant structure."[65]

Studies of subsequent efforts to enshrine Shakespeare according to some measure of lost scriptural perfection have tended to focus either on the fixing of Shakespeare's reputation, or on the fixing of his texts. Among the former, some critical studies of bardolatry have recognized the importance of books, publishing, and textual scholarship. As mentioned above, Linda Rozmovits's chapter on bardolatry is particularly useful, as is her argument that Victorian bardolatry was driven by a sense of moral obligation to acknowledge that "the Shakespearean text comes to approximate the status of the Bible—flawless, divinely authored, a book unlike all other books."[66] Charles LaPorte's more sustained analysis connects bardolatry with its anti-Stratfordian challengers, and in turn connects them both to the revolutionary possibilities opened up by the emergence of German higher criticism, in which the Bible and Shakespeare alike could be subjected to literary and philological inquiry.[67] As Geddes MacGregor describes the impact of higher criticism, "The work of the great nineteenth-century pioneers in modern biblical study had been conducted by men who regarded themselves as detached from partisan controversies in the Church. Their aim was analytical. They sought to do for the Bible what literary scholars were expected to do for Homer and Shakespeare."[68] Especially notable in LaPorte's argument is what he calls the distinctively "*textual* emphases of Victorian bardolatry," which often depended upon the book form to place fragments of Biblical and Shakespearean texts in synoptic configurations.[69] A desire to fix the text motivated a great deal of the earlier period, and other critics have focused on Shakespeare and the Bible in the editorial tradition. Simon Jarvis notes that "there has been almost no recognition of the relationship between scriptural and Shakespearian textual criticism," but establishes that Theobald, Warburton, and Johnson were all exposed to debates in Scriptural textual criticism of the time.[70] Marcus Walsh's book *Shakespeare, Milton, and Eighteenth-Century Literary Editing* makes a significant contribution toward filling the gap Jarvis identifies, with chapters on the editing of Scripture and Shakespeare and an insightful analysis of their cross-pollination.[71]

While such studies have been vital in opening up new areas of inquiry, our collection is the first to offer sustained attention to the intersecting histories of Shakespeare and the Bible from the perspective of the history of the material book. By focusing our inquiry not so much on sources as on interdependencies, we can begin to formulate new questions about the histories of these books (both material and metaphorical). How does Bible editing and reception shape concepts central to Shakespeare studies, such as canonicity, textual materiality, and authority? What sorts of cultural, political, and even religious implications does the importation of Biblical models into Shakespeare editing and criticism entail? To what extent are our received Shakespeare texts produced by an editorial and critical tradition with Biblical roots? How does the invocation of Shakespeare to defend certain notions of cultural heritage intersect with explicitly religious forms of social and cultural conservatism? If Shakespearean scripture is founded on the evidence of things not seen, what are its blind spots? The essays described in the next section explore possible answers, and raise new questions in turn.

IV CRITICAL INTERSECTIONS

The papers in this collection examine the ways the Bible and Shakespeare have been mediated and transmitted by particular material forms, how these particular forms have shaped these texts' cultural authority, and how these histories of transmission have intersected. One of the major issues the collection addresses is how such early modern developments as the scholarship of Renaissance humanism, Reformation Bible translation, and the mediation of the Word through theologically and politically charged marginalia and other paratexts shaped the reception of the Bible and Shakespeare's engagement with it.

In "Shakespeare Reads the Geneva Bible," Barbara Mowat addresses one of the most contested Bibles, the 1560 Geneva version, shedding new light on the importance of its elaborate paratextual mediations for Shakespeare's adaptations of Biblical material. Mowat uncovers how Shakespeare reproduced the language and political preoccupations of the Geneva interpretive glosses in his drama, positing that a number of Shakespeare's plays register the Geneva's framing of fraternal conflict in terms of the contemporary social problem of primogeniture. She also argues that his plays draw upon Scriptural intertexts established through the Geneva marginalia, particularly the antithetical approaches to judgment articulated in the Old and New Testaments. Mowat demonstrates how Shakespeare's dramaturgy depends on one of the most important of the Geneva's information technologies, its intertextual cross-referencing system. Mowat's chapter thus illuminates Shakespeare's "intensive reading" of a historically specific Bible whose paratextual mediations manifest themselves in surprisingly direct ways in the plays.

Like Mowat, in "Cain's Crime of Secrecy and the Unknowable Book of Life: The Complexities of Biblical Referencing in *Richard II*" Scott Schofield homes in on the historically specific ways the Bible was mediated for Shakespeare and his contemporaries. Schofield tacks back and forth between a reading of Biblical references in *Richard II* and an examination of evidence about the private libraries of Shakespeare's earliest readers. Modifying a traditional approach of Shakespeare scholarship, which tends to assume that Biblical allusions derive solely from one of the contemporary versions of the Bible, Schofield reveals how Biblical references in Shakespeare need to be considered additionally in terms of the period's extensive commentary tradition, constituted by exegetical texts, liturgy, sermons, polemics, and paratextual materials surrounding Bibles. Schofield's essay thus complements Mowat's by emphasizing the importance of an expansive culture of Biblical commentary in addition to the significance of Shakespeare's focused engagement with the Geneva marginal apparatus.

In "Paulina, Corinthian Women, and the Revisioning of Pauline and Early Modern Patriarchal Ideology in *The Winter's Tale*," Randall Martin shares Mowat's and Schofield's concern for how the complexities of Reformation

Bible-reading enter the space of Shakespeare's theatre. Martin explores the ways early modernity's rhetorical traditions and emergent historicizing approaches to the Bible, both of which were engaged by Shakespeare in his writing, would have enabled readers and theatregoers to construe an antipatriarchal critique of St Paul in the character Paulina in *The Winter's Tale.* Just as Mowat and Schofield contend that Shakespeare's Biblical references participate in a larger textual and cultural web than the term *allusion* implies, Martin too critiques the standard model of Shakespearean Biblical allusion. For Martin, concepts of adaptation and appropriation better capture *The Winter's Tale*'s invocation of the non-Judeo-Christian spirituality targeted by Paul in 1 Corinthians, a recuperation which exemplifies a rejection of the "closed book" of monumental Pauline authority in favor of a performative adaptation of a Biblical past.

Many previous studies of Shakespeare and the Bible limit themselves to the period of Shakespeare's agency as a playwright drawing upon the Bible. By contrast, this collection pursues the themes of cultural mediation, textual materiality, and instability described above into the interlocking reception histories of Shakespeare and the Bible. The 1623 Shakespeare First Folio serves as an essential bridge between Shakespearean production and reception, being at once a tomb/tome for the dead author and a source for new printed playtexts and Shakespeare's ensuing cultural authority.

In "The Tablets of the Law: Reading *Hamlet* with Scriptural Technologies," Alan Galey describes the folio format as a "scriptural technology": when Shakespeare is represented in a physical form typically associated with the Bible, this raises paradoxical cultural associations of unity and archival completeness on the one hand and the threat of information loss on the other. Memory is dramatically figured in Hamlet's use of writing in tablets, which, as many commentators have noted, evoke the Tablets of the Law that Moses receives from God in Exodus. Galey draws out the complex ways the Mosaic tablets are connected to narratives of divine inscription, memory, and even information loss, given the destruction of the original tablets. He proceeds to track informatic aspirations and anxieties, often directly represented in terms of the Sinai revelation, from *Hamlet* to the marketing of early modern wax tablets, to such recent media of inscription as the Apple iPad and the Kindle.

Galey's and Edward Pechter's chapters both deal with the imaginative power of literature, though in different ways. However, in "Shakespeare and the Bible: Against Textual Materialism" Pechter regards "textual materialism" as an obstacle to such engagement and criticizes the way scholars concerned with the text as material artifact often contextualize literature to the point that it becomes perceived as disconnected from the present. Pechter explores the relationship between Shakespeare and the Bible as one involving both persistent historical linkages as well as radical discontinuities, and as constituting a crucial nexus for what are often perceived as the contrary priorities of religious commitment and aesthetic experience.

Complementing Martin's focus on adaptation as a means by which the past lives in the present, Pechter urges scholars to resist merely debunking claims about continuities between the present and the cultural heritage and to consider ways to engage the reality of literary power. He concludes by raising the cultural significance of the enduring desire for continuity represented by various attempts to unify Shakespeare and the Bible.

In "Going Professional: William Aldis Wright on Shakespeare and the English Bible," Paul Werstine probes a similar disjuncture between historical scholarship and imaginative response produced by the cultural linkage between Shakespeare and the Bible. Werstine examines an important node of intersection in the histories of the Bible and the Shakespearean text: the work of a nineteenth-century editor, William Aldis Wright, who worked on both texts, at times simultaneously. Werstine's fine-grained history of Wright's scholarly milieu reveals that the latter's bibliographic and philological scholarship represents a high-water mark of historical rigor, yet, in his *Bible Word-Book* (1884), Wright anachronistically defers to Shakespearean usage when presenting the English Bible's linguistic history. Similarly, in his commentary on Shakespeare Wright anachronistically draws on the Authorized Version's usage. Werstine contends that such violations of Wright's normal practice illuminate how Shakespeare and the English Bible became constructed as mirroring authorities for early modern language use and that such violations are particularly revealing of the intensity of the Victorian tendency to elevate the two monuments alongside one another.

Andrew Murphy's "'Stick to Shakespeare and the Bible. They're the roots of civilisation': Nineteenth-Century Readers in Context" complements Werstine's examination of a newly professionalized and culturally elite nineteenth-century textual scholarship with a study of Victorian working-class educational institutions. Like Werstine, Murphy presents a history revelatory in powerful ways of just how naturalized the Shakespeare–Bible link was in the nineteenth century. He illuminates how working-class people perpetually registered a deep identification between the two texts and argues that this phenomenon's roots are in the combination of the newly expanded educational curriculum and the book market. For working-class people, the Bible was at the center of their education, given that early educational institutions were largely church run, and when these newly literate people went on to secular literature, Shakespeare, whose post-tercentenary status as national poet put him at the heart of the canon, was a natural choice. Shakespeare's cultural status was given material support by a book market flush with cheap reprints of older literature. Murphy also contends that the culture of Bible memorization, largely of the AV, meant that the encounter with Shakespeare involved a familiarity with an otherwise alien language, and that this too bolstered the sense of these texts' profound connection.

In "The Devotional Texts of Victorian Bardolatry," Charles LaPorte examines another facet to the Victorian conjoining of Shakespeare and

Scripture. His chapter takes up the printing of Shakespearean and Biblical passages alongside one another in Victorian miscellanies. Critiquing scholars' standard dismissive treatment of such pious recastings of Shakespeare, LaPorte claims that "devotional Shakespeare texts" exhibit a profoundly Scriptural mode of quotation in their disregard for the assumptions of modern textual scholarship and their emphasis on inspiration and textual unity. Drawing on Jerome McGann's notion of bibliographic codes, LaPorte reveals how the physical page of such works shape meaning and encourage certain reading practices: an equivalence between Shakespeare and Scripture is produced through the *mise-en-page* and the ways the physical book and its typefaces recall medieval breviaries.

Both Murphy and LaPorte are concerned with processes of secularization: Murphy with the decreasing presence of the Bible in education and its implications for literature, LaPorte with the blurring of boundaries between sacred and literary forms of inspiration in the post-Romantic era. Secularization is also a central issue in Travis DeCook's "Apocalyptic Archives: The Reformation Bible, Secularity, and the Text of Shakespearean Scripture." Like Galey, DeCook is concerned with the way the Biblical and Shakespearean texts become viewed as possessing an ideal archival completeness. Additionally, DeCook examines the ways apocalyptic narratives cluster around these "ideal archives": an examination of nineteenth-century cultural commentators and cryptographic analysts of the Shakespeare text reveals the recurring construction of the two texts as archives preserving the bases of civilization in the face of impending chaos. DeCook argues that a key historical analogue for such an imagined archive is the Bible as constructed during the Protestant Reformation and that this Reformation legacy not only imbues these modern ideal archives with a religious dimension, but also, paradoxically, carries with it a logic central to secular modernity. Specifically, this essay addresses a persistent "textual ontology" characterized by a conception of Scripture, and later Shakespeare, as self-grounding, univocal, and transhistorical.

Also engaging Reformation conceptions of Scripture, David Coleman's chapter, "Disintegrating the Rock: Ian Paisley, British Shakespeare, and Ulster Protestantism," examines the legacy of the early modern transformation of the Bible into a printed text, newly fragmented into numbered verses, which arguably encouraged a decontextualizing hermeneutic. He uncovers the persistence of this hermeneutic in the fiercely Protestant preacher and politician Ian Paisley, which is apparent both in his treatment of Scripture and his occasional attempts to yoke the early modern "Britishness" embodied in the English Bible to Shakespeare. Supplementing the more common analysis of Catholic engagement with "British" Shakespeare in the politicized field of Northern Ireland, Coleman provides a rare look at the rhetorical fusion of Scripture and Shakespeare in the Protestant milieu.

These chapters thus reveal how Shakespeare's textual afterlife has been intensely conditioned by the Bible: such material forms and practices as the early modern folio, the Reformation Bible and its paratexts, educational systems, the Victorian miscellany, editorial method, and nationalist speech have repackaged Shakespeare in explicitly scriptural terms. Yet the question of Shakespeare's scriptural repackaging cannot be considered apart from Shakespeare's repackaging of Scripture. As our authors show, the reciprocal nature of those questions elicits a greater level of attention to material context than the term *allusion* tends to entail. It is a mode of inquiry that reveals continuities and discontinuities alike. *Shakespeare, the Bible, and the Form of the Book* thus seeks to examine one of our most persistent cultural linkages, offering a crucial intervention into accounts of the interlocking history of Shakespeare and the Bible and their unique dual role in modern culture.

NOTES

1. George Bernard Shaw, *Everybody's Political What's What*, London: Constable, 1944, p. 181, italics added; Sharp qtd. in Charles Wordsworth, *On Shakspeare's Knowledge and Use of the Bible*, London: Smith, Elder, & Co., 1864, p. ix.
2. John Drakakis, "Theatre, Ideology, and Institution: Shakespeare and the Roadsweepers," in Graham Holderness (ed.) *The Shakespeare Myth*, Manchester: Manchester University Press, 1988, p. 25.
3. Wordsworth, *Shakespeare's Knowledge*, n.p.
4. Stephen Greenblatt, *Shakespearean Negotiations: The Circulation of Social Energy in Renaissance England*, Berkeley: University of California Press, 1988, p. 163.
5. Stephen Greenblatt, *Hamlet in Purgatory*, Princeton, NJ: Princeton University Press, 2001; *Will in the World: How Shakespeare Became Shakespeare*, New York: Norton, 2004.
6. For example, see the collection edited by Ewan Fernie, *Spiritual Shakespeares*, London: Routledge, 2005; on Shakespeare and theory's spiritual turn, see John D. Caputo's foreword to the volume, "Of Hyper-Reality," p. xvii, and Fernie's introduction, "Shakespeare, Spirituality, and Contemporary Criticism," p. 11.
7. Rudyard Kipling, "Proofs of Holy Writ," in *Strand Magazine*, April 1934, 350–8. See Philip Mason, "'Proofs of Holy Writ': An Introduction," *Kipling Journal*, 1988, vol. 62, no. 245, 33–7; and David Norton, *A History of the Bible as Literature*, vol. 2, Cambridge: Cambridge University Press, 1993, pp. 325–6.
8. The title comes from Iago's lines, "Trifles light as air / Are to the jealous confirmations strong / As proofs of holy writ," 3.3.323–5; Edward Pechter (ed.), *Othello*, New York: Norton, 2004.
9. Kipling, "Proofs," p. 353. In Anthony Burgess's literary reply to Kipling, "Will and Testament" (printed as a story-within-the-story in his novel *Enderby's Dark Lady*), the roles are reversed, with Jonson as the KJV scholars' contact and Shakespeare as the recruit (who allegedly encodes his name in the 46th Psalm); see Anthony Burgess, "Will and Testament," in *Enderby's Dark Lady*, London: Hutchinson, 1984, pp. 9–34.
10. Ibid., p. 358.
11. Ibid., p. 353.
12. Ibid.
13. Ibid., pp. 357–8.

14. Peter France, "Translation Studies and Translation Criticism," in France (ed.) *The Oxford Guide to Literature in English Translation*, Oxford: Oxford University Press, 2000, p. 3.
15. *The Holy Bible, conteyning the Old Testament, and the New*, London, 1611, sig. 3Q1v; accessed from the UPenn Libraries online facsimile at http://dewey.library.upenn.edu/sceti/ (accessed 13 June 2011).
16. Calling this story "a piece of translation criticism," France remarks on the differences but does not specify them (pp. 3–4). In verses 1 and 2, where Will prefers "Rise," "risen on thee," and "cloke the earth," the 1611 text has "Arise," "risen upon thee," and "cover the earth." Verse 19 also differs in the placement of several words, and, most interestingly, in verse 20 the 1611 text opts for the neuter reflexive pronoun "itself" to describe the moon, rejecting Will's personifying choice of "herself"—the moon in the King James Bible cannot also be Diana.
17. W.W. Greg, "The Rationale of Copy-Text," in Joseph Rosenblum (ed.) *Sir Walter Wilson Greg: A Collection of His Writings*, Lanham, MD: Scarecrow Press, 1998, pp. 213–28. Douglas Brooks notes that the story was written in "the heyday of the New Bibliography" in *From Playhouse to Printing House: Drama and Authorship in Early Modern England*, Cambridge: Cambridge University Press, 2000, p. 222.
18. Oddly enough, the version of Kipling's story printed in Maurice O'Sullivan's collection of Shakespeare-related fiction appears to correct the character Will by adding commas to the first quoted line, "To-morrow, and to-morrow, and to-morrow"—perhaps drawing on the commas in the unique Folio text as authority (though the Folio does not hyphenate the *to-morrow*s); see Rudyard Kipling, "Proofs of Holy Writ," in Maurice O'Sullivan, Jr. (ed.) *Shakespeare's Other Lives: Fictional Depictions of the Bard*, Jefferson, NC: McFarland, 1997, p. 152.
19. An unspecified book is also given iconographic pride of place in the illustration by A.R. Middleton Todd that appears on the story's opening pages in the *Strand* (also left out of reprinted versions).
20. Charlton Hinman (ed.) *The First Folio of Shakespeare*, 2nd ed., New York: Norton, 1996, sig. A3ʳ.
21. Kipling, "Proofs," p. 356.
22. Ibid., p. 353.
23. Ibid., p. 358.
24. Brooks, *Playhouse*, p. 222 (see note 17 above).
25. Peter Stallybrass, Roger Chartier, J. Franklin Mowery, and Heather Wolfe, "Hamlet's Tables and the Technologies of Writing in Renaissance England," *Shakespeare Quarterly*, 2004, vol. 55, no. 4, 379–419.
26. Qtd. in ibid., p. 380.
27. Ibid., pp. 414–5.
28. Ibid., p. 379.
29. Andrew Barnaby and Joan Wry, "Authorized Versions: *Measure for Measure* and the Politics of Biblical Translation," *Renaissance Quarterly*, 1998, vol. 51, no. 4, 1225–54, pp. 1232–3. For the history of the Bible in the English Reformation, see S.L. Greenslade, "English Versions of the Bible, 1525–1611," in P.R. Ackroyd and C.F. Evans (eds) *The Cambridge History of the Bible*, vol. 3, Cambridge: Cambridge University Press, 1963, pp. 141–74; and David Daniell, *The Bible in English: Its History and Influence*, New Haven, CT: Yale University Press, 2003. While Daniell provides a useful overview of the English Bible's history, caution must be taken given this book's strongly partisan nature, encapsulated by such brusque simplifications as "New Testament theology, particularly that of Paul, [. . .] became known as Calvinism" (p. 383). For a short version of this history, see Naseeb Shaheen, *Biblical References in Shakespeare's Comedies*, Newark, NJ: University of Delaware Press, 1993, pp. 15–22.

30. For example, see Charles Bullock's 1879 book, *Shakespeare's Debt to the Bible*, Folcroft, PA: Folcroft Press, 1970; and William Burgess, *The Bible in Shakespeare*, New York: Haskell, 1903.
31. Although scholars were locating Shakespeare's Bible references long before, one of the most important early studies is Richmond Noble, *Shakespeare's Biblical Knowledge and Use of the* Book of Common Prayer, New York: Macmillan, 1935.
32. Naseeb Shaheen, *Biblical References in Shakespeare's Plays*, Newark, NJ: University of Delaware Press, 1999.
33. Hannibal Hamlin, "William Shakespeare," in Rebecca Lemon, Emma Mason, Jonathan Roberts, and Christopher Rowland (eds) *The Blackwell Companion to the Bible in English Literature*, Oxford: Blackwell, 2009, pp. 225–6. See also Naseeb Shaheen, "Shakespeare's Knowledge of the Bible—How Acquired," *Shakespeare Studies*, 1988, vol. 20, 201–14.
34. Steven Marx, *Shakespeare and the Bible*, Oxford: Oxford University Press, 2000.
35. Beatrice Groves, *Texts and Traditions: Religion in Shakespeare 1592–1604*, Oxford: Oxford University Press, 2007.
36. Beatrice Groves, "Shakespeare's Sonnets and the Genevan Marginalia," *Essays in Criticism*, 2007, vol. 57, no. 2, 114–28.
37. James Black, *Edified by the Margent: Shakespeare and the Bible*, Calgary: Faculty of Humanities, University of Calgary, 1979.
38. Groves, "Shakespeare's Sonnets," p. 124.
39. Eleanor Marx-Aveling, "[Eleanor Marx on her Father]," in Eugene Kamenka (ed.) *The Portable Karl Marx*, New York: Viking, 1983, p. 50; Matthew Arnold, "A French Critic on Milton," in R.H. Super (ed.) *The Complete Prose Works of Matthew Arnold*, vol. 8, Ann Arbor: University of Michigan Press, 1972, p. 170. Ironically, Arnold goes on to claim that "The Bible and Shakespeare may be said to be imposed upon an Englishman as objects of his admiration; but as soon as the common Englishman, desiring culture, begins to choose for himself, he chooses Macaulay."
40. George Saintsbury, *A History of Elizabethan Literature*, London: Macmillan, 1887, p. 218.
41. Norton, *History*, p. 176.
42. Ibid., p. 180.
43. Norton phrases it this way in his single-volume abridgement, *A History of the English Bible as Literature*, Cambridge: Cambridge University Press, 2000, p. 318; see p. 210 in the two-volume edition.
44. Linda Rozmovits, *Shakespeare and the Politics of Culture in Late Victorian England*, Baltimore: Johns Hopkins University Press, 1998, p. 11.
45. On book history and the term *Nachleben*, see D.C. Greetham, "What Is Textual Scholarship?" in Simon Eliot and Jonathan Rose (eds) *A Companion to Book History*, Malden, MA: Wiley-Blackwell, 2009, p. 26; on the term's applicability to Shakespeare studies specifically, see Jonathan Bate, *Shakespearean Constitutions: Politics, Theatre, Criticism, 1730–1830*, Oxford: Clarendon Press, 1989, pp. 1–9.
46. Walter Benjamin, *The Arcades Project*, trans. Howard Eiland and Kevin McLaughlin, Cambridge, MA: Belknap Press, Harvard University Press, 1999, p. 460 [N2,3].
47. Graeme Gilloch, *Walter Benjamin: Critical Constellations*, Cambridge: Polity, 2002, p. 2.
48. Ibid., p. 4.
49. Gary Taylor, *Reinventing Shakespeare: A Cultural History from the Restoration to the Present*, London: Hogarth, 1990, p. 385.
50. David Scott Kastan, *Shakespeare and the Book*, Cambridge: Cambridge University Press, 2001, p. 97.

51. Ibid.
52. Louis Marder, *His Exits and Entrances: The Story of Shakespeare's Reputation*, Philadelphia: Lippincott, 1963, p. 18.
53. See Marcus Walsh, *Shakespeare, Milton, and Eighteenth-Century Literary Editing: The Beginnings of Interpretative Scholarship*, Cambridge: Cambridge University Press, 1997; Simon Jarvis, *Scholars and Gentlemen: Shakespearean Textual Criticism and Representations of Scholarly Labour, 1725–1765*, Oxford: Clarendon Press, 1995; and Margreta de Grazia, *Shakespeare Verbatim: The Reproduction of Authenticity and the 1790 Apparatus*, Oxford: Clarendon Press, 1991.
54. Norton, *History*, p. 269.
55. J.B. Stallo, George Hoadly, and Stanley Matthews, *Arguments Against the Use of the Bible in the Public Schools*, Cincinnati: Robert Clarke, 1870, p. 101; see also Norton, *History*, pp. 267–71.
56. Drakakis, "Theatre," p. 26.
57. Ibid., p. 25.
58. William Prynne, *Histrio-Mastix. The Players Scovrge, or Actors Tragaedie*, London, 1633, sig.**6ᵛ.
59. Andrew Murphy, *Shakespeare in Print: A History and Chronology of Shakespeare Publishing*, Cambridge: Cambridge University Press, 2003, p. 208.
60. Henry Morley, *A First Sketch of English Literature*, 10th ed., London: Cassell, 1883, p. 902.
61. Joss Marsh, *Word Crimes: Blasphemy, Culture, and Literature in Nineteenth-Century England*, Chicago: University of Chicago Press, 1998, p. 112.
62. See esp. the section on "The Shakespearean Touch," which includes a discussion of Kipling's "Proofs of Holy Writ": Norton, *History*, pp. 323–6; see also Daniell, *Bible in English*, pp. xiv–xv.
63. In addition to the relatively brief but provocative discussions in Drakakis, Brooks, and Kastan, cited above, see also Paul Franssen, "The Bard, the Bible, and the Desert Island," in Franssen and Ton Hoenselaars (eds) *The Author as Character: Representing Historical Writers in Western Literature*, Madison, WI: Fairleigh Dickinson University Press, 1999, pp. 106–17.
64. Graham Holderness, Stanley E. Porter, and Carol Banks, "Biblebable," in Andrew Murphy (ed.) *The Renaissance Text: Theory, Editing, Textuality*, Manchester: Manchester University Press, 2000, p. 154.
65. Ibid., p. 172.
66. Rozmovits, *Politics of Culture*, p. 22.
67. Represented most by Benjamin Jowett's 1860 essay "On the Interpretation of Scripture," which offered the controversial precept, "*Interpret the Scripture like any other book*"; in Victor Shea and William Whitla (eds) *Essays and Reviews: The 1860 Text and Its Reading*, Charlottesville: University of Virginia Press, 2000, p. 504, emphasis in original.
68. Geddes MacGregor, *A Literary History of the Bible: From the Middle Ages to the Present Day*, Nashville: Abingdon Press, 1968, p. 326.
69. Charles LaPorte, "The Bard, The Bible, and the Victorian Shakespeare Question," *English Literary History*, 2007, vol. 74, no. 3, 609–28, p. 610, emphasis added.
70. Jarvis, *Scholars*, pp. 17–19.
71. Walsh, *Shakespeare*, pp. 116–19.

2   Shakespeare Reads the Geneva Bible

Barbara A. Mowat

That Shakespeare's plays allude throughout to the Bible is old news. Nor is it exactly new news that Shakespeare acquired most of his Biblical knowledge through private reading of the Bible (rather than from what he heard in church) or that his favorite Bible was apparently the Geneva—either the 1560 edition or one or more of its later incarnations.[1] What is arguably new is that we can discover much about how Shakespeare read this Bible, about his habits of reading in general, and about his dramatic craftsmanship when we closely study the Geneva Bible as it is reflected in his plays; also arguably new is the light that such study sheds on our awareness of how thoroughly steeped in Biblical story and language Londoners of the late-sixteenth- and early-seventeenth centuries seem to have been—this despite the fact that less than a century had passed since congregations first heard the Bible read aloud in English and that only since 1575 had a reader-friendly English Bible—the Geneva—been published in England and therefore been widely available for private reading.[2]

I

Scholars who have studied Shakespeare's reading and those who have analyzed his quotations of the Bible agree that Shakespeare's reading was remarkable for its breadth. S. Schoenbaum expressed himself "astonished by the range of Shakespeare's reading," and F. P. Wilson saw Shakespeare as a man who "read widely . . . with a darting intelligence."[3] This characterization of Shakespeare as a reader seems to be supported by his pattern of quotations from the Bible. Naseeb Shaheen's "Index to Shakespeare's Biblical References," for example, links Shakespeare's text to 39 of the 40 books in the Christian Old Testament, to 12 of the 14 books in the Apocrypha, and to 27 of the 29 books in the New Testament.[4]

When we look, though, at Shakespeare's allusions to and borrowings from actual *stories* in the Bible, as well as in, for example, Ovid's *Metamorphoses* or Virgil's *Aeneid,* we discover to our surprise that, along with reading broadly in these works, Shakespeare also returned frequently to seemingly favorite narratives. The stories to which he repeatedly alludes in the *Aeneid,* for instance, cluster in its first few books, and the stories he cites again and again from Ovid's *Metamorphoses* are found in books 3 through 7 and book 13. And the Biblical stories that seem most to have captured his interest—or, perhaps, that he found most useful in his writing—are found in specific chapters in the Book of Genesis and the Gospel according to Saint Luke.

It should not surprise us that, of all the books of the Bible, Shakespeare would have been especially attracted to Genesis and to Luke's Gospel. As Stephen Marx notes, Genesis is filled with "mythic, legendary, and novelistic" stories that display, in Robert Alter's words, the "brilliantly laconic style, [and the] uncanny ability to intimate psychological and thematic complexities" characteristic of "the golden age of Hebrew narrative."[5] From the gripping story of the creation and the Garden of Eden, through that of Noah and the flood, and on through the cycles of stories of Abraham, Isaac, Jacob, and Joseph, Genesis offers, in Alter's words, an "extraordinary . . . representation of actions, character, speech, and motive." And St Luke's Gospel, written by a supreme storyteller, is filled with parables not of the generally allegorical kind found in St Mark's and St Matthew's Gospels, but appealingly "lucid and realistic tales"—stories such as that of the Good Samaritan and the Prodigal Son. John Drury notes that Luke's great section of parables is "as full of domestic detail as a Dutch painting [and] draws its characters with [rare] subtlety."[6]

To cite the literary appeal of Genesis and Luke as an explanation of Shakespeare's attraction to these books is, of course, to speculate. That he returns to these books repeatedly in crafting his plays, though, is simple fact. He cites the Genesis stories about Jacob (Genesis 25:23–49:33), for instance, 19 times, with one of the stories—Jacob's stealing of Esau's blessing (Genesis 27:1–46)—recalled in three of his plays. From Luke's Gospel, one sequence of three parables feeds into play after play. Eleven plays allude to the parable of the Prodigal Son (Luke 15:11–31), while the parable that immediately follows it, that of "the clever [or the unjust] Steward"[7] (Luke 16:1–13) appears in six different plays, and the parable that follows—that of the rich man and Lazarus the beggar (Luke 16:19–31)—is cited in ten plays, often more than once.[8]

The most potent Biblical story in Shakespeare's plays, though, is that of Cain and Abel. This story, found at Genesis 4:1–16, is cited in nine plays, each citation bringing with it the full weight of the "primal eldest" sin of fratricide. The interaction of the plays and these sixteen verses illuminates both Shakespeare's intensive reading habits and the process through which such reading informs his writing.[9] As is customary in Genesis, the Cain and Abel story is presented in a powerful combination of narrative and direct speech. The first four verses of the story briefly narrate the birth of Cain, then of Abel, and then tell how, "in process of time," the brothers brought their offerings to God, who "had respect unto Abel and to his offering" but "unto Cain and his offering he had no regard."[10] In response to Cain's "exceeding wroth," God speaks directly to Cain, enumerating the consequences if Cain acts violently against his brother, promising him future prosperity if he behaves well. Then follows the single narrative verse (verse 8) into which the story's central action is crowded: "Then Cain spake to Abel his brother. And when they were in the field, Cain rose up against Abel his brother and slew him." This verse is followed in turn by dialogue between God and Cain (verses 9–15), with the story wrapped up in a final narrative sentence: "Then Cain went out from the presence of the Lord and dwelt in the land of Nod toward the Eastside of Eden."

As brief as is this story, the plays make clear that Shakespeare was most engaged with particular verses. He sometimes refers to the entire story of the murder and its consequences—as, for example, when he has Northumberland call down chaos on the world by saying "Let one spirit of the first-born Cain/ Reign in all bosoms."[11] But more often Shakespeare focuses on specific verses, a habit that reveals the importance of the particular Bible he chose to read. The Geneva Bible, published on the continent in 1560, and, beginning in 1575, repeatedly reprinted in England, was designed for use by lay readers: "Instead of the large unwieldy folio volumes that had been common, the new Bible was instead a handy quarto" (see Figure 2.1). Further, "it was the first English Bible to be printed in roman type rather than black letter." [12] Another of its important innovations was the division of the Scripture into verses, a feature that, according to the translators, aided the memory and made it possible for the reader to move easily between the concordance and the text. To further aid the reader, the translators provided "marginal commentary, both textual and explanatory, 'upon all the hard places,'"[13] along with two "tables"—the first of which gave "The Interpretation of the Proper Names" and the second a concordance "of the principal things that are contained in the Bible."[14]

The "useful information technology which we find in the apparatus of the Geneva Bible" (to quote Patrick Collinson[15]) not only made the Geneva Bible the most popular of English translations of the Bible well into the seventeenth century, but also provided a working playwright with remarkably helpful tools. We can see this in his handling of specific verses and their marginal explanatory comments. For example, while he seems to have found especially potent God's words to Cain just after the murder, "'The voice of thy brother's blood crieth unto me from the ground. Now therefore thou art cursed from the earth, which hath opened her mouth to receive thy brother's blood from thine hand'" (verses 10–11), he seems at least equally drawn to the marginal gloss on the words "the voice of thy brother's blood crieth unto me," a gloss which reads "the iniquity itself crieth for vengeance" (see Figure 2.2). He blends words from the text—*blood crieth unto me*—with words from the gloss—*crieth for vengeance*—to create an image that appears in eight of his plays, the image of spilled blood crying for vengeance. While it appears most baldly in *Richard II,* where the blood of the

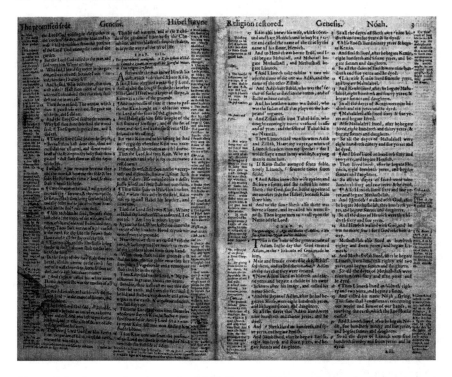

Figure 2.1   An opening from the 1560 Geneva Bible, with marginal glosses and commentary. Image courtesy of the Thomas Fisher Rare Book Library, University of Toronto.

Duke of Gloucester, "like sacrificing Abel's, cries/ Even from the tongueless caverns of the earth/ . . . for justice and rough chastisement" (1.1.104–06), it is also found in plays that span his writing career, from the very early *1 Henry VI*, where it is Joan of Arc's "maiden blood" that "will cry for vengeance at the gates of heaven" (5.4.52–53) to the very late *Henry VIII*, where it is the condemned Buckingham's "guiltless blood" that will "cry against" his enemies and "make 'em one day groan" (2.1.68, 105).[16]

Shakespeare's conjoining of text and gloss from various moments in the Cain and Abel story produces some of his most potent images and themes. Verse 12, which concludes God's curse on Cain—"a vagabond and a renegade shalt thou be in the earth"—is twice alluded to in *Richard II,* as when Bolingbroke banishes King Richard's murderer with the words "With Cain go wander thorough shades of night" (5.6.43) and it makes its way surreptitiously into *A Midsummer Night's Dream,* as Hermia echoes Genesis in her own curse on Demetrius: "Hast thou slain him then?/ Henceforth be never numbered among men" (3.2.66–67). But the curse of exile and vagabondage appears more powerfully when Shakespeare combines it with its marginal gloss—"Thou shalt never have rest: for thine heart shall be in

6 Then the Lord said vnto Káin, Why art thou wroth? and why is thy countenance cast downe?

7 If thou do wel, shalt thou not be e accepted? and if thou doest not wel, sinne lieth at the f dore: also vnto thee his g desire shalbe subiect, and thou shalt rule ouer him.

8 ¶ Then Káin spake to Hábel his brother. And * when they were in the field, Káin rose vp against Hábel his brother, and slewe him.

9 Then the Lord said vnto Káin, Where is Hábel thy brother? Who answered, I cã not tel. h Am I my brothers keper?

10 Againe he said, What hast thou done? the i voyce of thy brothers blood cryeth vnto me from the grounde.

11 Now therefore thou art cursed k frõ the earth, w hathe opened her mouth to receiue thy brothers blood from thine hand.

12 When thou shalt til the grounde, it shal not henceforthe yelde vnto thee her strength: a l vagabonde and a rennegate shalt thou be in the earth.

13 Then Káin said to the Lord, m My punishment is greater, then I can beare.

14 Beholde, thou hast cast me out this day from the earth, and from thy face shal I be hid, and shalbe a vagabonde and a rennegate in the earth & whosoeuer findeth me, shal slaye me.

15 Then the Lord said vnto him, Douteles whosoeuer slayeth Káin, he shalbe o punished seuen folde. And ∮ Lord set a o marke vpon Káin, lest anie man finding him shulde kil him.

16 Then Káin went out from the presence of the Lord and dwelt in the land of Nod towarde the Eastside of Eden.

the tre of life.
Ebr.11,4.
d Because he was an hypocrite and offred onely for an outwarde shew without sinceritie of heart.
e Bothe thou and thy sacrifice shalbe acceptable to me.
f Sinne shal stil torment thy conscience.
g The dignitie of ∮ first borne is giuen to Káin ouer Hábel.
Wisd.10,3.
mat.23,35.
1.ioh.3,13.
iud.11.
h This is the nature of the reprobate whẽ thei are reproued of their hypocrisie, eue to neglect God and despite him.
i God reuengeth ∮ wrõgs of his Saints, thogh none cõplaine: for the iniquitie it self cryeth for vengeance.
k The earth shalbe a witnes agaist thee which mercifully receiued that blood, w thou most cruelly shed.
l Thou shalt haue no rest: for thine heart shalbe in continual feare & care.
m He burdeneth God as a cruel iudge.

because he did punish him so sharpely. *Or, my sinne is greater then can be pardoned.* n Not for the loue he bare to Káin, but to suppresse murther. o A visible signe of Gods iudgement that others shulde feare.

Figure 2.2 Marginal glosses to Genesis 4:6–16 from the 1560 Geneva Bible. Image courtesy of the Thomas Fisher Rare Book Library, University of Toronto.

continual fear and care"–and with verse 7 and its gloss—"if thou doest not well, sin lieth at the door," a warning that the gloss rephrases as "Sin shall still torment thy conscience" (see Figure 2.2). These two verses and their glosses, when combined, constitute a grim warning that the wages of mur-der—or, perhaps more specifically, the wages of the murder of a kinsman—are continual fear and a tormented conscience. On Shakespeare's stage, the truth of that warning is enacted vividly as early as the nightmare visions of Richard III, as centrally as Claudius's anguished attempt to repent, and as late as Macbeth's and Lady Macbeth's scorpion-filled minds, ghost-plagued banquets, and blood-spotted hands.

The paratextual apparatus of the Geneva Bible provided its readers, including William Shakespeare, not only with the kind of interpretive glosses mentioned above, but also with what William Slights calls "intertex-tual cross-references"—i.e., both marginal notes that link the text to other places in the Bible and detailed indices.[17] Sometimes the cross-references lead elsewhere in the Bible, to material that itself serves as significant inter-pretive commentary. For example, the cryptic words "Cain rose up against Abel his brother and slew him" are provided with two different kinds of cross-reference—one in the margin, and one in the concordance under the name "Kain"—both of which direct the reader to the first epistle of John 3:12, which reads: "Cain . . . was of the wicked, and slew his brother. And wherefore slew he him? because his own works were evil and his brother's good."[18] This passage provides a motive for Cain's murder of Abel not to be found in Genesis, but arguably crucial to Shakespeare's thinking about male—and especially brother-on-brother—violence. As Cain slew Abel because Abel's works made Cain's "evil," so, in Shakespeare's plays, more than one male character seeks to destroy another because the potential victim's virtues make the destroyer feel inferior or evil by comparison.[19] Shakespeare has Iago state this motive clearly in explaining why Cassio must die: "He hath a daily beauty in his life that makes me ugly" (5.1.19). In *As You Like It*, when Oliver sets up the murder of his brother Orlando, he expresses at length this same hatred of a rival whose goodness contrasts so clearly with his own moral ugliness, making him "altogether misprized" (1.1.156–61). And one may suspect a similar motivation behind the unex-plained malice of other villainous brothers—for example, Don John in *Much Ado about Nothing* and Edmund in *King Lear*—as well as in Iago's unconvincingly rationalized hatred of Othello.

The translators of the Geneva Bible account for their interpretive glosses as follows: "considering how hard a thing it is to understand the holy Scriptures . . . we have . . . endeavored . . . to gather brief annotations upon all the hard places, as well for the understanding of such words as are obscure, and for the declaration [i.e., elucidation, interpretation] of the text . . . "[20] One notable gloss appended to the Cain and Abel story in the Geneva margins goes far beyond the translators' expressed goals, elucidat-ing the text in a way that fixes the story—and the plays that allude to the story—firmly in early modern English culture. At verse 7, God promises Cain "if thou do well [i.e., if you do not kill Abel] . . . unto thee his desire shall be subject, and thou shalt rule over him." The interpretive marginal gloss to this line reads "The dignity of the firstborn is given to Cain over Abel." The key phrase in this gloss—"the dignity of the firstborn"—in effect sets the world's first sibling rivalry and fratricide in the unexpected context of the rights of inheritance and blessing that go to the firstborn son. For Cain and Abel, the question of the inherited rights of the firstborn almost immediately becomes moot, because Cain does not "do well" and Abel, the threatening younger brother, is eliminated.[21] But the theme of brother striving with brother for "the dignity of the firstborn," introduced in this gloss, goes on to dominate the book of Genesis. Indeed, Robert Alter argues that "the entire Book of Genesis is about the reversal of the iron law of primogeniture."[22] The series of stories of such reversals begins in chapter 21, when Abraham's firstborn son, Ishmael, is cast out so that the younger son Isaac can inherit Abraham's property and his blessing. (As Isaac's mother Sarah explains: "the son of this bondwoman [Hagar] shall not be heir with my son Isaac" [21:10]) When Isaac himself grows up and his wife Rebekkah is pregnant with Jacob and Esau, the twins engage in a mighty struggle in her womb. Esau manages to be born first, but Jacob buys Esau's birthright and then, using disguise and trickery, steals the blessing that belongs to the eldest son, thus making Jacob Esau's "lord." Esau, when he realizes what has happened, cries out, "'[Jacob] hath deceived me these two times: he took my birthright, and lo, now hath he taken my blessing' . . . Therefore Esau hated Jacob . . . and . . . thought in his mind . . . 'I will slay my brother Jacob'" (27:34–41). The fratricide is prevented when their mother warns Jacob and helps him escape, but Jacob's life is thenceforth haunted by his fear of Esau's threatened revenge. Stories of violent struggles between brothers and stories of the passing over or casting out of the firstborn for the rights of inheritance continue up to the very end of Genesis: Jacob bestows his blessing not on his firstborn Reuben but on the fourthborn, Judah, and then, as the book ends, when blessing his grandsons, Jacob crosses his hands so that his blessing goes not to Joseph's eldest but to his second-born son.

In Shakespeare's plays, as in the book of Genesis, we find an extensive collection of rival brothers caught up in stories reminiscent of that of Isaac and Ishmael, or Jacob and Esau—that is, stories in which the younger brother usurps the dignity of the firstborn by displacing his elder and seizing his inheritance.[23] In *Richard III*, Richard kills Clarence as the first step toward acquiring "the dignity of the firstborn"—here, the crown. In *As You Like It*, Frederick, the younger brother, rules the dukedom after having ousted his older brother Duke Senior, whose name never lets us forget that he is Frederick's elder and therefore the rightful ruler; in *King Lear*, Edmund supplants the older, and legitimate, Edgar. *The Tempest* features two such pairs of brothers; in the background story, Antonio has disposed of the firstborn Prospero and taken over his dukedom, and, in the play's action, Sebastian attempts to kill his older brother Alonso in order to replace him as king of Naples. Even the two sets of twins in *A Comedy of Errors,* strange as it may seem, belong among Shakespeare's stories of younger brothers replacing elders. The play puts considerable emphasis on which of the twins was "the latter born"—a fact that leads Patricia Parker to argue convincingly that the twins are significantly connected to "the quintessential Biblical elder and younger sons," Esau and Jacob.[24] The play's emphasis on birth-order highlights the fact that it was the younger Antipholus and Dromio who come to Ephesus and, for a while, supplant their older brothers, both in the lives of their women and in the eyes of the city.

While there is no way to demonstrate that it was the gloss at Genesis 4:7 contextualizing the Cain and Abel story in terms of primogeniture which led Shakespeare to connect Cain and Abel to Genesis's series of stories of rival brothers, that he did see them as connected is strongly suggested by *Hamlet.* This play, the action of which is triggered by the violent overthrow of an elder brother by a younger, is structured around allusions not to Ishmael and Isaac or Esau and Jacob, as we might expect, but to Cain and Abel. Claudius rules Denmark in the place of his recently dead older brother and has taken that brother's wife as his queen. When he consoles his grieving nephew, he does so with an allusion to Abel, saying that death has been inevitable "from the first corpse till he that died today" (1.2.105). When Hamlet later meets his father's ghost, we learn how appropriate it was for Claudius to talk about his brother's death in terms of that first fratricide: as the ghost explains, King Hamlet was "by a brother's hand,/ Of life, of crown, of queen at once dispatched" (1.5.75–76). And, when Claudius, at midplay, tries to repent of the murder, he specifically links it to Cain's killing of Abel: "my offense is rank!" he says: "It hath the primal eldest curse upon't,/ A brother's murder" (3.3.36–38). He himself recognizes that he is another Cain, cursed and marked. He then discovers that he cannot repent because through the murder he has achieved the "dignity of the firstborn," along with the firstborn's queen, and he is not willing to give them up (ll. 52–56).

These are not the only references in *Hamlet* to Cain and Abel, nor the only allusions to brotherly rivalry and violence. The final act, for example, features a duel between quasi-brothers and includes a prominent reference to "Cain's jawbone, that did the first murder" (5.1.77). But we can already see how Shakespeare's intensive reading of the book of Genesis and its glosses gave him a way of rethinking and transforming the old Amleth fable, adding remarkable resonance to what had been little more than a primitive revenge story. We can also imagine how the rival-brother stories in *Hamlet* as in other plays might have spoken to audiences in the early 1600s, audiences no doubt filled with younger sons essentially disinherited through primogeniture, along with a few firstborn sons sitting in expensive seats their impoverished younger brothers could not afford.[25] In other words, Shakespeare's use of ancient stories from a time when religious law specified that the largest share of the father's property and dominion over younger brothers went to the firstborn son (Genesis 27:37) would not only have given a mythic resonance to his plays, but would also have doubtless sparked a powerful interest in an audience once again in the thrall of the law of primogeniture. Since, in the heated debates in Shakespeare's day about this mode of inheritance, supporters of both elder and younger sons appealed to the story of Jacob and Esau to support their argument,[26] it is likely that such audiences and contemporary readers would have recognized his allusions to the book of Genesis and would have heard echoes of the stories behind the one being enacted.

II

In the plays thus far considered, Shakespeare's pattern of reading in the intensive mode is reflected in the way he used Biblical narratives. But his reading of the Geneva Bible intensively, it turns out, pertains even when story *per se* is not involved—as, for example, in *Measure for Measure*. This play is an anomaly in that, as Louise Schleiner notes, "in no other [Shakespeare] play do the central characters evoke specific Biblical passages and theological concepts to explain their crucial deeds."[27] The title of the play is, of course, itself a Biblical allusion, one that finally leads us to Jesus' Sermon on the Mount, with its "Judge not, that ye be not judged; for with what judgment ye judge, ye shall be judged, and with what measure ye mete, it shall be measured to you again" (Matthew 7:1–2). However, when Shakespeare introduces the phrase "measure . . . for measure" into the dialogue at a crucial moment in act 5, the context and the syntax take us initially to a familiar Old Testament injunction and its reversal in the Gospels. Josephine Waters Bennett, commenting on the Duke's urging Isabella "to demand 'An Angelo for Claudio, death for death,'" points out that "When the Duke goes on to say 'Haste still pays haste, and measure still for measure,' this is the 'measure for measure' of the Old Law of 'an eye for an eye, a tooth for a tooth.'"[28]

This "Old Law" version of "measure for measure" is found first in Exodus, where God, speaking to (and through) Moses, instructs magistrates and judges that, should one man do violence to another, he should "pay life for life, eye for eye, tooth for tooth, hand for hand, foot for foot, burning for burning, wound for wound, stripe for stripe" (Exodus 21:23–5). In the Geneva Bible, a marginal citation on this passage leads the reader to Leviticus 24:20, and then to Deuteronomy 19:20 (see Figure 2.3), which reads, at verse 21, "thine eye [i.e., the eye of the judge] shall have no compassion, but life for life, eye for eye . . . " In this context, when the Duke says to Isabella, "The very mercy of the law cries out . . . / 'An Angelo for Claudio, death for death.'/ Haste still pays haste, . . . / . . . and measure still for measure"

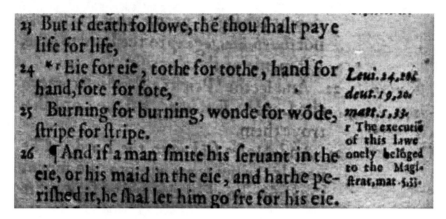

23 But if death followe, thē thou ſhalt pay e
life for life,
24 *r Eie for eie, tothe for tothe, hand for   *Leui.24,25.*
hand, fote for fote,   *deut.19,20.*
25 Burning for burning, wonde for wōde,   *matt.5,35.*
ſtripe for ſtripe.   *r The executiō
of this lawe
26 ¶ And if a man ſmite his ſeruant in the *onely belōged
eie, or his maid in the eie, and hathe pe- *to the Magi-*
riſhed it, he ſhal let him go fre for his eie. *ſtrat, mat.5,35.*

Figure 2.3   Marginal glosses to Exodus 21:23–5 from the 1560 Geneva Bible. Image courtesy of the Thomas Fisher Library, University of Toronto.

(5.1.415–18), he alludes, as Bennett notes, to the ancient, thrice-repeated Mosaic injunction that calls for retributive justice.

But marginal citations attached to the passages in Exodus, Leviticus, and Deuteronomy also lead the reader directly to the passage in the gospel of Matthew where Jesus, in his Sermon on the Mount (Matthew 5–7), says "Ye have heard that it hath been said, An eye for an eye, and a tooth for a tooth.[29] But I say unto you, Resist not evil, but whosoever shall smite thee on the right cheek, turn to him the other also" (5:39). In the margin beside Jesus' words one finds links back to the passages in Exodus, Leviticus, and Deuteronomy and forward to Luke 6:29. The apparatus in the Geneva Bible, in other words, does not let the reader forget that this matter of punishment of offenders has been addressed in the Bible in diametrically opposite ways—first, as a matter of untempered justice and then as a matter of unqualified mercy. Bennett is not alone in thinking that when the Duke says to Isabella, "an Angelo for Claudio, . . . measure still for measure," he is using language that encourages revenge, perhaps as a way of testing her. I would argue that it is equally likely that his language tests her in a more subtle way, carrying within it an inevitable reminder of Jesus' injunction that a victim respond with forgiveness and mercy. The Duke's interesting phrase "the very mercy of the law," along with the sequence of marginal Geneva glosses that take one back and forth between Exodus and Matthew, give some support to this conjecture.

While the syntactic pattern of the Duke's message to Isabella—"'An Angelo for Claudio, death for death . . . and measure . . . for measure'"— seems designed to lead us to the Mosaic injunctions and their reversal in Matthew 5, the actual words "measure for measure," as noted earlier, occur later in that sermon, where Jesus says (in the less familiar but more interesting account by Luke), "Give and it shall be given unto you; a good measure, pressed down, shaken together and running over shall men give into your bosom: for with what measure ye mete, with the same shall men mete to you again" (6:38). This New Law version of "measure for measure" is, in part, a warning that those who impose penalties on others should first reflect on their own faults and their own dependence on divine mercy, a message to which the play more than once alludes in regards to the harsh and deeply flawed Angelo. The Duke at 3.2.249–51, to cite a single example, notes that "If [Angelo's] own life answer the straitness of his proceeding, it shall become him well; wherein if he chance to fail, he hath sentenced himself."[30] The Biblical echoes of "judge not that ye be not judged" that resonate within comments to and about Angelo leave no doubt that Angelo's conduct as a judge has rendered him subject to harsh and punitive judgment. However, how the complicated Isabella—devout, grief-stricken, deeply wronged and humiliated—will hear the Duke's words "An Angelo for Claudio . . . ; measure . . . for measure" is far from predictable. And for a Biblically knowledgeable audience, the suspense lies in whether she will choose mercy or retribution and, as a consequence, to which version of "measure for measure" the play finally alludes.

While *Measure for Measure* does not employ Biblical story, it seems clear that in writing this play, pondering Mosaic injunction and its reversal in Jesus' sermon, Shakespeare once again moved from passage to passage in the Geneva Bible, following the lead of marginal citations, absorbing language and meaning and using them centrally in the play. It also seems likely that, just as, for example, *As You Like It* seems to speak with special clarity to a social world caught up in the ramifications of the law of primogeniture, so *Measure for Measure* addresses a world in which theological and ecclesiastical debate had recently surged into new prominence. King James's accession in 1603 had led almost immediately to the 1604 Hampton Court Conference, where the future of the Church of England was debated and where the decision about a new translation of the Bible was made; hopes and fears around James's accession, along with James's own theological bent, had led as well to heated debates about religion and moral conduct, in both sermons and in print.[31] It should not surprise us, then, that a play presented at James's court in December of 1604 should be suffused with matters of keen current interest, namely, Biblical texts and glosses and matters theological.

III

I suggested at the outset that Shakespeare's use of Biblical story and allusion indicates that playgoers in Shakespeare's London were steeped in the Bible's stories and language. Such a suggestion, so phrased, is highly vulnerable to attack: we cannot know how audience member's responded to Shakespeare's plays, nor can we rationally argue that knowledge of the

Bible was a necessary precondition for enjoying *As You Like it* or *Hamlet* or *Measure for Measure.* What we can assert, though, is that considerable evidence exists that, by the late sixteenth century, English men and women knew their Bible well. From print runs of English Bibles to anecdotes in Foxe and elsewhere of Bible readers, to accounts of trials for heresy, to reports about "prophesyings" (local gatherings that "spent whole days each week, from early morning to late at night, reading and studying the Bible"[32]), all support David Daniell's assessment that "the Bible for the Tudors . . . was the life-blood, the daily, even hourly, nourishment of the nation and of ordinary men and women. It was known with a thoroughness that is, simply, astonishing."[33]

We can also assert that Shakespeare's elaborate intertextual structuring of Biblical allusions—whether of repeated citations of particular stories or of dramatic playings-out of Biblical warnings and promises—suggests an assumption on his part that a significant portion of his audience shared with him a linguistic and narrative world, one made possible by the Geneva Bible—or, better, by the availability of the Bible in English in a format designed for individual and domestic reading.[34] When his intertext was, e.g., Holinshed's *Chronicles,* he needed to consider (and, in *Henry V,* actually address) both those in the audience "who have not read the story" and those who "have" (*Henry V,* 5.0.1–2). When his intertext was the Bible, he could assume a shared familiar and resonant linguistic world. And because Shakespeare, along with his audience, depended on a still-extant scholarly Bible, we can, with pleasure, trace him from the text and margins of his reading to the dialogue of his writing, watching a master dramatic craftsman weaving Biblical language and story into his "Comedies, Histories, and Tragedies" as he created plays that spoke directly to his chronological moment and that speak just as compellingly today.

NOTES

1. See Naseeb Shaheen, "Shakespeare's Knowledge of the Bible—How Acquired," *Shakespeare Studies* 20, 1988, 201–14; David Daniell, "Reading the Bible," in David Scott Kastan (ed.) *A Companion to Shakespeare,* Oxford: Blackwell, 1999, pp. 158–71, esp. pp. 165–6; Lee W. Gibbs, "Biblical Interpretation in Medieval England and the English Reformation," in Alan J. Hauser and Duane F. Watson (eds) *A History of Biblical Interpretation,* vol. 2: *The Medieval through the Reformation Periods,* Cambridge: William B. Eerdsman, 2009, vol. 2, pp. 372–402, esp. pp. 389–91; Lynne Long, "Scriptures in the Vernacular Up to 1800," in Hauser and Watson, *A History of Biblical Interpretation,* vol. 2, pp. 450–81, esp. pp. 465–7.
2. The "reader-friendly" characteristics of the Geneva Bible will be discussed below.
3. S. Schoenbaum, "Shakespeare and the Book," in *Shakespeare and Others,* Washington, DC: Folger Shakespeare Library, 1985, p. 25; F.P. Wilson, "Shakespeare's Reading," *Shakespeare Survey* 3, 1950, pp. 17–8. See also Leonard Barkan, "What Did Shakespeare Read?" in Margreta de Grazia and Stanley

Wells (eds) *The Cambridge Companion to Shakespeare*, Cambridge: Cambridge University Press, 2001, pp. 31–47, esp. p. 40.

4. Naseeb Shaheen, "Index to Shakespeare's Biblical References," in *Biblical References in Shakespeare's Plays*, Newark, NJ: University of Delaware Press, 1999, pp. 769–826.

5. Stephen Marx, *Shakespeare and The Bible*, Oxford and New York: Oxford University Press, 2000, p. 40; Robert Alter, "Introduction to the Old Testament," in Robert Alter and Frank Kermode (eds) *The Literary Guide to the Bible*, Cambridge, MA: Harvard University Press, 1987, p. 30. See also Robert Alter, *The World of Biblical Literature*, New York: Basic Books, 1992, p. 77.

6. John Drury, "Luke," in Alter and Kermode, *The Literary Guide to the Bible*, pp. 432, 434.

7. Drury suggests that "clever" is the better characterization (p. 434). Luke 16:8 reads, "the Lord commended the unjust steward because he had done wisely."

8. Shaheen, "Index," pp. 769–826.

9. The term *intensive* is taken from Heidi Brayman Hackel, who defines it as a "mode of reading based upon repeated encounters with a text" ("The 'Great Variety' of Readers and Early Modern Reading Practices," in Kastan, *A Companion to Shakespeare*, p. 149).

10. All Biblical quotations are from the 1560 edition of the Geneva Bible, with spelling modernized. (Because the Shakespeare text is modernized, to retain early modern spelling for the Bible would create a misleading chronological gap between the two texts.) We do not know which version of the Geneva Shakespeare read, but the text and paratextual matter which I examine, although clearly reset in the later editions, is essentially unchanged from the 1560 through the 1599 edition. The famous (or infamous) marginal notes that were added by Tomson (1587) and by Junius (1599) are found primarily in the New Testament and especially in Revelation. They do not affect the passages I cite.

11. *Henry IV, Part 2*, 1.1.157–58, in David Bevington (ed.) *The Complete Works of Shakespeare*, 5th ed., New York: Longman, 2003. All quotations from Shakespeare's plays will be from this edition, and will be cited parenthetically.

12. Lloyd E. Berry, "Introduction to the Facsimile Edition," in *The Geneva Bible: A Facsimile of the 1560 Edition*, Peabody, MA: Hendrickson, 2007, p. 12. See also Gibbs and Long.

13. Berry, "Introduction," p. 12.

14. Some of these prominent helpful features of the Geneva Bible in its English incarnation drew from French Bibles published in Geneva in the late 1550s, especially the landmark edition of 1559. See Francis Higman, "'Without Great Effort, and with Pleasure': Sixteenth-Century Geneva Bibles and Reading Practices," in Orlaith O'Sullivan (ed.) *The Bible as Book: The Reformation*, London: The British Library and Oak Knoll Press, 2000, pp. 115–22; Basil Hall, "The Geneva Version of the English Bible: Its Aims and Achievements," in W. P. Stephens (ed.) *The Bible, the Reformation and the Church: Essays in Honour of James Atkinson*, Sheffield: Sheffield Academic Press, 1995, pp. 124–49, esp. 140–3. See also S.L. Greenslade, "English Versions of the Bible, 1525–1611," in S.L. Greenslade (ed.) *Cambridge History of the Bible: The West from the Reformation to the Present Day*, Cambridge: Cambridge University Press, 1963, pp. 141–74, esp. pp. 156–8.

15. Patrick Collinson, "The Coherence of the Text: How it Hangeth Together: The Bible in Reformation England," in Stephens, *The Bible, the Reformation and the Church*, p. 94.

16. While Buckingham does not quote Genesis precisely, editors hear the words as a citation. David Bevington, e.g., glosses the lines as saying "Buckingham's shed blood will cry out from the grave for vengeance" (2.1.106 note).
17. William Slights, "'Marginall Notes That Spoile the Text': Scriptural Annotation in the English Renaissance," in his *Managing Readers: Printed Marginalia in English Renaissance Books*, Ann Arbor: University of Michigan Press, 2001, p. 105.
18. The 1599 edition of the Geneva Bible adds, at Genesis 4:7, a marginal reference to the Index itself. Otherwise, as noted above, the text and the glosses for Genesis 4:1–16 are the same in the 1560 and the 1599 editions.
19. While the language of John 3:12 does not state explicitly that Cain found his own works evil *in comparison to* the good works of Abel, that comparison is implied. There is nothing in the Genesis story that suggests that Cain's offerings were in any way objectively evil; they simply weren't preferred by God.
20. "To Our Beloved in the Lord. . . . From Geneva, 10 April, 1560," *The Geneva Bible*, iiii–iiii^v.
21. Because Cain is banished, the inheritance, though, does in fact descend through a later-born brother.
22. Robert Alter, *The Art of Biblical Narrative*, New York: Basic Books, 1992, p. 6. Among the many other scholars who have noted Genesis's repeated subversion of primogeniture, see, e.g., Northrop Frye, *The Great Code: The Bible and Literature*, New York: Harcourt Brace Jovanovich, 1982, pp. 180–1; Tibor Fabiny, "Brothers as Doubles: Birthright and Rivalry of 'Brothers' in Genesis and Shakespeare," in Gabor Ittzes and Andras Kisery (eds) *Elaborate Trifles*, Piliscsaba: Pazmany Peter Katolikus Egyetem, 2002, pp. 35–47.
23. One apparent exception to this pattern is that of Oliver and Orlando in *As You Like It*, where, to quote Russell Fraser, "Wicked Oliver is . . . the Cain-like older brother who pursues his brother's life" ("Shakespeare's Book of Genesis," *Comparative Drama*, 1991, vol. 25, no. 2, 121–8, p. 126). However, even this pair of brothers finally reflects the reverse primogeniture pattern, since the younger brother Orlando, by play's end, is destined for a higher status than Oliver's.
24. Patricia Parker, *Shakespeare from the Margins: Language, Culture, Context*, Chicago: University of Chicago Press, 1996, pp. 56–82. See also p. 25 and pp. 283–4, notes 15, 17.
25. See Louis Adrian Montrose, "'The Place of a Brother' in *As You Like It*: Social Process and Comic Form," *Shakespeare Quarterly*, 1981, vol. 32, no. 1, pp. 33–4.
26. Parker, *Shakespeare*, p. 63 and note 16.
27. Schleiner adds, "[T]his is Shakespeare's most theological play" ("Providential Improvisation in *Measure for Measure*," *PMLA*, 1982, vol. 97, no. 2, 227–36, esp. p. 227).
28. Josephine Waters Bennett, Measure for Measure *as Royal Entertainment*, New York: Columbia University Press, 1966, pp. 72–3.
29. In the margin of Jesus' quotation of "an eye for an eye," one finds the comment "Albeit this was spoken for the judges, yet every man applied it to revenge his private quarrel."
30. See also Escalus's comment to Angelo at 2.1.9–17 and the Duke's reflection at 4.2.86–92.
31. For a most helpful analysis of the religious and political climate of England in 1603–4, see Lori Anne Ferrell, *Government by Polemic: James I, the King's Preachers, and the Rhetorics of Conformity, 1603–1625*, Stanford: Stanford University Press, 1998, esp. pp. 9–13, 46–7, 146–50, 168. See also Andrew

Barnaby and Joan Wry, "Authorized Versions: *Measure for Measure* and the Politics of Biblical Translation," *Renaissance Quarterly*, 1998, vol. 51, no. 4, 1225–54, esp. 1228–34. James's theological proclivities were well understood at the time. The Bishop of Winchester, in the preface to the *Works of James I* (1616), wrote that "Anciently Kings drempt dreames and saw visions; and Prophets expounded them./ In this age, Prophets have written Visions, and Kings have expounded them." I am grateful to Dr Owen Williams for this quotation and for helpful conversations on this topic

32. Daniell, "Reading the Bible," p. 169. Vincent Strudwick, pointing out that "the Geneva Bibles were the main resource for 'prophesyings,'" notes that Queen Elizabeth tried to suppress the group Bible studies, without success, and quotes a description of such a group, observed sometime in the decade between 1588 and 1598: "Each of them had his own Bible and assiduously turned pages and looked up the text cited by the preachers, discussing the passages among themselves to see whether they had quoted them to the point and accurately" ("English Fears of Social Disintegration and Modes of Control, 1533–1611," in Richard Griffiths [ed.] *The Bible in the Renaissance: Essays on Biblical Commentary and Translation in the Fifteenth and Sixteenth Centuries*, Aldershot: Ashgate, 2001, p. 142). The account of the prophesying which Strudwick quotes was written by William Weston in his autobiography published in 1611.

33. Daniell, "Reading the Bible," pp. 168–70.

34. As David Daniell puts it, " . . . Shakespeare makes large assumptions about the biblical understanding of his ordinary hearers and readers" ("Reading the Bible," p. 159).

3 Cain's Crime of Secrecy and the Unknowable Book of Life

The Complexities of Biblical Referencing in *Richard II*

Scott Schofield

The first of several Biblical allusions in Shakespeare's *Richard II* comes at the midpoint of the play's opening scene when Henry Bolingbroke accuses Thomas Mowbray of murdering the Duke of Gloucester:

> That he did plot the Duke of Gloucester's death,
> Suggest his soon-believing adversaries,
> And consequently, like a traitor coward,
> Sluiced out his innocent soul through streams of blood:
> Which blood, like sacrificing Abel's, cries,
> Even from the tongueless caverns of the earth,
> To me for justice and rough chastisement;
> And, by the glorious worth of my descent,
> This arm shall do it, or this life be spent. (1.1.100–8)[1]

Bolingbroke's accusation comes as part of a ritualistic exchange wherein the king acts as judge before presiding representatives from the Houses of York (Mowbray) and Lancaster (Bolingbroke and Gaunt). Since Bolingbroke assumes the role of appellant and Mowbray that of defendant, it is to be expected that Bolingbroke will *accuse* Mowbray. But how he accuses him is what is of interest to us here. By comparing the death of Gloucester to that of the Old Testament Abel, Bolingbroke forces us to read this particular medieval encounter in Biblical terms. Indeed, Shakespeare's decision to use this well-known moment from the Bible invites his readers to reevaluate the passage above and the larger Cain-Abel narrative in relation to several important themes from the first act. In this instance, readers are being asked not simply to recall the particulars of Genesis 4:8–10, but also to consider the larger commentary tradition behind this Biblical passage. By the late sixteenth century that commentary tradition was widespread in England, transmitted through the various editions of the Bible, as well as a range of printed genres including liturgies, catechisms, sermons, and polemics. When we attend to this tradition we begin to see the play differently. And when we accept that the Biblical allusions in *Richard II* are an essential part of the play's trajectory it is because we imagine the work as designed for readers well versed in early modern Biblical culture.

With this argument in mind let us return now to the Biblical allusion just cited, and let us begin where most critics do, with the unfinished analogue. If, according to the above passage, Gloucester is Abel, then who is Cain? The obvious answer is Mowbray, the *he* at whom Bolingbroke directs his accusation; however, there is good reason to think that Bolingbroke refers to Richard. One scene later Bolingbroke's father, John of Gaunt, will acknowledge Richard's complicity in the act during his argument with the Duchess of Gloucester. Is Gaunt's son really unaware of the king's involvement in the murder of Woodstock in the opening scene? I think not. Either way, one thing is certain: Shakespeare's contemporaries knew full well that while Mowbray was likely involved with the killing of Gloucester, it was Richard who was ultimately responsible for ordering the Duke's death.[2] In other words, while Bolingbroke may be pointing his finger at Mowbray, and all the while thinking of Richard's involvement in the crime, Shakespeare's readers would have had their sights set firmly on the king.

Turning to those sixteenth-century English works that deal with the Cain and Abel story provides additional evidence for making the Richard-Cain connection. Looking to these texts may seem obvious, but much of the criticism dealing with religion in the play, and particularly those studies examining Biblical allusion in *Richard II*, fail to engage adequately with these works and therefore ignore the precise cultural conditions in which readers of the time received the story. J.A. Bryant's and Stanley R. Maveety's important treatments of Biblical allusion in the play rightly use the Geneva Bible as a source for contextualizing the play, but they do not consider that Bible's printed marginalia, that is, its commentary, and therefore ignore what was an essential feature of the text.[3] Neither critic, moreover, has referenced any of the English printed commentaries on Genesis available at the time the play was produced, despite the fact that most of the editions of the Geneva Bible produced after 1579 advised readers to do so (as I will discuss below). In other words, while critics often consider a Biblical tradition in their readings of the play, that tradition is rarely explored with enough cultural specificity.

One way of alleviating this problem is by working closely with the range of religious genres available to Shakespeare and his readers in the 1590s, and in particular, by paying close attention to the paratexts found in these works, especially those notes and prefaces offering advice on how to read and apply the Scriptures. In looking more closely at the *mise-en-page* of the Geneva Bible in order to contextualize the Biblical allusions found in *Richard II*, this chapter follows Barbara Mowat's suggestion that we must pay close attention to "the particular Bible [Shakespeare] chose to read," and "the intensive mode" he employed when reading it.[4] This chapter complements Mowat's argument by turning to the separately printed Biblical commentaries and other overtly religious genres printed in England in the sixteenth-century, contending that the Geneva Bible and its apparati represent a vital starting point for Shakespeare and his readers.

I CAIN'S SINS AND GOD'S RESPONSE:
SECRECY, JUSTICE, AND EXILE

In the Geneva Bible the killing of Abel and the subsequent call to revenge his death takes place over two verses in Book 4 of Genesis: "And when they were in the fielde, Kain rose up against Habel his brother, and slew him" (4:8), and "the voice of thy brothers blood crieth unto me from the earth" (4:10).[5] These are the precise moments Bolingbroke alludes to in his commentary on the death of Gloucester. To read these verses in isolation is to confront a story of fratricide. One brother kills another, and consequently, revenge is sought. But the Cain and Abel story is more than a story of murder; it is also a story about justice, exile, and most of all secrecy. To identify Richard with Cain requires that we look to the whole of the Biblical story, and not just that moment explicitly alluded to in the play.

The strife between Cain and Abel is rooted in secrecy. God shows favor towards Abel, "the keeper of sheepe" over Cain, the "tiller of the ground" (4:2), because while Cain "brought an oblation vnto the Lorde, of the fruite of the ground," Abel [gave] the "first fruites of his sheepe and of the fat of them" (3–4). That God shows "no regard" (5) for Cain is not because of the size of the offering, but rather because of the spirit in which the offering is given. As the marginal note to "no regard" explains: "Because he was an hypocrite and offered onely for an outward shew without sinceritie of heart" (note d). While God will proceed to give Cain a chance to redeem himself, explaining that his offering will be accepted if Cain "do well" (7), Cain ignores God and kills his brother. Finally, when God questions Cain about his brother's whereabouts, he responds, with the most famous line from the story: "I cannot tell am I my brothers keeper?" (9). Although Cain's refusal to come clean about the killing marks the ultimate act of deception, what the commentator explains as "the nature of the reprobate . . . to neglect God and despite him" (note h), it is but one among many of Cain's acts of secrecy and concealment.

This concern over the secrecy of Cain's action, conveyed in the story and especially the notes of the Geneva Bible, is more strongly reiterated in the printed commentaries of the period. It makes sense to turn to these commentaries not least because it was suggested that readers do so in order to better understand the Scriptures. One of the Geneva Bible's paratexts, entitled "Howe to take profite by reading of the holy Scriptures," provides seven recommendations for users. Among these are guidelines for how readers should log, annotate, and apply the Scriptures. The seventh and final guideline in the list, and the one most relevant to my chapter, reads: "Take opportunitie to Reade interpreters[,] Conferre with such as can open the Scriptures[,] Heare preaching."[6] (See Figure 3.1) Such instructions were confirmed in the commentaries. In the preface to Gervase Babington's commentary on Genesis, which I discuss in more detail below, Miles Smith notes "I graunt the notes that we haue vpon our English Bybles are most sound and profitable: but they want applycation for the most part" (sig. a3v). In other words, readers of the Geneva Bible were expected to examine the text and notes on the page, but this was only a first step in the process. In an ideal scenario, readers would supplement their notes with lengthier exegesis. In order to "open the Scriptures," readers had to confer with printed commentaries or "interpreters" and attend sermons, i.e. "preaching."

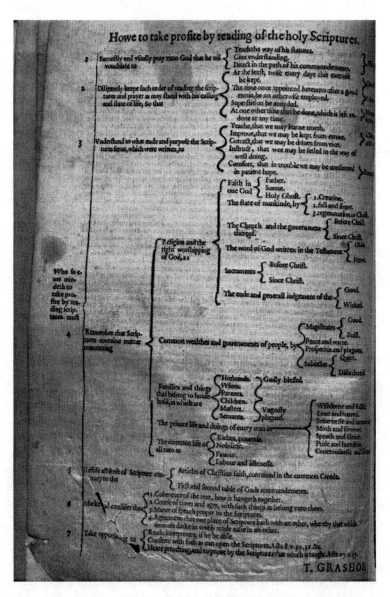

Figure 3.1   Paratextual advice on scriptural reading practices found in the Geneva Bible (London, 1594). Image courtesy of the Thomas Fisher Rare Book Library, University of Toronto.

Babington's commentary on the famous passage from Genesis 4:10, *Thy brothers bloud cryeth to mee (sayeth God) out of the earth*, provides a case in point. He writes:

> And doe wee hope secresie for want of witnesses? Alas wee are de-
> ceyued. The wickednesse it selfe will torment vs, as if a thousand
> knewe it. The conscience cannot be bribed to holde his peace, it will
> giue euidence do what we can. And the verie deede we haue doone
> will giue God no rest, but crie against vs till it be reuenged and we
> punished. If you knew your secret sinnes should bee cryed at the mar-
> ket crosse assoone as you haue doone them, you would bee afraide to
> sinne and take no comfort in the wante of witnesses, nor hope of rest
> by the secresie.[7]

Babington concludes: "Care not then for secresie if it bee euill: for if God see it and heare it, hee is priuie that can doe more to you then any man, euen Kill the soule as well as the body, and cast them both into Hell fire."[8] What is most fascinating here is that Babington all but ignores the act of murder. There is no commandment against killing, no moralizing over the immensity of the crime; instead the passage focuses entirely on the secrecy of Cain's actions and the subsequent suffering resulting from his defiance of God. Calvin's commentary on Genesis, first translated in 1578, simi-larly focuses on the secrecy of Cain's actions, indexed in the English edi-tion as "the colouring of Cain's fault."[9] In other words, when Bolingbroke evokes history's first murder he is reminding those present that the blood cries not only for revenge, but also because the crime remains shrouded in secrecy. When considered in this context Bolingbroke's allusion is directed squarely at the conscience of the king.

This point is reinforced by the fact that Bolingbroke assumes the role of God, or at least, as Harry Berger Jr. notes, "his surrogate."[10] Indeed, Bolingbroke's reference of "to me" in the quotation echoes the text of Genesis 4:10, which reads, "The voice of thy brothers blood cryeth vnto me from the grounde." Given the larger context of the play Bolingbroke's "to me" is ironic, for he will replace Richard as king and thus become, like the Genesis God evoked, administer of justice. Bolingbroke-God punishes Richard-Cain for the killing of Gloucester-Abel. Still, such divine aspira-tions are troubling, for by appropriating God's words, and particularly his right to revenge, Bolingbroke "presumes to do something that even as *microchristus* he could not expect to accomplish without committing the same sin he would avenge."[11] At the end of the play, as he wrestles with the part he plays in the death of Richard, he once again assumes the role of God from the Cain-Abel narrative, condemning Exton, "With Cain go wander through shades of night/ And never show thy head by day nor light" (5.6.43–4). The references to the Cain-Abel story do not end here; indeed, much of the first act is structured by it. Just as God punishes Cain with exile, so Richard banishes Mowbray and Bolingbroke. In *Richard II*, the Cain and Abel narrative is a global referent.[12]

Critical interest in the play's Biblical allusions is well established, and those scholars interested in the play's religion have routinely assessed the references cited above. What they have been less likely to do is look at the larger panorama of religious texts available to Shakespeare's readers in 1597, the year the first quarto of the play was printed. It is one thing to investigate the Biblical tradition behind the Cain and Abel story. It is quite another thing to examine that tradition by looking at the actual books available to Shakespeare's readers at the time: the text and sidenotes of the 1594 edition of the Geneva Bible and the exegesis provided by Calvin and Babington. Before I turn to the other Biblical allusions in *Richard II*, I want to consider some recent work on Shakespeare, religion, and the history of the book in order to probe the difficult question of how we measure reader reception of Shakespeare's plays in this period.

II SHAKESPEARE READING, READING SHAKESPEARE

When we envision Shakespeare working on his English history plays we usually imagine him sitting at a large desk surrounded by chronicles in both prose and verse—*The Mirror for Magistrates*, Samuel Daniel's *Civil Wars*, and Edward Halle's *Union of the Two Noble Families*, and at the center of the table the three-volume revised edition of Holinshed's *Chronicles of England, Scotland, and Ireland*. There is good reason to imagine this scenario, as we know Shakespeare consulted, borrowed, paraphrased, and reworked passages from these works for his drama. The evidence, here, is irrefutable: Shakespeare turned to the major English printed chronicles of his day for the central material required to write his medieval history plays.

But I want to consider a different scenario for Shakespeare as a reader working on *Richard II*. In this scenario, the chronicles have been shelved to make room for a new set of books. At the center of the table is a series of English Bibles, copies of each of the Geneva and Bishops' translations, and a copy of the Rheims New Testament. On one side of the Bibles lie a range of religious books: a copy of the *Book of Common Prayer*, the *Homilies*, the metrical psalms, as well as various commentaries and sermons; and on the other side of these books lie a range of political-religious imprints, including controversies and other polemics. In this imagined scenario Shakespeare is not borrowing material *per se*, except, of course for his Biblical citations, most of which derive, in modified form, from the Geneva Bible.[13] No, in this scenario Shakespeare is simply reading for ideas to help shape his play. When we imagine Shakespeare reading in this way we are simply acknowledging that he was, like many of the more educated playgoers and readers of his plays, one who read and engaged with the vast array of religious publications produced in early modern England.

That Shakespeare knew the Bible and repeatedly turned to it for his plays and poems is undeniable. But just how he processed the Scripture he received is more difficult to ascertain. Robert S. Miola speaks to this uncertainty in his more general comments on Shakespeare's reading: "Did Shakespeare remember the whole text and content or just a few lines? Did he, in the age of collection, commonplace, and anthology, ever read the whole text at all? Did some intermediary recall the original and pass it on to Shakespeare?"[14] Miola is not alone. Leonard Barkan reaches a similar conclusion when he exclaims, "we have no hard facts about Shakespeare the reader: no personal documents, no inventories, and no annotated volumes with his bookplate,"[15] and Jeff Dolven and Sean Keilen repeat the point by reminding us how little we know about the "physical particulars," the where, when, and how of Shakespeare's reading.[16]

The point here is clear: we don't know; we can't know. And while the admission is important, it doesn't stop us from attempting to recreate the scene. Miola, Barkan, Dolven, and Keilen all attempt to do so, even as they acknowledge the speculative nature of the pursuit. Indeed, some of the most provocative work in Shakespeare studies of late has focused on reconstructing early modern reading practices. Peter Stallybrass, in collaboration with others, has repeatedly turned to Shakespeare's plays and poems for such evidence. In what has become a seminal article on the subject, Stallybrass et al. offer a materialist explanation for Hamlet's famous reference to the "tables of my memory."[17] "Tables," in their argument, is a reference to early modern table books, those compact and erasable notebooks often bound with almanacs. The reference is important for it replaces a figurative reference with a materialist one. Hamlet's allusion to his tables reminds us of the object itself, a book where information is gathered and arranged to assist in the reading process. Stallybrass returned to *Hamlet* again with Zachary Lesser in 2008, but this time to examine the printed commas used as commonplace markers found in the first quarto of 1603.[18] Here again he showed how a Shakespeare play quarto was deliberately designed for readers. In using these markers for the speeches of Corambis/Polonius, for example, the text reminded readers of what was memorable and, in the commonplace tradition, what was worth noting. In both instances, Stallybrass has turned to material evidence to connect particular early modern reading practices to Shakespeare's plays. One of the reasons Shakespeare alluded to tablebooks and commonplace books in his plays may be because he used them himself; what is certain, however, is that many of his contemporaries certainly did. Before I return to the Biblical allusions in the play, I want to end this section by considering the prevalence of religious publications in those early modern libraries containing plays and poems of Shakespeare. Simply put, what else was the sixteenth-century reader of Shakespeare reading?

We must not forget that in England religious books formed the "single most important component of the publishing trade, comprising around half of the output of the industry."[19] While part of that output was produced by and for religious professionals—the bishops, ministers, and other church officials who constituted the church hierarchy—many of these printed books were marketed for those who comprised the remainder of the demographic. Those who read and purchased literary works, Shakespeare and his readers included, also read and purchased religious works. In other words, many of those who read *Richard II* in 1597 would have been familiar with the interpretations of Genesis previously discussed, and while not all readers of the first quarto of *Richard II* would have had the commentaries of Babington, Calvin, and Perkins in front of them as they read the play, most would have been familiar, like Shakespeare, with the exegesis of these books.

How then do we test this assertion? One way is by looking to the private libraries of Shakespeare's contemporaries, particularly those individuals who owned literary works, and especially those who owned the plays and or poems of Shakespeare. Edward Dering,[20] for example, owned two copies of Shakespeare's plays (1623), Jonson's *Works* (1616), a copy of both Sidney's *Arcadia* and Chaucer's *Works,* and no less than two hundred unspecified "playbooks." Needless to say, Dering liked his literature, but looking at the remainder of the more than 600 books in the inventory we discover that Dering also liked his religion—religion makes up the highest percentage of books from his library. Included among these books are Bibles, New and Old Testaments, multiple copies of the *Book of Common Prayer,* a copy of the Homilies, a concordance, several different surveys of church history, patristic writings, as well as a range of sermons, dialogues and polemics. While Dering owned books that defended the Elizabethan church settlement, including copies of Whitgift's *Defense* and Hooker's *Ecclessiastical Polity*, he also owned tracts by Catholic recusants, including the writings of Robert Parsons and Richard Verstegan. His religious reading was extensive, but also diverse.

Richard Stonley, "one of the four Tellers of the Exchequer of Receipt from 1554–1600," offers another good example.[21] Stonley's books, like Dering's, are recorded in multiple sources, including an inventory of 1597 and a series of account books with chronological entries for the years 1581–1582, 1593–1594, and 1597–1598. Interest in Stonley's library has resulted in part because he purchased a copy of *Venus and Adonis* only two months after it had been entered in the Stationers' Register.[22] While there are no other titles by Shakespeare in Stonley's lists, there are multiple entries simply marked pamphlets, and one for interludes and comedies;[23] thus, it is more than possible that other Shakespeare titles were part of his library. What is certain is that he read other literature, as he owned copies of works by Greene, Lodge, and Gascoigne, editions of Virgil and Cicero in both English and Latin, and a number of literary works in French, Italian, and Spanish.[24] And also like Dering, Stonley's library was "dominated by spiritual concerns," with Bibles, commentaries, and other religious books making up no less than 40 per cent of the 413 books.[25] Finally, while the majority of Stonley's religious books aligned with the official church orthodoxy, others, especially the imprints authored by Catholic writers, did not.[26]

And Dering and Stonley were not alone. Many of those who collected the plays of Shakespeare and his contemporaries, including John Harrington, Scipio Squyer, Thomas Barrington, and Robert Burton, also owned numerous religious imprints.[27] A number of these collectors often catalogued their religious imprints alongside playbooks and other seemingly less-serious reading mater.[28] This physical arrangement is important, for it reminds us of the predisciplinarity of the early modern English library.

Since the inventories of private libraries were produced largely by nobility, they provide us with only partial evidence for measuring the readership and collecting habits of early modern English society as a whole; they take no account of the "middling sort"—that large segment of the English population who purchased play quartos but did not catalogue them. And yet these inventories do confirm that the plays and poems were in the hands of educated readers. One of those readers, Gabriel Harvey, has reminded us, in a now-famous line that he inscribed in his copy of Thomas Speght's edition of Chaucer's *Workes* (London, 1598), that Shakespeare did qualify as serious reading: "his Lucrece, & his tragedie of Hamlet, prince of Denmark, have it in them, to please the wiser sort."[29] This comment is significant not least because it is one of the earliest references to the reception of Shakespeare's works, and while Shakespeareans often cite it, they often forget that Harvey made similar comments on philosophers, astronomers, and religious divines. The same Harvey who praised Shakespeare and other poets also, for example, praised John Jewel and Thomas Harding as "two thundring and lightning Orators in diuinity."[30] In focusing entirely on Harvey's reference to Shakespeare literary scholars reduce a polymath to a literary footnote.

Having said that, it is more than possible that Harvey was interested primarily in the literary merits of Shakespeare's plays and poems. At least one early reader of *Richard II* examined the play in these terms. Writing in the late 1590s, William Scot's treatise on poetry examines the conceits, allusions, and other aspects of poetic style in *Richard II*, sometimes disdainfully, in what Stanley Wells has described as "the earliest precise close criticism of Shakespeare's style."[31] That other readers of the period approached the play in these terms is likely. Some readers of *Richard II*, for example, might have been reminded by analogues in the recent work of Shakespeare, including his *Lucrece* (1594). The reference to Abel's blood crying from the earth is reminiscent of Lucrece's suicidal blood as it, too, serves as a testimonial of the crime committed against her.[32] Similarly, references to blotting in *Richard II*, which I discuss in the next section in relation to the Biblical book of life, find an echo in Tarquin's consideration of the long-term consequences of rape, especially when he imagines his coat of arms being blotted by the cipher as punishment for the crime. That some readers read *Richard II* this way is more than conceivable.

Reading by its very nature is both idiosyncratic and culturally informed. My point is simply that those sixteenth- and early seventeenth-century readers of Shakespeare's plays and poems were the same men and women who read the Bible and other religious publications and listened to sermons at church and in open pulpits. The question then is not if, but rather how and to what extent did this constant exposure to religion influence reading of all kinds in the period, including plays. In the final section of this paper I will return to another recurring Biblical allusion in *Richard II*, but this time I will examine one that is more complicated than the Cain and Abel reference I started with. As I return to the relationship between *Richard II* and the Scriptures, I do so with the readers previously cited in mind; I turn to the play as Richard Stonley would, as one who in cataloguing his books made no attempt to separate his literature from his religion. But first I begin with Shakespeare as Biblical reader.

III   MY NAME BE BLOTTED FROM THE BOOK OF LIFE

In act 1 scene 3, just moments after Richard has banished Mowbray and Bolingbroke, Bolingbroke makes one final plea to Mowbray to come clean and confess his crimes.

> As now our flesh is banished from this land.
> Confess thy treasons ere thou fly the realm.
> Since thou hast far to go, bear not along
> The clogging burthen of a guilty soul.

Mowbray replies,

> No, Bolingbroke. If ever I were traitor,
> My name be blotted from the book of life,
> And I from heaven banished as from hence!
> But what thou art, God, thou and I do know;
> And all too soon, I fear, the king shall rue. (1.3.197–205)

Mowbray's Biblical reference is well chosen, for in evoking the book of life he complements Richard's earthly exile with a spiritual equivalent. Later in the play, Richard will allude to the same Biblical image, "Marked with a blot, damned in the book of heaven" (4.1.236), during the pivotal scene when Northumberland asks him to recount his crimes. Picking up on the cultural resonances of the passage, I want to consider three interrelated questions. Where does the reference derive from in the Bible; how was it interpreted in commentaries of the period; and how do the answers to these two questions change the way we interpret the scene?

Unlike the Genesis story of Cain and Abel, Mowbray's reference to the book of life is more difficult to pinpoint in the Bible. There are at least three places in Scripture from where it may derive, two from the Old Testament and one from the New:

Exodus 32:33	Then the Lord sayd to Moses, Whosoeuer hath sinned against me, I will put him out of my booke.
Psalms 69:28	Let them bee put out of the booke of life, neither let them be written with the righteous.
Revelation 3:5	He that ouercommeth shalbe clothed in white aray, and I will not put out his name out of the Booke of life, but I will confesse his Name before my Father, and before his Angels.[33]

Most critics contend that since Shakespeare uses the word "blotted" here he must have the verse from Revelation in mind. The reasoning is based on the fact that while Shakespeare turned repeatedly to the Geneva translation when paraphrasing Scripture in the play, in this one instance he used the Bishops' Bible, for only there could he find the word blot. "I will not put out his name" in the Geneva is replaced by "I will not blot out his name" in the Bishops'. (See Figures 3.2 and 3.3)[34] As Hannibal Hamlin summarizes,

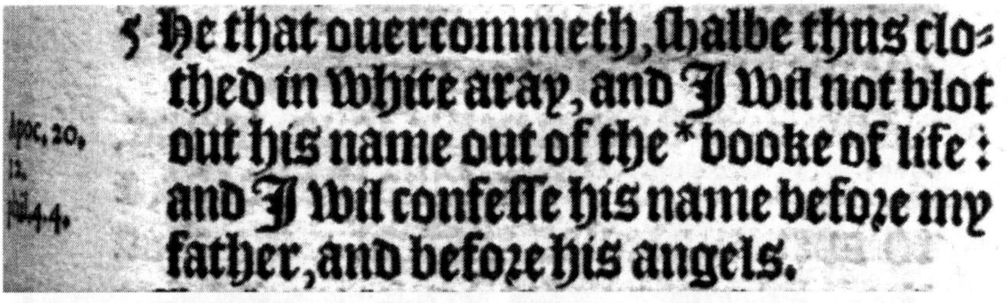
5 He that ouercommeth, shalbe thus clo-
thed in white aray, and I wil not blot
out his name out of the *booke of life:
and I wil confesse his name before my
father, and before his angels.

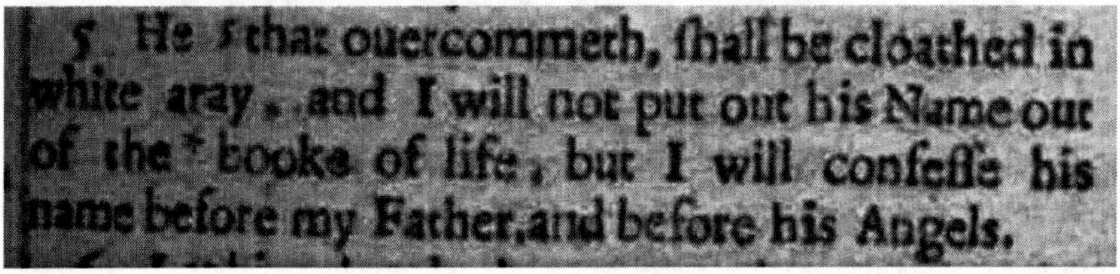
5 He that ouercommeth, shall be cloathed in
white aray, and I will not put out his Name out
of the * booke of life, but I will confesse his
name before my Father, and before his Angels.

Figure 3.2 and 3.3 From Revelation 3.5. Upper image with *blot out* from the Bishops' translation (London, 1585) and lower image with *put out* from the Geneva translation (London, 1594). Both images courtesy of the Thomas Fisher Rare Book Library.

"It is clear therefore that Shakespeare was reading the Bible on his own in the Geneva translation, but also hearing the Bishops in church."[35] Hamlin's logic makes sense. The Bishops' Bible—so called because it was overseen by Matthew Parker and other Church of England officials—was the Bible placed in all English churches and therefore the Bible read aloud to parishioners. It is a large and expensive folio, which unlike the Geneva Bible, was not suitable for private study.[36] The only way a layperson like Shakespeare could access the Bishops' translation of "blot out his name" was by hearing it in church.

This theory rests on a well-worn assumption that asserts that when Shakespeare needed a Biblical reference he turned to the various English translations of the Bible, compared them, and then chose which was best. The problem with this theory is it ignores the range of religious publications available to Shakespeare at the time, the printed commentaries, sermons, and other religious works of the period that often present translations of Scripture that differ from those found in the Bibles of the day. Was Shakespeare unaware of these alternative translations? I think not, and to prove this point I want to examine the prevalence of the phrase *blotted* in conjunction with *book of life* as found in English sixteenth-century religious works. A quick search of EEBO offers surprising discoveries. Not only had these phrases been used in tandem prior to the Bishops' translation, and not only had they been used regularly in connection with the Exodus, Psalms, and Revelation verses cited above, but they also had been used largely by authors with Calvinist leanings, those individuals whom we would expect to rely on the Geneva translation.

The phrase *blotted out of the book of life* first appears in the 1530s, in two works by George Joye: his polemical response to Thomas More and his edition of the psalter.[37] Both occurrences are noteworthy, for while they predate the Bishops' reading by more than thirty years, neither of them is made in relation to Revelation. Joye alludes to Exodus 32:33 when using the phrase in his polemical tract (sig. H4v) and offers the following translation in his edition of the psalter: "Let them be blotted oute of the boke of lyfe /& let them in no wise be written with the rightwyse" (sig. H3r). Subsequent adoptions of the phrasing appeared occasionally in works over the next three decades, one of the most interesting coming in 1561 as part of the first translation of Calvin's *The Institvtion of Christian Religion*. In a reference to Psalm 69:28, the translator, Thomas Norton, offers the following: "Wherefore Dauid coulde not deuise a more greuous curse than this: Let them be blotted out of the boke of life, and not be written with the righteous" (K2r).[38] (See Figure 3.4) How did Norton come up with the phrase? Did he know of Joye's edition of the Psalms? If he consulted the Geneva Bible, first published one year earlier, he clearly ignored its use of *put*; moreover, in choosing *blot* he opted for a distinctively English word, one that differed from Calvin's French *effacez* and Latin *deleantur*.[39]

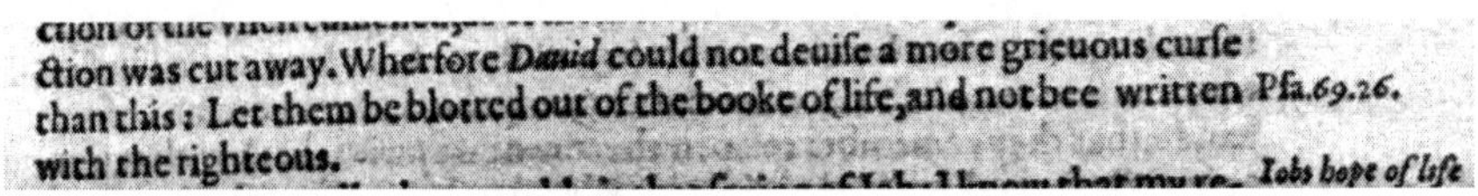

> &ction was cut away.Wherfore *Dauid* could not deuiſe a more grieuous curſe
> than this : Let them be blotted out of the booke of life,and not bee written Pſa.69.26.
> with the righteous.   *Iobs hope of life*

Figure 3.4   From Thomas Norton's translation of Calvin's *The institution of Christian religion* (London, 1587). The phrase *blotted from the booke of life* appeared in the first edition of 1561 and all subsequent editions. Image courtesy of the Thomas Fisher Rare Book Library.

We will never know exactly why Norton or Shakespeare chose the word *blotted*, nor exactly where they turned to for it; what we do know, however, is that they did not have to read or listen to the Bible to find the phrase *blotted out of the book of life*, for this particular Biblical rendering matched those found in other printed religious genres of the day. Simply, then, the Bible in Early Modern England was not limited to a select number of editions; it was everywhere in print, scattered, paraphrased, and often newly translated by any author guiding readers to the Scriptures.

I want to conclude by looking at how the *book of life* was typically interpreted by exegetes in the period and how these interpretations influence our reading of the passages on the book of life in the play. In his *Sermons vpon the Whole Booke of the Reuelation*[40] George Gifford questioned the very logic of Revelation 3:5, particularly the conditional nature of the book of life by arguing that "the saying here vsed may seeme to be superfluous . . . seeing Gods decree is vnchangeable, and no one of Gods elect, whose names are written up, can be blotted out" (G5r). Calvin would make a similar claim in his commentaries on the Psalms when he noted:

> the booke of lyfe is nothing else, then the eternall purpose of GOD, whereby he hath predestinate his children to saluacion. Sure it is, that nothing can be chaunged in it. Agein, wee knowe, that those, which are adopted too the hope of saluacion, were written before the creation of the world. (KK6v–KK7r)[41]

In line with Calvin's interpretation, William Perkins questions the reasoning behind David's wish for "his enemies to be blotted out of the booke of life" by replying, "Davids enemies had not their names written in the booke of life, but only in the iudgement of men" (Y6r).[42] Whether they referenced Revelation 3:5 or Psalms 69:28, most English commentators emphasized the Calvinist underpinnings connected to the book of life, particularly that the elect have been predestined and thus chosen by God at the beginning of time. Any gestures to being removed from the book, be they spoken by Moses, David, or God himself, thus cannot be understood literally.

How then do we interpret Mowbray's "No, Bolingbroke. If ever I were traitor,/ My name be blotted from the book of life,/ And I from heaven banished as from hence!" Read within the Calvinist tradition, such a remark could be read as fraudulent rhetoric, as a false promise, since any attempt at deciphering what the book of life is and who belongs within it is beyond human comprehension. But if seen in Catholic terms, terms that imagine salvation through works, then Mowbray's remark is legitimate. As the annotation to this passage in the Rheims edition explains:

> In al these speaches to diuers Bishops and their Churches, he continu-
> ally encourageth them to constancie in faith and good life, by setting
> before their eies the revvard of the next life. And yet the Caluinists
> vvould haue no man do good in respect of such revvard. (4v1v)[43]

Read in either Catholic or Calvinist terms, one thing is for certain: comments on the book of life were readily made in the wide range of religious publications of the day—so available that any reader of the play alert to its Biblical resonances could not ignore the larger exegesis circulating in print at the time.

This paper has argued that if we are to understand the function of Biblical allusion in *Richard II* we must look not only at the Bibles of the period, but other religious genres as well. The commentaries by Babington, Calvin, and Gifford, for example, provided readers of the time access to a more extensive and complex exegetical frame of reference than that offered in even the most annotated of editions available at the time. The fact that readers of Shakespeare often owned and read such religious works is reason enough for us to look to these genres as a possible key to elucidate certain moments in the play. These commentaries, moreover, sometimes offered their own distinct Biblical readings which differed from those found in the Bibles of the day, thus reminding us how these genres participated in the act of Biblical translation. When we imagine a reader, circa 1597, sitting down to read *Richard II,* we need not think of him or her consulting religious works as he reads, but we should think of that reader as one who was aware of the rich interpretative contexts of both Cain's crime of secrecy and the unknowable essence of the book of life.

NOTES

1. This and all subsequent references to the play are from Charles Forker (ed.) *Richard II*, London: Arden, 2002.
2. See for example Raphael Holinshed, *Chronicles*, vol. 3, London, 1587, pp. 488–9.
3. J.A. Bryant, "The Linked Analogies of *Richard II*," *Sewanee Review*, 1957, vol. 65, no. 3, 420–33; Stanley R. Maveety, "A Second Fall of Cursed Man: The Bold Metaphor in *Richard II*," *Journal of English and Germanic Philology*, 1973, vol. 72, no. 2, 175–93. One important exception is Adrian Streete's chapter on political typology in *Richard II*. Streete considers both Calvin's sermons and his commentaries in a compelling examination of the Biblical allusions in the play. See Adrian Streete, "Shakespeare on Golgotha: Political Typology in *Richard II*," in *Protestantism and Drama in Early Modern England*, Cambridge: Cambridge University Press, 2009, pp. 162–99.

4. See, in this volume, "Shakespeare Reads the Geneva Bible," [INTERNAL REF: pp. 27, 33].
5. This and all subsequent references are to the 1594 edition of *The Bible*, London, 1594, STC 2163.
6. This paratext was included in select editions of the Geneva Bible after 1579, including the 1594 edition I have been citing. See sig. pi2v. William Sherman discusses this paratext and other forms of instruction in his chapter on Biblical reading in the early modern period. See his *Used Books: Marking Readers in Renaissance England*, Philadelphia: University of Pennsylvania Press, 2008, pp. 71–85.
7. Gervase Babington, *Certaine plaine, briefe, and comfortable notes, vpon euerie chapter of Genesis . . . in sundry places enlarged with some additions*, London, 1596, STC 1087, sig. E1r. An earlier edition of this work appeared in 1592.
8. Ibid., sig. E1r.
9. See *A commentarie of Iohn Caluine, vpon the first booke of Moses called Genesis: translated out of Latine into English, by Thomas Tymme*, London, 1578, esp. sig. I5v–I6v.
10. For this comment and his extensive reading of the opening scenes of the play, see Harry Berger Jr., "Psychoanalyzing the Shakespeare Text: The First Three Scenes of the 'Henriad'" in *Making Trifles of Terrors: Redistributing Complicities in Shakespeare*, ed. Peter Erickson, Stanford: Stanford University Press, 1997, pp. 148–167, p. 154.
11. Bryant, "Linked Analogies," p. 431. Stanley R. Maveety similarly notes that Bolingbroke "takes upon himself the administration of justice appropriate only for God." See his "A Second Fall," p. 179.
12. Steven Marx's comments on allusion are appropriate here: "In either alluding or evoked text, the link may apply only to a phrase or globally to the work's overall theme and structure." (*Shakespeare and the Bible*, Oxford: Oxford University Press, 2000, p. 13.)
13. On the relationship between misquotation and poetic style in Shakespeare's plays, see Julie Maxwell, "How the Renaissance (Mis)Used Sources: The Art of Misquotation," in Laurie Maguire (ed.) *How to do Things with Shakespeare: New Approaches, New Essays*, Oxford: Blackwell, 2009, pp. 54–76; on Shakespeare's misquoting of the Bible see esp. pp. 63–70.
14. Robert S. Miola, *Shakespeare's Reading*, Oxford: Oxford University Press, 2001, pp. 13–14.
15. Leonard Balkan, "What did Shakespeare Read?" in Margreta de Grazia and Stanley Wells (eds) *The Cambridge Companion to Shakespeare*, Cambridge: Cambridge University Press, 2001, p. 31.
16. Jeff Dolven and Sean Keilen, "Shakespeare's Reading," in Margreta de Grazia and Stanley Wells (eds) *The New Cambridge Companion to Shakespeare*, 2nd ed., Cambridge: Cambridge University Press, 2010, p. 28.
17. Peter Stallybrass, Roger Chartier, John Franklin Mowery and Heather Wolfe, "Hamlet's Tables and the Technologies of Writing in Renaissance England," *Shakespeare Quarterly*, 2004, vol. 55, no. 4, 379–419.
18. Zachary Lesser and Peter Stallybrass, "The First Literary *Hamlet* and the Commonplacing of Professional Plays," *Shakespeare Quarterly*, 2008, vol. 59, no. 4, 371–420.
19. Patrick Collinson, Alexandra Walsham, and Arnold Hunt, "Religious Publishing in England, 1557–1640," in John Barnard and D.F. McKenzie (eds) *The Cambridge History of the Book in Britain*, vol. IV: *1557–1695*, Cambridge: Cambridge University Press, 2002, p. 29.

20. Nati H. Krivatsy and Laetitia Yeandle, "Books of Sir Edward Dering of Kent (1598–1644)," in R.J. Feherenbach and E.S. Leedham-Green (eds) *Private Libraries of Renaissance England (PLRE): A Collection and Catalogue of Tudor and Early Stuart Book-Lists*, vol. 4, Binghamton, NY: Medieval and Renaissance Texts and Studies, 1995, pp. 136–269.

21. Jason Scott-Warren, "Books in the Bedchamber: Religion, Accounting and the Library of Richard Stonley," in John N. King (ed.) *Tudor Books and Readers: Materiality and the Construction of Meaning*, Cambridge: Cambridge University Press, 2010, p. 236.

22. Ibid.

23. Ibid., pp. 238–9.

24. Ibid., pp. 238–42.

25. Ibid., p. 239.

26. Ibid., pp. 245–6.

27. For a fuller discussion of early modern English collectors of playtexts, see Lukas Erne, *Shakespeare as Literary Dramatist*, Cambridge: Cambridge University Press, 2003, pp. 12–4, and Alan H. Nelson, "Shakespeare and the Bibliophiles: From the Earliest Years to 1616," in Robin Myers, Michael Harris, and Giles Mandelbrote (eds) *Owners, Annotators and the Signs of Reading*, New Castle: Oak Knoll Press, and and London: British Library, 2005, pp. 49–73.

28. Erne, *Shakespeare*, p. 14 and Scott-Warren, "Books in the Bedchamber," pp. 238, 240.

29. BL Add. MS.42518, f. 422v. See http://www.bl.uk/treasures/shakespeare/playhamlet.html. Accessed 10 May 2011. The shelfmark and website are taken from Lesser and Stallybrass, "The First Literary *Hamlet*," p. 394.

30. See *Pierces Supererogation or A New Prayse of the Old Asse*, London, 1593, sig. B4r. Harvey would praise Jewel on a subsequent occasion by placing him among the likes of Chaucer. The comment, which comes in a marginal note to his copy of Quintillian, is cited in Virginia F. Stern, *Gabriel Harvey: His Life, Marginalia and Library*, Oxford: Clarendon Press, 1979, p. 149.

31. Stanley Wells discusses the recently rediscovered manuscript in his essay "A New Early Reader of Shakespeare," in Richard Meek, Jane Rickard, and Richard Wilson (eds) *Shakespeare's Book: Essays in Reading, Writing and Reception*, Manchester: Manchester University Press, 2008, p. 236.

32. On this point, see William P. Weaver, "'O teach me how to make mine own excuse': Forensic Performance in *Lucrece*," *Shakespeare Quarterly*, 2008, vol. 59, no. 4, 421–49.

33. All references are to the Geneva translation.

34. For a list of the Biblical references in the play see Naseeb Shaheen, *Biblical References in Shakespeare's Plays*, Newark, NJ: University of Delaware Press, 1999, pp. 360–89. Charles Forker lists all three of the above passages as possible referents for Shakespeare's two allusions to the book of life, but he leans towards Revelation as the most likely referent. See Forker's note to 4.1.l.236.

35. Hannibal Hamlin, "William Shakespeare," in Rebecca Lemon et al. (eds) *The Blackwell Companion to the Bible in English Literature*, Oxford: Blackwell, 2009, p. 226; Shaheen, *Biblical References* pp. 41–2.

36. An inscription in one of the copies of the Bishops' Bible, London, 1585, STC 2143 at the Thomas Fisher Rare Book Library at the University of Toronto testifies to this fact. It reads "This Byble was bought in Aprill in the xxixth yere of the reigne of [her] most gracious majesty Queene Elizabeth an[n]o d[omi]ni 1587 and yt cost xliiiis. Thomas Warylow and John Parker." Sig. 2Y3r. Shelfmark: knox f00303.

37. *The Subuersio[n] of Moris False Foundacion* [Antwerp] 1534. STC 14829; *The Psalter of Dauid in Englyshe* [London] 1534. STC 2371.

38. London, 1561. STC 4415.

39. *Institution de la Religion Chrestienne*, [Geneve], 1564, sig. q5r; *Institutio Christianae Religionis* [Geneve], 1561, sig. r6r.

40. London, 1596. STC 11866.

41. *The Psalmes of Dauid and others*, [London], 1571. STC 4395.

42. *An Exposition of the Symbole or Creede of the Apostles*, Cambridge, 1596. STC 19704.

43. *The Nevv Testament of Iesus Christ*, Rheims, 1582. STC 2884.

4 Paulina, Corinthian Women, and the Revisioning of Pauline and Early Modern Patriarchal Ideology in *The Winter's Tale*

Randall Martin

Among Shakespeare's periodic references to St Paul, Paulina in *The Winter's Tale* may be the most complex and revealing. An invented character with no equivalent in the play's source, Robert Greene's *Pandosto*, she becomes Shakespeare's main voice of rational moral authority: first as she defends Hermione against the sexual slander of Leontes; and then, after the king has belatedly acknowledged his error, as his political and spiritual counselor in anticipation of a spectacular reconciliation with his "dead" wife and abandoned daughter. In appearing prominently towards the end of Shakespeare's career in a play that self-consciously re-examines many of the themes and structures of his earlier works, Paulina has the potential to illuminate the interpretive significance of other Shakespearian allusions to Paul, and the nature of the playwright's imaginative and critical engagements with scripture in general.

Leontes's violent antagonism towards Hermione and Paulina reflects issues of female public speech, sexual chastity, and their regulation by male authorities that directly connect the play to late sixteenth- and early seventeenth-century controversies over women's conduct and alleged encroachment on masculine roles. As members of Shakespeare's audience knew from these and other debates of the period, one repeatedly cited authority for restricting female behavior was Paul. Spectators or readers of *The Winter's Tale* would have quickly recognized that Shakespeare's decision to choose a woman named Paulina to oppose Leontes's Pauline-related misogyny was deliberately provocative.

Beyond cheekily inverting Paul, however, it becomes less clear what possible effects this recognition could have had in terms of redrawing the traditional image of Paul's negativity towards women and the patriarchal ideology it authorized by virtue of scripture's status as divine revelation. Since Leontes is representative of Pauline-derived opinions but also obviously mistaken in his jealousy, his dramatic function as a divinely rebuked tyrant would seem to contain any culturally transformative work that Paulina's and Hermione's subversion of patriarchal assumptions might achieve amongst original or later audiences. This delimited situation appears to persist into the play's final act. The gendered hostility characterizing

Leontes and Paulina's encounters recedes in favor of the latter's demonstration through Hermione of the healing powers of visual art and the affective female body—subjects not commonly associated with Paul. Moreover, Leontes's power as king is not only restored but also seems to resume arbitrary sway in commanding Paulina's marriage to Camillo.

To reach beyond the play's apparent containment of Pauline subversion, audiences would have to perceive that Leontes is not merely a tragic-comic exaggeration of Pauline attitudes, or Paulina simply an ironic device to correct them before a chastened but still-dominant patriarchal order is reinstalled. Rather they would have to recognize that the play's gender conflicts originate in contradictions in scripture itself, and that these discrepancies call into question the culturally constructed authority of Paul's antipathy to women and the suppression of early modern female speech it sanctioned. These insights would involve turning Paulina's words and actions into an analytical tool for re-examining Paul's letters—not as revealed-for-all-time doctrines mandating universal female subordination, but as contingent arguments made in response to situations of local resistance to Paul's commands. This historicizing epistemology would also convert Paul's apostolic author-function into a discursively generative one open to critical reinvention.[1]

This essay will explore the ways in which *The Winter's Tale* invited early modern readers and spectators to reread both Paul's letters and paratextual discourses such as the Geneva bible's marginalia from these controversial perspectives. Paulina's exchanges with Leontes both mimic and subvert Paul's objections to the public conduct of first-century women in 1 Corinthians and other New Testament letters. Rhetorically the play's connections to Paul's words and ideas take dramatically reworked forms such as parody, inversion, and paradox. Thus, in terms of its relationship to scripture, *The Winter's Tale*'s references to Paul operate not simply as allusions or citations but as adaptations signifying both similarities to and departures from his writings and the early modern social order authorized by them. The conventional term *allusion* suggests a unidirectional relationship between the biblical source and Shakespeare's text. It also implies interpretive deference towards Paul's writings based on the received understanding of scripture as a transcendent unifying hermeneutic (i.e., the Word of God). This traditional interpretive practice constructs the material and semantic form of Paul's "book" as a closed, static, and authoritarian monument. By contrast the adaptive mode, as modern theorists have shown, is intertextually dialogic. It aims for an "open book" that resists interpretive closure and reconceives source-use and reception as starting-points for a process of interdependent re-creation. Shakespeare's dramatic adaptations of Pauline discourse accordingly heighten the visibility of the rhetorically patterned and historically contingent scriptural text, defamiliarize its ideologically occluding modes of signification, and challenge its revelatory authority as apostolic discourse.[2]

At the same time the adaptive mode establishes the possibility of seeing the wider action of *The Winter's Tale* as a re-visioning of Paul's rhetoric and ideology that articulates the alternative integrity of his Corinthian opponents. Just as they asserted the freedom and sanctity of the female body through their ecstatic worship, Paulina's presentation of Hermione combines boldness of female speech with affective corporality to overturn Paul's objections to both as patriarchally subversive and inherently idolatrous. Analogizing the assumptions of first-century women in Corinth, Ephesus, and other Mediterranean centers of cross-cultural spirituality, Paulina and Hermione reconnect the regenerative powers of the female body to spiritual (re-)creation in the physical world through the kinetic energy and affective performativity of their stage action. Their holistic practice is symbolically enabled by the statue's coming-to-life in Paulina's chapel. As a space of domestic worship, it recalls the first-century house-churches under female leadership mentioned by Paul in Corinthians and elsewhere, but whose varying customs he viewed as threats to his centralizing authority. While directing spectators and readers to rediscover the textually subordinated but retrievable evidence of Corinthian practices, Hermione and Paulina rejoin free speech and physical expression as truth to the female body. Their actions reverse the dematerializing logocentrism of Paul and his traditional interpreters that dissociate women from unmediated or authentic access to grace and political power. They also negotiate Sicily's formal reversion to patriarchal kingship on the new basis of collaboratively reinterpreting the past to arrive at a more equitably determining social narrative in the present. By inviting readers and spectators to join them in reassessing scriptural textuality through adaptation, Paulina and Hermione also encourage present-day critics to remodel the conventionally undynamic concept of Shakespearian biblical allusion.

I

From the outset *The Winter's Tale* makes clear the relationship between persuasive speech and social power; from Polixenes's opening response to Leontes's request to stay longer ("There is no tongue that moves, none, none i'th'world, / So soon as yours could win me"); to Leontes's transfer of this task to Hermione ("Tongue-tied, our queen? Speak you"); to Hermione's claim to equal powers of verbal authority ("a lady's 'verily' 's / As potent as a lord's) (1.2.20–1, 27, 49–50). Hermione convinces Polixenes to extend his visit through her articulate wit and bodily presence as a late-term pregnant queen (1.2). Her verbal and physical charisma recalls both the Humanist paradigm of the "learned lady" and the performative imperatives of courtesy theory, both of which encouraged displays of female learning and rhetorical skill in particular social contexts such as religious writing or participation in court activities.[3] But either in print or at court such displays also breached traditional restrictions on female public display that served as a register of masculine honor. Hermione transgresses conventional early modern ideals of chastity and silence by playfully pretending to misunderstand Leontes's implied call to bring her opening conversation with Polixenes to a close, and then by soliciting an unlooked-for show of prowess from her husband as a verbal competitor:

Leontes:	Hermione, my dearest, thou never spok'st
	To better purpose.
Hermione:	Never?
Leontes:	Never but once.
Hermione:	What, have I twice said well? When was't before?
	I prithee tell me; cram's with praise, and make's
	As fat as tame things . . . (1.2.87–91)

This verbal dare also inadvertently emblematizes the link between fulsome female speech and sexual heat when Hermione returns to chatting and holding hands with Polixenes. In the first of three increasingly twisted monologues ("Too hot, too hot!), Leontes reads her conduct as signs of mingling "friendship" and "bloods" (1.2.108). He attempts to rechannel his suspicions in an awkwardly playful but reproving conversation with Mamillus full of patrilineal anxiety, but again slips into another self-tormenting rumination ("Affection!—thy intention stabs the centre" [1.2.138]). Visually his brooding looks startle Hermione and Polixenes out of their conversation and implicitly seek to reestablish control over his wife's speech.[4] But Hermione continues her unselfconscious banter with Polixenes in the garden, leaving Leontes to justify his full-blown jealousy after the manner of Shakespearian misogynists such as Iago and Angelo and theological ones such as Paul and Augustine: Hermione's "infidelity" represents the "destined livery" of womankind, with husbands becoming the victims of their irrepressible appetites.

Although Leontes's jealousy is rationally unfounded, its prejudices were consistent with what Stephen Orgel terms "the cultural currency of the age, articulated continually in sermons and pamphlets."[5] Such publications looked to traditional interpretations of St Paul's letters, with whose social contexts—Hellenistic Judaism and first-century Greek and Roman society—Jacobean England shared highly negative views of unregulated female behavior. As Karen Jo Torjesen explains of Hellenistic Mediterranean culture:

A woman's reputation rested on her sexuality, on a public demonstration that she was sexually exclusive. Shame[fastness], the defining quality of womanhood, meant that a woman understood her sexual vulnerability and was careful to avoid all appearances of sexual indiscretion.[6]

Fearing that English women were violating the same decorum, King James commanded public "tirades against 'the insolency of our women'" through the Bishop of London and his clergy.[7] Paul was their natural model, since he had associated female speech and physical display with threats to patriarchal authority and denounced local women on these grounds in early Christian communities. The most famous of these reproofs was addressed to Corinth:

> Let your women kepe silence in the Churches: for it is not permitted vnto them to speake: but *they oght* to be subiect, as also the Law saith.
>   And if thei wil learne anie thing, let them aske their housbands at home: for it is a shame for women to speake in ye Church. (14.34–5; original italics)[8]

After separating Mamillus from his mother, Leontes tries to compensate for the shame he feels as a husband and a king by mimicking the same rebuking mode, lashing Hermione with vehement speeches (and Shakespeare neologisms; *viz.* "bed-swerver," "[names] even as bad as those / That vulgars give bold'st titles" [2.1.93–4]). After having Hermione arrested as a traitor and dispatching Cleomenes and Dion to Delphos for a judgement to ratify his treason charges, Leontes confronts Paulina, presenting his newborn daughter, with an even broader catalogue of anti-female commonplaces (e.g., "intelligencing bawd"; "callet/ Of boundless tongue"; "lewd-tongued wife"; "gross hag!"; and "mankind witch"), whose underlying assumptions are all traceable to Pauline allegations of female vices.[9]

II

But while Leontes's misogyny is related to Paul's in force and opinion, it differs in rhetorical authority, for reasons partly illuminated by the Geneva Bible gloss to 1 Corinthians 14: "Because this disorder was in the Church, that women usurped what was peculiar to the men, the Apostle showeth what is more to be done and what is not" (note 14.x). The Geneva editors here avoided explaining the historical causes or context of this "disorder," instead using the politicized early modern language of usurpation to make its transgressive implications appear self-evident. The basis of their interpretation rested on the closed hermeneutic of Paul's author-function as an apostle and the patriarchal ideology empowered by it. This situation mirrors the force of Leontes's political will rather than any real impropriety or discursive logic, and whose "divinity" as king he counts on the oracle at Delphos confirming. As David Schalkwyk observes, Leontes's jealousy represents "a structural feature of a political order" related to Hermione's double bind as a wife enjoined to speak and as a woman forbidden to do so. His "personal motivation . . . resides in the suprapersonal sphere, in an ideological perception of the instability and transgressive openness . . . of both woman's body and her word."[10]

Paulina's resistance to Leontes, by contrast, appropriates the interpersonal rhetorical mode that characterizes much of Paul's writings and subjectivity in 1 Corinthians and other New Testament letters: *parrhèsia*, which Michel Foucault calls "fearless speech." Parrhesia is a paradoxical speech act because it is in fact anti-rhetorical, avoiding rhetorical colors in favor of plain and forceful words that directly express the speaker's heart and mind as truthful opinions to a hostile and/or higher-ranking audience. At the same time, parrhesiastic speech interpellates the speaker's subjectivity according to the public convictions he enunciates.[11] Foucault traces the use of parrhesia back to a wide range of ancient Greek and Hellenistic sources (including the New Testament), where it represents a privileged right of male citizens to voice criticism of rulers or close male friends, and accredits social capital to persons whose public standing is weak or limited. Because parrhesia opposes opinions held by the speaker's more powerful interlocutors, it is dangerous speech that runs the risk of arousing anger and punishment.[12]

For Shakespeare's early modern readers and audiences, models of fearless speech were familiar from several different sources related to Paul. One was the Greek New Testament itself and its vernacular translations, in which parrhesia serves to express Christian ethics. As David Colclough demonstrates in *Freedom of Speech in Early Stuart England*, parrhesia characterizes the language of Christ and the apostles in contexts where they defend themselves from accusers or interrogators. And in Paul's letters it underpins his blunt corrections of alleged faults in recipient communities. Early modern English bibles translate parrhesia as "boldness of speech."[13] Among its overlapping range of meanings with Greek secular uses, it signifies the speaker's independent access to grace and personal conviction as a self-constituting subjectivity.[14]

Parrhesiastic speech was also familiar from Humanist pedagogy, which drew on classical and biblical models to disseminate knowledge of rhetorical strategies serving as persuasive speech to successive generations of early modern readers and writers, including Shakespeare.[15] With Paul's example partly in mind, Erasmus promoted letter-writing as a practical means of deploying this knowledge in a wide range of institutional and political contexts. In his widely used *De Conscribendi Epistolaris*, he shifted the medieval emphasis on learning epistolary forms for the sake of stylistic emulation and deferential propriety to practising the arts of rhetoric in personal correspondence in order to change personal opinions. In *Shakespeare and Social Dialogue* Lynne Magnusson argues that Erasmian epistolary pedagogy also sought to level disparities in rank among correspondents of varying backgrounds, thereby opening up avenues for social interaction and cultural transformation, particularly among the generation of Humanist-educated men whose social or artistic aspirations were authorized by schooling and interpersonal relationships and not by traditional privileges of class and wealth.

Erasmus's systematic refiguring of letter-writing as persuasive speech entailed venturing into the high-risk territory of correcting faults or advising friends or superiors to adopt new courses of action. In his discussion of letters of advice, for example, Erasmus cites Plutarch's "How to tell a flatterer from a friend" to support his wider argument that frank speech was the authentic mark and office of a friend. (This is also Foucault's exemplary text for parrhesia.)[16] In the context of letter-writing as socially enabling discourse, it became a tactical option for Humanist letter-writers whose lower status made them vulnerable to the power of their higher-ranking recipients. Moreover, as Erasmus was aware from his scriptural scholarship and translations of Plutarch, the latter's commendation of parrhesia was paralleled by Paul's characteristic mode of reproof against women in 1 Corinthians and other letters, with righteous but ostensibly "charitable" correction corresponding to the Ciceronian ideal of authentic (male) friendship.

Paulina's adoption of fearless speech to correct Leontes thus represents a conscientious duty related positively in form and speaking-position to Paul in 1 Corinthians:

> These dangerous, unsafe lunes i'th'King, beshrew them!
> He must be told on't, and he shall; the office
> Becomes a woman best. I'll take't upon me;
> If I prove honey-mouthed, let my tongue blister,
> And never to my red-looked anger be
> The trumpet any more (2.2.29–34)

This risky outspokenness contrasts with Hermione's earlier speech, whose persuasive force Shakespeare tropes as spontaneously gracious and charismatic in its fully embodied affectivity. Hermione is also the daughter of an emperor and a royal consort, and therefore privileged to speak—an entitlement she takes up robustly in her cogent self-defense during Leontes's state trial (3.2). Paulina, on the other hand, challenges Leontes from the subordinate position of a subject and woman. Her vulnerable social standing recalls the physical weaknesses Paul tactically emphasizes at many points in his letters so that he may play up the strength of his conviction and authority as an apostle (e.g., 1 Corinthians 1:27–8). Paulina similarly defends her faith in Hermione's innocence by emphasizing her relative powerlessness as a woman in a society that, like Paul's, associates female speech with folly and shame:

> Paulina: Good my liege, I come—
> And I beseech you hear me, who professes
> Myself your loyal servant, your physician,
> Your most obedient counsellor; yet that dares

                    Less appear so in comforting your evils
                    Than such as most seem yours—I say I come
                    From your good Queen.
Leontes: Good Queen!
Paulina: Good Queen, my lord, good Queen, I say good Queen,
           And would by combat make her good, so were I
           A man the worst about you! (2.3.52–61)

Yet because Paulina usurps the masculine privilege of parrhesia and presumes to reprove Leontes as a woman, her relationship to Paul is profoundly ambiguous. To Leontes her "audacity" sounds like a nightmare
version of everything Paul—or King James—objected to in women. By
speaking "shamelessly," however, Paulina lays down a self-reflexive challenge to Humanist pedagogy to open its male-centered social agenda to
women as equal practitioners, with the same potential for acquiring cultural capital through their rhetorical skills as men—opportunities the
period's women were beginning to seize as published writers (as we shall
see in the next section).

    Paulina's appropriation of parrhesia's gender exclusions also draws
spectators' and readers' attention back to the form and context of Paul's
rebukes. This reorientation dovetailed with wider Humanist and post-
Reformation principles encouraging lay-readers to rediscover what the
original scriptural texts actually said.[17] An awareness of the play's critical adaptations of Pauline discourse invited them to consider these textual
relationships as more than unobjectionable allusions. Instead they became
reversible modes, returning audiences to scripture with new eyes for gen-
erating rhetorized and historicized readings that diversified the closed circuit of orthodox interpretation. Readers with knowledge of classical and
Humanist paradigms of rhetorical persuasion used in letter-writing and
other forms of social communication possessed especially powerful analytical knowledge for evaluating patterns of claim and counterclaim in letters
such as 1 Corinthians and for questioning their "natural" restrictions on
both early Christian and early modern female speech and bodies.

III

In 1 Corinthians chapter 14, Paul's famous reproof of local women, cited
above, is followed by a series of rhetorical questions:

    Came the worde of God out from you? ether came it vnto you onely?
    (14:36)

These shift the basis of Paul's opposition from rational argument to externally sanctioned authority, by which his voice personally represents the

"commandements of the Lord" (14:37). Yet these questions also implicitly acknowledge the existence of opinions contrary to Paul's, and they anticipate resistance to this chapter's concluding command to "Let all things be done honestly and by order" (14:40). The Geneva marginal note to chapter 14 (x), also cited earlier, reminds readers that Paul "mencioned this abuse afore," and refers them back to the second "disorder" Paul alleges against Corinthian women in chapter 11: uncovered and loose hair, which accompanies their uninhibited prophesying (i.e., speaking in tongues and expressing their spirituality through ecstatic physical gestures). Whereas men praying with uncovered heads is dishonorable, Paul asserts that "euerie woman that prayeth or prophecieth bareheaded, dishonoreth her head;"

> Therefore if the woman be not couered, let her also be shorne: and if it be shame for a woman to be shorne or shauen, let her be couered (14:6)

Another Geneva note interprets "covered" to mean bound up in a particular style:

> For God hathe giuen to woman longer heere then vnto the man, to the end she shulde trusse it vp about [sic] her head . . . (note 15–16.l).

In 1 Corinthians freedom of words and physical expression in worship are the two main faults that Paul rebukes and seeks to regulate as emblematic "sign[s] of [female] subiection."[18]

According to Elisabeth Schüssler Fiorenza, the historical background of this dispute pertained to Corinthian women eclectically adapting Hellenistic religious practices. These included extra-verbal gestural language such as letting down hair and uninhibited bodily expression associated with prominent first-century Mediterranean religions of Isis or Artemis that gave equal power to women and men. In Corinth or Ephesus these practices mingled with pre-Pauline understandings of the new Christian faith based on Hellenistic-Jewish spirit-wisdom, or Sophia, theology.[19] Paul's background as a Palestinian Jew and Roman citizen led him to dismiss such liturgical syncretism as inauthentic: "But if any man luste to be contentious, [I say] we have no suche custome, nether ye Churches of God [elsewhere in the Mediterranean basin]" (11:16).

Even without access to this kind of historical information, early modern readers attending to the rhetorical patterns of Paul's arguments and their doctrinal interpretation by the Geneva editors could have made distinctions between their logical gaps or internal weaknesses and the externally directed appeals to patriarchal values and divine revelation Paul urges to justify his personal rejection of local customs. For like Leontes, who after hurling ineffectual verbal abuse must resort to coercive force ("On your allegiance,/ Out of the chamber with her!" [2.3.120–1]), Paul ultimately rests his case for female subordination on his personal authority as an apostle, both in the passage quoted above and in its corresponding one in chapter 14:

> If anie man thinke him self to be a Prophet, or spiritual, let him acknowledge, that the things, that I write vnto you, are the commandments of the Lord. And if any man be ignorant [of my authority], let him be ignorant [i.e., ignored in his claim] (37–8).[20]

Humanist readers educated in the epistolary arts of respectfully levelling hierarchical differences between correspondents in favor of reasoned argument would have recognized that, by pulling rank, Paul was implicitly admitting a certain degree of rational weakness in his imposed regulations governing female physical decency and subordinate conduct. As Schüssler Fiorenza observes, these were "not specific[ally] Christian" but cultural values derived from Hellenistic Jewish and Greco-Roman patriarchy.[21]

Scripturally knowledgeable readers would likewise have noticed internal contradictions between Paul's sex-specific and hierarchically ordered restrictions and his equally famous declarations abolishing distinctions of gender, race, religion, and class among Christians:

> There is nether Iewe nor Grecian: there is nether bonde nor fre: there is nether male nor female: for ye are all one in Christ Iesus. (Galatians 3:28)[22]

This radical model of social equality and freedom gave women in Corinth and other first-century Christian communities an incentive to adopt diasporic Jewish customs and female-centered rituals associated with Hellenistic deities. The Corinthians did not believe their local worship insulted masculine honor or was (as Paul's tradition deemed) inherently idolatrous. Instead they allowed for physically and verbally ebullient access to the divine as well as women's public leadership in the local community (of which more in section 4 below). This may explain Paul's omission of the category of gender in another version of the Galatians equality-formula in 1 Corinthians 12:13.[23]

Some early modern readers recognized that the liberating implications of these verses contradicted the subordination Paul prescribes at other points and chose to follow the scriptural passages authorizing freedom of female public expression. One such woman was the militant Protestant writer Anne Dowriche. In 1589 she published *The French History*, a verse account of the persecution and martyrdom of Huguenots (French Protestants) leading up to the Bartholomew's Day Massacre in 1572. Her Epistle to the Reader opens by citing 1 Corinthians 14:26, in which Paul encourages equality of expression ("*according as* euerie one of you hathe a psalme, *or* hathe doctrine, *or* hath a tongue, *or* hathe reuelacion, *or* hathe interpretacion" [original italics]) in name of "edifying," or building up, the church.[24] As we have seen, Paul then goes on to exclude women from this freedom by silencing and domesticating them. For Dowriche writing publicly as a woman, this created a problem, which she acknowledged—like Paulina addressing Leontes and other early modern women anticipating skeptical readers—by conventionally disabling her abilities in a Dedicatory Epistle to her brother: "If you finde anie thing that fits not your liking, remember, I pray, that it is a womans doing" (sig. A2v). Dowriche evidently solved the cultural dilemma of women's teaching by asserting her right to interpret both scripture and contemporary European history independently according to her own conscience while tacitly subordinating Paul's restrictions on female speech.[25] In other words she recognized the textual slippages in scripture and selectively adapted their inconsistencies to authorize public circulation of her work.

To return to 1 Corinthians, when viewed as part of the rhetorical patterning of these local controversies, Paul's arguments in the intervening chapters of Corinthians (12–13) seem like attempts to shore up his overbearing reproofs based on their allegedly transcendent authority. In chapter 12 (echoed and parodied by Bottom in *A Midsummer Night's Dream*),[26] Paul compares members of the Christian community to parts of the human body, metaphorically ranking apostles such as himself as the head and prophets, teachers, miracle-workers, healers, helpers, governors, and speakers-in-tongues in descending order below. Within the wider context of this letter, the low priority he assigns to speaking in tongues appears to be a calculated snub to the Corinthians, who clearly valued this form of religious expression but which Paul mistrusted and sought to regulate. In chapter 13 he follows these hierarchalizing maneuvers with his famous hymn to charity (or love)[27] as self-sacrifice and other-centeredness. Although traditionally understood as a universal ideal, the chapter takes on more self-interested overtones when viewed as part of Paul's strategic attack on freedom of female speech and corporal worship in Corinth. Antoinette Clark Wire remarks that it represents Paul's substitution of self-subordination for the local Corinthian practice of holistically embodied self-rejoicing that signifies an alternative concept of moral and theological integrity.[28]

IV

The Humanist paradigm of contextual and reconstructive reading I have been positing from the practices of early modern writers such as Anne Dowriche and from Shakespeare's intertextual adaptations of Paul anticipates the philological and historical criticism of later biblical and Shakespearian textual scholarship, including that of present-day New Testament theologians.[29] Originally it would have shaped the Jacobean audience's understanding of *The Winter's Tale*'s final act, and above all the statue scene, as positive reinventions of transgressive female conduct.

Conceptually these represent a movement from what Julie Sanders (following Adrienne Rich) calls adaptation into appropriation. The latter mode extends adaptation's ideological challenge into more radical territory, writing back and "re-visioning" the source text's patriarchal assumptions in innovative genres and cultural paradigms.[30]

After Leontes has submitted to the oracle's judgement, he adopts Paulina as his mentor and exchanges subject-positions with her. She now speaks with the personal and political authority she previously lacked, whereas Leontes adopts her Pauline strategy of playing up personal weakness—*viz.* his fatally mistaken jealousy—in order to authenticate his new subjectivity predicated on devotion to Hermione's memory and the strength of his penitent conviction.

Paulina also claims substantial new power from staging the statue scene in her house and chapel. Leontes expects to find the statue in her "gallery" with other artworks in her collection (5.3.9–14), a detail that implicitly links Paulina's broader knowledge of curatorial art with the theatrical artistry she will demonstrate in this scene.[31] But Paulina has set the statue itself "lonely "and "apart" in a space not designated by particular religious furnishings but produced by the interactive rituals that construct its social identity. Their meaning is now often related to early modern debates over mimetic versus metaphorical representations of the divine and their respective claims to legitimacy. Perdita herself draws attention to the impressions of "superstition" and outlawed Marian worship that her kneeling to the statue may create:

> give me leave,
> And do not say 'tis superstition, that
> I kneel and implore her blessing. (5.3.42–4)

Huston Diehl is representative of recent Protestant-oriented commentators who link Perdita's anxieties to Reformation rejection of image-worship and Puritan condemnations of the theatre as subversively feminine and idolatrous.[32] C.L. Barber and later scholars have argued that the early modern theater reassembled the symbolic language, communal rituals, and hunger for real presence characteristic of pre-Reformation religion as a secularized experience of transcendence.[33] Michael O'Connell is representative of a long line of Catholic-oriented critics who regard the scene as a visual affirmation of incarnation theology and/or a nostalgic restaging of officially abandoned but surreptitiously practised English Catholic worship.

For spectators with either Protestant or Catholic allegiances, the scene's Marian overtones might have elicited either of these binarized perspectives. Seen from the viewpoint of the play's intertextual relationship between Paulina and her scriptural namesake, however, Paulina's space of domestic worship recalls first-century house-churches in which women exercised independent moral and social authority in communities such as Corinth and Ephesus. New Testament references indicate that house-churches were centers of physical and spiritual sustenance, often organized and led by higher-status women. At the end of 1 Corinthians, for instance, Paul conveys greetings from the house-church of Aquila and Priscilla (or Prisca) in Ephesus, from where he writes to the Corinthians (16:19–20). Priscilla is the New Testament woman most frequently mentioned in Paul's letters and the Acts of the Apostles. Acts states that she and her husband Aquila instructed Paul's powerful competitor at Corinth, the Alexandrian Jew Apollos, while he was in Ephesus (Acts 18:26, 1 Corinthians 1:12). Like Paul they travelled as independent teachers between their house-churches in Ephesus, Corinth, and perhaps Rome (Romans 16:4).[34] Their freedom and authority further contextualizes while not resolving the fundamental contradiction in 1 Corinthians with Paul's commands for female silence in public and for women to be instructed at home by their husbands. This conflict rehistoricizes Leontes's sarcastic references to Paulina as "Dame Partlet" and "Lady Margery, your midwife"—traditional symbols of the "unroosting woman" who turns the patriarchal household upside down (2.3.74–5, 159).

Women leaders of house-churches mentioned in 1 Corinthians and elsewhere in the New Testament also analogize Paulina's boldness in taking up Pauline-restricted roles as teacher, physician, prophet, and political counsellor in Leontes's court, and later as the healer of his body and soul in her chapel. There she exercises charismatic authority over the participants akin to that which Hermione expressed unselfconsciously at the beginning of the play:

> Paulina: Shall I draw the curtain?
> Leontes: No, not these twenty years.
> Perdita: So long could I
> Stand by, a looker-on.
> Paulina: Either forbear,
> Or quit presently the chapel, or resolve you
> For more amazement. (5.3.83–7)

The statue of Hermione elicits in her onlookers a complex somatic and pneumatic experience suggestive of the integrated physical and spiritual plenitude to which Corinthian women aspired and which the shepherds' and shepherdesses' enraptured reception of Autolycus's ballads humorously anticipates (4.4.592–614).

For Paul, as we have seen, the original physical emblem of female unchastity and disobedience was uncovered and unbound hair, which he invoked from the Jewish tradition of female uncleanness.[35] Paul also related loose hair to a symbolic violation of the hierarchy (based on the gendered human ontology of Genesis 2:7) of God, Christ, Angels, Man, and Woman, in which one order of being acted as the head of the one immediately below. For women, covered or bound hair was the sign of their proper subjection to men, whereas neglect was tantamount to idolatry.[36] Spectators recalling these conflicts between Paul and his local female opponents might have arrived at an equally radical understanding of Hermione's and Paulina's performances as a Corinthian challenge to Pauline anti-female discourse. Hermione's "statue" deliberately risks exposing her body to immodest display and corrective discipline. Leontes observes the queen's "veins . . . bear[ing] blood," and Polixenes "the very life . . . warm upon her lip" (5.3.63–6). Even as "stone" the statue remains ambiguously vulnerable: ruddy and still wet with "oily painting," the "royal piece" is threatened by Leontes's desire to kiss it, which Paulina successfully averts. The king's urge to merge his body with that of the image suggests a deeper struggle to reconcile his painful memories with the visual "rebuke" he feels afresh. In that conjoined experience his sense of shame recalls the earlier Pauline-related understanding of female speech as an embarrassing violation of patriarchal privilege. But here it also intensifies the lack of a fully harmonized response to the memory of his wife's death that he has yearned for but failed to achieve over sixteen years. As Leontes gradually integrates sub-articulate and not fully controlled (i.e., incipiently "usurping" and "disordered") emotion into his "afflicted" memory, the experience creates positive effects of "cordial comfort" and "wonder." According to early modern physiological theory, wonder, while momentarily immobilizing onlookers in a state of ethical and kinetic indeterminacy, also marked their imaginative opening to new epistemological horizons.[37] Together these impulses create an unwonted rational affect that heals the feelings of "tremor cordis" associated earlier with Leontes's overheated fantasy of sexual transgression and its corresponding suppression of female speech. They also mark his advance into the imaginative receptivity that Paulina's leap of faith ultimately requires.

Hermione's coming-to-life and the enthralled responses of on- and off-stage spectators enacts a fleshly version of the parrhesiastic mode heard in the play's first half and its scriptural avatar, the fearlessly expressive tongues and full-body worship of Corinthian women. The spectacle not only rewrites Leontes's tragic narrative, completing (as many critics have discussed) the regenerative process initiated by oracle's judgement and the pastoral scenes of act 4, but also transvaluing the misogynist labels and suppressive tropes of Leontes's Pauline discourse. One of these was the stereotypical "midwife" and "gossip," conveying old wives' secrets of the womb threatening to patrilineal legitimacy. Hermione and Paulina instead reinstall the maternal wisdom of the "great goddess," the classical earth-mother deities of nature, fertility, and spirituality. Like Paulina's intercultural mingling of Hellenistic and Christian gestures, the creative energies of Isis, Artemis, Demeter and Persephone, and other Mediterranean goddesses continually recirculated from heaven to earth and back again. This movement included passage through the prophetic bodies and voices of Corinthian women without ideological injury to the latest revelation of "the good goddess Nature" represented by the Christ-event (2.3.103, 185–6).

Similarly when Paulina brings Hermione to life, her imperative commands

> Music; awake her—strike!
> 'Tis time; descend; be stone no more;
> Strike all that look upon with marvel . . . (5.3.98–100)

transform the parrhesiastic rebuke, which to Leontes made Paulina sound like a "scold" and "crone," into corporeal mediations of grace. Her "spell" converts Leontes's former association of female speech and unregulated physical expression with witchcraft into theatrical conviction, "as lawful as eating." Like that of other spectators, the king's recognition occurs on more than a level of verbal significance alone. Audiences experience the moment as a live process of emotional, somatic, and verbal semiosis through their bodies and intellects.[38] Paulina and Hermione stage an adaptive demonstration of Corinthian practice by remediating the transgressive but repressed instability of Paul's female body and word as a fearlessly epiphenomenal body. As a discursively and affectively remembered event, it continues to signify productively in the hearts and minds of audiences in the theatre and beyond.

As she draws the spectacle to a close, Paulina's adoption of Corinthian discourse also challenges the privileged apostolic language and author-function of Paul himself. Appropriating one his characteristic images of athletes competing in a race to the present moment of equally earned rewards among participants, Paulina charges the chapel's male and female initiates with personally "evangelizing" the event:

> Go together,
> You precious winners all; your exultation
> Partake to everyone. (5.3.130–2)

Acknowledging this new order, Leontes relinquishes his absolute control. He asks Paulina to lead the gathering off in a spirit of historically reconstructive and multivoiced interpretation:

> Good Paulina,
> Lead us from hence, where we may leisurely
> Each one demand and answer to his part
> Performed in this wide gap of time . . . (5.3.151–4)

Implicitly this narrativizing process will pluralize rather than suppress or hierarchalize individual explanations of events "since first/ We were dissevered." It also resituates the "justifying" authority of royal patriarchy, which motivates Leontes's last-minute proposal of marriage between Paulina and Camillo, back into diachronic contingency subject to a range of individual desires.

In *The Winter's Tale* Shakespeare rewrites the traditional logocentric image of Paul through Paulina and Hermione's intertextual appropriations of scripturally restricted verbal and physical female expression. Their revisioning performances open up the self-authorizing hermeneutic that traditionally constitutes Paul's apostolic author-function, transforming it into a new rhetorized and historicized discourse, commonly sourced by spectators, readers, and writers for divergent uses. From the perspective of contemporary critical practice, recognition of these possibilities expands the horizons of Shakespearian scriptural allusion. Currently in Shakespeare studies, biblical texts tend to be treated as semantically stable and critically underproductive, except perhaps to support speculation about Shakespeare's religious beliefs. Yet scriptural scholarship, like Shakespeare criticism and textual studies in particular, has always been a controversial practice related to changing social and political contexts. Interpretations of Paul's life and writings are no more universally fixed in our time than they were in Shakespeare's. As early modern Humanist and Reformation cultures of vernacular translation, polemical commentary, and print technology began to draw attention to the rhetorically and historically constructed status of Paul's "book," they revealed the discursive faultlines of its authorship and ideology to Shakespeare and his audiences. Through Paulina and Hermione, *The Winter's Tale* actively reinstates this intertextual dynamism. The play shows Shakespeare using the Bible with the same bold freedom as his other favorite primary sources—Ovid, Holinshed, Plutarch, and Montaigne. It therein provides us with a productive model for reassessing the intercultural relationships between scriptural references and Shakespearian adaptations in other plays as well.

NOTES

1. Michel Foucault discusses the emergence of the discursively generative author-function in "What Is an Author?" in Josué V. Harari (ed.) *Textual Strategies: Perspectives in Post-Structuralist Criticism*, Ithaca: Cornell University Press, 1979, pp. 141–60.
2. Christy Desmet, "Introduction," in Desmet and Rob Sawyer (eds) *Shakespeare and Appropriation*, New York and London: Routledge, 1999, pp. 1–4; Daniel Fischlin and Mark Fortier, "Introduction," in Fischlin and Fortier (eds) *Adaptations of Shakespeare: A Critical Anthology of Plays from the Seventeenth Century to the Present*, London and New York: Routledge, 2000, pp. 1–11; Sonia Massai, "Defining Local Shakespeares," in Massai (ed.) *World-Wide Shakespeares: Local Appropriations in Film and Performance*, London and New York: Routledge, 2005, pp. 5–7; Julie Sanders, *Adaptation and Appropriation*, London and New York: Routledge, 2006, p. 21 and *passim*; Linda Hutcheon, *A Theory of Adaptation*, New York and London: Routledge, 2006,

p. 3 and *passim*; Margaret Jane Kidnie, *Shakespeare and the Problem of Adaptation*, London and New York: Routledge, 2009, pp. 8–9.

3. Martine Van Elk, "'Our Praises Are Our Wages': Courtly Exchange, Social Mobility, and Female Speech in *The Winter's Tale*," *Philological Quarterly*, 2000, vol. 79, no. 4, 429–58, p. 430.

4. Van Elk, "Our Praises," 435.

5. Stephen Orgel (ed.) "Introduction," *The Winter's Tale*, Oxford: Oxford University Press, 1996, pp. 27–8. All quotations from the play are taken from this edition.

6. Karen Jo Torjesen, "Reconstruction of Women's Early Christian History," in Elisabeth Schüssler Fiorenza (ed.) *Searching the Scriptures: A Feminist Introduction*, vol. 1, New York: Crossroad Publishing, 1993, p. 302.

7. Orgel, "Introduction," 26, citing Norman E. McClure (ed.) *The Letters of John Chamberlain*, Philadelphia: American Philosophical Society, 1939, pp. 286–7.

8. Some modern scholars now think this verse is not authentically Pauline but a later interpolation, like other passages advocating female silence and gender subordination in his letters. See Raymond Edward Brown, Joseph A. Fitzmyer, and Roland Edmund Murphy (eds) *The New Jerome Bible Commentary*, New York: Prentice-Hall, 1990, p. 811. See also 1 Timothy 2:11–2. Although humanist scholars such as Erasmus had begun to draw lay-readers' attention to the possibility of non-Pauline authorship of certain letters such as Hebrews and to textual instabilities created by secretarial transmission, possible co-authorship, and the material practices of first-century letter-writing (e.g., in the prefaces to Erasmus's officially distributed and widely read *Paraphrase upon the New Testament*), most Elizabethan readers would have understood the letters as single-authored and would have had to grapple with the inconsistencies that 1 Corinthians 14:34 created with other passages. See below.

9. As Orgel again observes, it is not the specific charge (and falsity) of Leontes's charge of witchcraft here that is paramount, but its symbolically metonymic relationship to the threat of female power to the social and political order by women as a group (Orgel, "Introduction," p. 58).

10. David Schalkwyk, "'A Lady's "Verily" Is as Potent as a Lord's': Women, Word, and Witchcraft in *The Winter's Tale*," *English Literary Renaissance*, 1992, vol. 22, no. 2, 242–72, p. 248; Van Elk, "Our Praises," p. 436. Schalkwyk cites Peter Stallybrass, "Patriarchal Territories: The Body Enclosed," in Margaret W. Ferguson, Maureen Quilligan, and Nancy J. Vickers (eds) *Rewriting the Renaissance: The Discourses of Sexual Difference in Early Modern Europe*, Chicago and London: University of Chicago Press, 1986, pp. 129–30, on the "Renaissance homology between chastity and silence." Schalkwyk's stimulating article concludes that Leontes's reestablished patriarchal authority at the end of the play silences Paulina's oppositional voice. By contrast I argue that the reinterpretive process underlying her adaptive appropriation of scripture contests Paul's arguments in ways that fundamentally question their transcendent authorization of patriarchy, first-century and early modern. This process is affective and somatic as well as textual. Words alone are only part of the audience's experience on and off stage of Paulina and Hermione's dramatic signification.

11. Michel Foucault, in Joseph Pearson (ed.) *Fearless Speech*, Los Angeles: Semiotext(e), 2001, pp. 9–24.

12. Not surprisingly for a book of rhetoric commenting on an anti-rhetorical style, George Puttenham's well-known *Art of English Poesy*, 1589, defines "*Parisia, or the Licentious*" as speeches that declare the mind of the "fine and

subtle persuader" in "broad and liberal" manner, but offers only one example of how to avoid giving offense by prefacing such speeches with politely
deferential deflection, which undermines the device's intent and effect in the
terms Erasmus, Foucault, and others understand it.

13. For example: 2 Corinthians 3:12 (Geneva).
14. As Huston Diehl has also shown, Paul's bold rebukes of erring behaviour
    became a model for zealous protestant reformers, whom she relates to Paulina
    in *The Winter's Tale*. See Huston Diehl, "'Does Not the Stone Rebuke Me?':
    The Pauline Rebuke and Paulina's Lawful Magic in *The Winter's Tale*," in
    Paul Yachnin and Patricia Badir (eds) *Shakespeare and the Cultures of Per-
    formance*, Aldershot and Burlington, VT: Ashgate Press, pp. 79–80.
15. T.W. Baldwin, *William Shakspere's Small Latine and Less Greeke*, 2 vols.,
    Urbana: University of Illinois Press, 1944.
16. Plutarch, "How to Tell a Flatterer from A Friend," trans. Frank Cole, *Mora-
    lia*, vol. 1, Loeb Classical Library, Cambridge, MA: Harvard, and London:
    Heineman, 1927, pp. 263–95. This essay is explicitly concerned with defin-
    ing parrhesia. See Foucault, *Fearless Speech*, pp. 133–8.
17. John William Aldridge shows that Erasmian textual and historical criticism
    was founded upon the idea of returning to the original texts ("ad fontes")
    studied in relation to non-scriptural writings and philology. This approach
    constitutes an anthropological concept of natural revelation reminiscent of
    Montaigne in his later *Essays* ("One comes nearer to perceiving the sense of
    Scripture if [the reader] considers not only the situation and what is said, but
    also by whom it is said, to whom it is said, the words that are said, what time,
    what occasion, what precedes and what follows" [Aldridge, p. 61, note 11]).
    Rather than being focused exclusively on moral or theological meaning, the
    Erasmian hermeneutic is a process of interdependent dialogue with the origi-
    nal texts from the diverse perspectives of present-day readers: "The sources
    are no longer speaking for themselves, but have become subject to the period
    in which they are interpreted." John William Aldridge, *The Hermeneutic of
    Erasmus*, Richmond, VA: The John Knox Press, 1966, pp. 63.
18. See also headnote to Geneva chapter 11, and marginal notes to verses 11.f,
    14.y.
19. Elisabeth Schüssler Fiorenza, "Women in the Pre-Pauline and Pauline
    Churches," *Union Theological Seminary Quarterly Review*, 1978, vol. 33,
    158–9.
20. The Geneva marginal note 14.[2] glosses this cryptic passage: "I speake of
    the Spirit of God, and so let him obey."
21. Schüssler Fiorenza, "Women in the Pre-Pauline," pp. 155, 158–59.
22. This letter immediately follows 2 Corinthians. It exemplifies Paul's charac-
    teristic use of the parrhesiastic rebuke ("O Foolish Galatians, whoe hath
    bewitched you that ye shulde not obey the trueth" [3:1]), and his strategy
    of covering potential weaknesses in his rational arguments with appeals to
    personally revealed authority ("[I was] taught . . . by the reuelation of Iesus
    Christ" ["By an extraordinarie reuelation"] [1:12 and Geneva gloss]).
23. "For by one Spirit we are all baptized into one bodie, whether *we be* Iewes
    or Grecians, whether *we be* bonde, or fre, and haue bene all made to drinke
    into one Spirit" (original italics). Paul's rhetorical bias may also explain his
    erasure of women from his account of Christ's post-resurrection appear-
    ances, notwithstanding the Gospels' and later traditions of the three Marys
    greeting Jesus at the tomb and carrying the news to other apostles and sup-
    porters. See Schüssler Fiorenza, *In Memory of Her: A Feminist Theological
    Reconstruction of Christian Origins*, New York: Crossroad Publishing, pp.
    97–241.

24. "Amongst manie excellent precepts which Saint Paul gave vnto the Church, this is to be considered; Let al things be done vnto edifying" (sig. A3v). See also Anne Dowriche, "Epistle to the Reader, from *The French History* (1589)," in Randall Martin (ed.) *Women Writers in Renaissance England*, 1997, London: Longmans, 2010, p. 27. For a discussion of the Reformation theme of edification, see John Coolidge, *The Pauline Renaissance in England: Puritanism and the Bible*, Oxford: Clarendon Press, 1970.

25. Micheline White has linked Dowriche to a group of religious women writing in the West of England at this time. See Micheline White, "Women Writers and Literary-Religious Circles in the Elizabethan West Country: Anne Dowriche, Anne Lock Prowse, Anne Lock Moyle, Ursula Fulford, and Elizabeth Rous," *Modern Philology*, 2005, vol. 103, no. 2, 187–214.

26. Verses 14–22; *The Winter's Tale* 4.1.211–4.

27. This word was the focus of fierce early modern contention related to the ideologically inflected English translation of the Vulgate's *caritas* and the Greek text's *agape*.

28. Antoinette Clark Wire, *The Corinthian Women Prophets: A Reconstruction through Paul's Rhetoric*, Minneapolis: Fortress Press, 1990, pp. 135–58, 183–4.

29. On the rhetoric of Paul's letters, for example, which "betray[s] evidence of a solid classical education" that Humanist-educated members of Shakespeare's audience would have shared, see Jerome Murphy-O'Connor, "Organizing a Letter," in *Paul the Letter-Writer: His World, His Options, His Skills*, Collegeville, MN: The Liturgical Press, 1995, pp. 42–113, p. 44.

30. Sanders, *Adaptation and Appropriation*, 26; Adrienne Rich, "When We Dead Awaken: Writing as Re-vision," *College English*, Oct. 1972, vol. 34, no. 1, 18–30.

31. Orgel, pp. 53–62.

32. Diehl, "'Does not the stone rebuke me?,'" p. 80.

33. Diehl argues that Shakespeare answers these objections by relating Paulina's actions to early modern Protestant discourses praising "Paul . . . as a man of 'miracles.'" C.L. Barber, *The Whole Journey: Shakespeare's Power of Development*, Richard P. Wheeler (ed.) Berkeley: University of California Press, 1986; Richard P. Wheeler (ed.) *Creating Elizabethan Tragedy: The Theater of Marlowe and Kyd*, Chicago and London: University of Chicago Press, 1988; Louis Montrose, *The Purpose of Playing: Shakespeare and the Cultural Politics of the Elizabethan Theatre*, Chicago: University of Chicago Press, 1996, pp. 30–2. Walter S.H. Lim, and Anthony B. Dawson put forward related arguments that the scene adapts vestigial Catholic discourses to create a theatricalized version of a faith-event in tension with contemporary discourses of empirical scepticism and secularization, whereas Julia Reinhard Lupton sees the play constructing an "iconology of idolatry," a "visual and critical analysis of the religious image in a secular world," from intersecting Catholic, Protestant, Jewish, and Greco-Roman traditions. See Walter S.H. Lim, "Knowledge and Belief in *The Winter's Tale*," *Studies in English Literature*, 2001, vol. 41, no. 2, 317–334; Anthony B. Dawson, "Shakespeare and Secular Performance," in Paul Yachnin and Patricia Badir (eds) *Shakespeare and the Cultures of Performance*, Aldershot and Burlington, VT: Ashgate Press, 2008, pp. 83–97; Julia Reinhard Lupton, "'*The Winter's Tale*' and the Gods: Iconographies of Idolatry," in *Afterlives of the Saints: Hagiography, Typology, and Renaissance Literature*, Stanford: Stanford University Press, 1996, pp. 175–218.

34. Where, like 2 Timothy 4:19 (another passage conveying greetings) and Acts 18:26, Prisca is mentioned before her husband Aquila. As Schüssler Fiorenza

notes further, they shared Paul's trade as tentmakers; their leadership of house-churches and missionary work was paralleled by that of Andronicus and Junia (Julia), described as apostles before Paul in Romans 16:7; the rich cloth-merchant Lydia of Thyatira (Acts 16:14); Apphia (Philemon 2); Nympha of Laodicea (Colossians 4:15). Also Phoebe of Cenchreae (Romans 16:1). See Schüssler Fiorenza, "Women in The Pre-Pauline," pp. 156–8. See also Torjesen, "Reconstruction," pp. 304–7.

35. Schüssler Fiorenza, "Women in the Pre-Pauline," p. 160; Numbers 4:8. The same tradition of female "uncleanness" underlies the *Book of Common Prayer's* liturgy of the churching of women.
36. Wire, *The Corinthian Women Prophets*, pp. 120–8.
37. Stephen Greenblatt, *Marvelous Possessions: The Wonder of the New World*, Chicago: University of Chicago Press, 1991, pp. 19–22, 79–80.
38. On the physical and cultural inscription of the live performance-text, see James C. Bulman, "Introduction: Shakespeare and Performance Theory," *Shakespeare, Theory and Performance*, London and New York: Routledge, 1996, pp. 1–11.

5 The Tablets of the Law
Reading *Hamlet* with Scriptural Technologies

Alan Galey

I SCENES OF WRITING

> Last time there was this much excitement about a tablet, it had some commandments written on it.
>
> *Wall Street Journal* (30 December 2009)[1]

This chapter considers how material inscriptions become transcendental scripture in iconic scenes of writing in *Hamlet*, Exodus, and, to begin with, a more recent episode involving a tablet. When Steve Jobs presented the Apple iPad to the world in a rollout event in January of 2010, he and his new device entered a long iconographic tradition of reading, writing, and memory.[2] Consider the coincidental symbolism as we observe Jobs's performance: a lone figure in black on a nearly bare stage, enthralling an audience with the disclosure of a closely guarded secret, simulating private acts of reading while self-consciously under the scrutiny of others ("words, words, words"), and brandishing a tablet that serves as symbol of, and prosthesis for, one's innermost memories. If Jobs may unintentionally evoke *Hamlet* at this moment, it is because the play has proven especially amenable to the themes of memory and mediation, along the lines of adaptations such as Michael Almereyda's 2000 film.[3] But the iPad rollout made even more pointed use of scriptural symbolism. On the screen behind Jobs at the presentation's opening appeared the *Wall Street Journal* quotation above, accompanied by Gustave Doré's engraving of Moses holding the Tablets of the Law (see Figure 5.1).[4] With that image, the Apple demo gave us a Moses drawn like a literary illustration: not the cinematic Moses of the twentieth century but a bookish Moses of the nineteenth. The Doré image stands within a tradition populated by his other illustrations for works like Coleridge's *Rime of the Ancient Mariner*, Poe's *The Raven*, and Shakespeare's *The Tempest*. Given the rich intertextuality of this performance, Jobs's offhand comment on the Moses comparison, "I chuckled when I saw this," belies the intensity of the cultural coding of this demonstration of a new reading technology. What does it mean to read *Hamlet*, or the Bible for that matter, on a digital device that could be presented to the world as a symbolic descendent of the Tablets of the Law?

Figure 5.1   Moses's destruction of the first Tablets of the Law, from *The Holy Bible, with Illustrations by Gustav Doré* (London, ca. 1866). Image courtesy of the E.J. Pratt Library, Victoria College, University of Toronto.

The Biblical episode of Moses and the tablets, one of writing's iconic scenes, emblematizes continuity in the transmission of texts. The brief timeline of Apple devices that follows the Moses reference in the iPad rollout implicitly places all these technologies in a progression whose originary moment is specifically Biblical. The trope of Biblical chronology lends itself to representations of technology and writing, as Michael Joyce echoes when he comments that orthodox accounts of the development of hypertext "take on the old testamentary feel of the Book of Numbers," as the technological advances of Vannevar Bush beget those of Douglas Engelbart, which beget those of Ted Nelson, and so on.[5] Indeed, Jobs was hardly the first to invoke Moses in advertising a writing-tablet technology. A figure of Moses pointing to his own tablets appears on the title page of Frank Adams and Robert Triplet's 1584 *Writing Tables with a Kalender for xxiiii. yeeres, with sundry necessarie rules*, a kind of early modern paper computer which bound an almanac together with erasable writing surfaces.[6] It would seem that not only technologies of writing, but also the ways we talk about them, tend to evoke the scriptural.

That scriptural trope for new technologies runs through Shakespeare as well. As suggested by the title of one self-help book for the always-on generation, *Hamlet's BlackBerry*, Shakespeare's depiction of writing tables serves as an imaginative early-modern forerunner of the present's mobile devices.[7] This book draws its analogy to the BlackBerry from act 1, scene 5, in which Hamlet responds to the Ghost's commands:

> HAMLET.   [. . .] Remember thee?
> Ay, thou poor ghost, whiles memory holds a seat
> In this distracted globe. Remember thee?
> Yea, from the table of my memory
> I'll wipe away all trivial fond records,
> All saws of books, all forms, all pressures past
> That youth and observation copied there,
> And thy commandment all alone shall live
> Within the book and volume of my brain,
> Unmix'd with baser matter. Yes, by heaven!
> O most pernicious woman!
> O villain, villain, smiling damned villain!
> My tables. Meet it is I set it down
> That one may smile, and smile, and be a villain—
> At least I am sure it may be so in Denmark.   [*Writes.*]
> So, uncle, there you are. Now to my word.
> It is "Adieu, adieu, remember me."
> I have sworn't. (1.5.95–112)[8]

Hamlet's motific connection to documents throughout the play begins with this speech, as does the perceived problem of Hamlet's delayed revenge. Hamlet himself repeatedly circles back to this moment of realization, and critics have similarly circled around what may or may not have happened on Shakespeare's stage in early productions. There is at least one ambiguous embedded stage direction, in lines 107–10 where Hamlet appears to manipulate writing materials on stage, calling for a prop to physicalize a complex metaphor for the operation of memory. As we shall see, Hamlet's speech on memory coordinates a complex set of desires and apprehensions about memory, writing, and the reproducibility of texts.

Hamlet's avowal that the Ghost's words alone shall be inscribed within the "book and volume" of his brain and Hamlet's choice of the words "tablet" and "commandment" tie his speech back to the Tablets of the Law. The symbolic link between the tablets of Hamlet and Moses has been noted before, and this chapter contributes to a discussion already begun by others including Marjorie Garber, P.K. Ayers, and most recently Peter Stallybrass, Roger Chartier, J. Franklin Mowrey, and Heather Wolfe in an article on "Hamlet's Tables and the Technologies of Writing in Renaissance England."[9] As the authors of the latter article point out, Hamlet's writing tables may well have been real inscription technologies, not just a metaphor, to the play's first audiences. In their investigation into the kinds of writing tables Shakespeare may have had in mind for Hamlet's speech, Stallybrass and his co-authors offer a valuable account of the erasable writing surfaces that generally use a stylus rather than ink to record signs on paper, parchment, or wax. Used in tandem with commonplace books— themselves often organized according to the topoi of rhetorical training that have much in common with mnemonic systems—writing tables were a normal part of early modern information management.[10] Stallybrass and his co-authors cite Philip Melanchthon's advice that writing tables should be used to record information to be organized later and sifted by recopying into a commonplace book. The division of the system into erasable table and permanent book would help prevent the "mere accumulation" and "copia [that] can actually threaten memory."[11]

An awareness of the duality of memory and forgetting, materialized in erasable writing tables of the kind published by Adams and Triplet, changes the way we read Hamlet's speech, as Stallybrass and his co-authors have demonstrated in their widely cited article (which appears to have inspired the title and central conceit of *Hamlet's BlackBerry*). As they point out, "It is surely because there could be no less suitable technology than erasable tables for a permanent remembrance that Hamlet metamorphoses the 'Table of . . . Memory' into the quite different 'Booke and Volume' of his brain, which he imagines as a place of indelible writing."[12] The opposition seems stable enough, but the paradoxical condition of all substrates becomes evident in their reading: "Hamlet first imagines the tables as figuring a mind from which the past can be erased so as to store a present memory. But the present memory is in turn vulnerable to the material form on which it is inscribed: an erasable surface, from which the present 'command' can be wiped out as easily as the trivial records of the past."[13]

Inscription and erasure are often dual operations within the same system, both technically and symbolically.

It is worth emphasizing the importance of this type of observation in recent scholarship that deals with memory and the materiality of texts in the Renaissance. Although the argument made by Stallybrass et al. may be expressed in simple terms—"A technology of memory, [. . .] tables are also a technology of erasure"[14]—the acknowledgement of erasure as an active, constitutive presence distinguishes their work from most studies of memory that came before. Frances Yates, by contrast, limits her scope to the history of ideas, omitting the material history of documents and the cultural practices that attended them, with the result that her otherwise exhaustive study in *The Art of Memory* envisions only how memory systems work productively, not how they fail productively.[15] With that idea in mind, I suggest that any discussion of Hamlet's tables is incomplete without serious consideration of how writing technologies signify in the present, and how the fears and desires associated with digital texts permeate the topic unavoidably. In that light, this chapter uses e-books to triangulate the relationship between memory and writing in *Hamlet* and Exodus, since all of these elements are part of the discourse about the transmission of culture and its material forms.

This chapter turns first to a discussion of the Mosaic tablets and their connection to concepts of scripture, inscription and erasure. It then considers Hamlet's speech in connection with the closest Shakespearean counterpart to the Mosaic tables, the 1623 First Folio. In a physical "book and volume" that deploys strong archival connotations of its own, the images of erasure and inscription in *Hamlet* carry a force in the Folio they would not have in another book. The Folio enables the fantasy of texts inscribed, as it were, by the finger of Shakespeare, and have functioned in some traditions of reception as though they form what Gary Taylor has called "an autonomous unit of bibliographical production," which he distinguishes from the heterogeneous disunity of its texts.[16] Put another way, the Folio's illusion of scriptural unity represents what Wilfred Cantwell Smith describes as "a widespread tendency to treat texts in a 'scripture-like' way: a human propensity to scripturalize," a phenomenon made possible by the belief that "being scripture is not a quality inherent in any given text, or type of text, so much as an interpretive relation between that text and a community of persons."[17] Like the received Bible, the cultural and material contexts of reading construct Shakespeare's gathered plays as a scriptural unity corresponding to the codicological unit of the Folio itself. Scriptural technologies are those which enable the fantasy that human writing can aspire to permanence, and the example of the iPad as a Mosaic tablet computer suggests that scriptural tropes have lost none of their imaginative power with digital textuality. With these contexts in mind, the chapter concludes by considering how the metaphor of the scriptural Shakespeare text translates to the reading device at the center of Steve Jobs's performance.

II   SCRIPTURE, INSCRIPTION AND ERASURE

> The former *Tables* of the Law were broken,
> And left no Monuments of themselves, no token
> No signe that ever such things were: But marke,
> The *later* were kept holy in the *Arke.*
>
>   Francis Quarles, "On the old and new tables"[18]

Let us begin by reviewing the story from Exodus. Moses first receives the tablets bearing the ten commandments directly from God in Exodus 31:18 as a divine inscription, "written with the finger of God," unmediated by anything except the tablets themselves: "The tablets were the work of God, and the writing was the writing of God, graven upon the tables" (32:16).[19] Moses descends from Mount Sinai and, upon seeing his people worshipping a false idol, destroys the tablets and must go back and ask God for another copy. Seeking atonement, Moses continues the theme of writing when he says to God, "blot me, I pray thee, out of thy book which thou hast written," if God will not forgive him (32:32).[20] In a significant act of repetition—but with a difference—God instructs Moses to fashion tablets from the local stone and to transcribe the commandments from dictation (34:1). Moses then returns with the renewed tablets, after which an Ark is constructed (38:1–5) and the Tablets placed inside them (40:20).

Doré illustrated Moses with the tablets twice, the first time returning from the mountain with the tablets in his arms, and the second time with his arms upraised to destroy the tablets as described in 32:15–19.[21] The first image would have made a better complement to the *Wall Street Journal* quotation and the comical subtext of Jobs as a digital-age Moses—the leader of a chosen people known for giving commandments from on high (thou shalt not support Flash). Curiously, the image used in the iPad demo is the second one, depicting the moment of the tablets' destruction, which means that the iPad presentation begins with an image not of transmission, but of erasure. This possibly unintentional but revealing choice of image in the demo reminds us that the questions of permanence and loss that inevitably shadow digital media are old indeed.

For example, in their discussion of the 1584 *Writing Tables* volume mentioned above, Stallybrass and his co-authors read the Mosaic tablets and the printed volume that depicts them as examples of permanent inscription to early modern eyes, set against the erasable tables that were bound with the book. Despite having been recopied by God's "amanuensis," Moses, "the second tables that God gave to Moses not only endured, but their endurance also came to signify the permanence of the Father's 'command.'"[22] Yet, as Francis Quarles implies in his epigram "On the old and new tables" (quoted above), the victory of permanent inscription in the Exodus story nevertheless carries with it the shadow of loss, since the original tablets "left no Monuments of themselves, [. . .] No signe that ever such things were." The Mosaic tablets can be at best a conflicted symbol of permanence since they are always doubled images: in any given depiction of Moses and the tablets, such as the title page of *Writing Tables*, how are we to know which set Moses is holding, the (destroyed) originals or the (preserved) copy? Doré's Bible helpfully disambiguates by illustrating both in separate images, but as a generalized symbol the tablets always harbor this irreducible ambiguity.

In this sense the Mosaic tablets represent what Jacques Derrida in *Archive Fever* calls the archiviolithic tendency, the informatic death drive that archives conceal within themselves. As he explains, archiviolithism depends upon the link between inscription and repetition:

> if there is no archive without consignation in an *external place* which assures the possibility of memorization, of repetition, of reproduction, or of reimpression, then we must also remember that repetition itself, the logic of repetition, indeed the repetition compulsion, remains, according to Freud, indissociable from the death drive. And thus from destruction.[23]

The tablets survived because they were copied, but they survived only as copies that were a further remove from their divine origin: Moses's writing on stone cut from the mountain rather than God's writing on material presumably not of this earth. This is the crux formed by the terms *inscription* and *scripture*.

The former term, *inscription*, has become a keyword in fields such as critical theory, media studies, and science and technology studies, through the work of N. Katherine Hayles, Lisa Gitelman, and Bruno Latour in particular. Inscription serves to distinguish categories of media in both their actual and imagined operations. Hayles offers a useful definition of the category: "to count as an inscription technology, a device must initiate material changes that can be read as marks"; examples would include both printed books (presumably letterpress and photo-offset) and computers.[24] Notably, Hayles and other practitioners of media-specific analysis emphasize inscription not to separate out devices like the iPad from traditional writing technologies, as many hypertext theorists have done, but rather to point out continuities. As Hayles explains, a digital computer depends upon inscriptions "because it changes electric polarities and correlates these changes with binary code, higher-level languages such as C++ and Java, and the phosphor gleams of the cathode ray tube."[25] In this sense an iPad is no less an inscription technology than a stone tablet, though the inscriptions may work in different ways.

What matters in contexts like the iPad demo, however, is the symbolic function of inscription. Gitelman elaborates:

> Like other media, inscriptive media represent, but the representations they entail and circulate are crucially material as well as semiotic.

Unlike radio signals, for instance, inscriptions are stable and savable. [. . .] The difference seems obvious, but it is important to note that the stability and savability of inscriptions are qualities that arise socially as well as perceptually.[26]

Gitelman's emphasis on the social nature and function of inscription echoes Cantwell Smith's point, quoted above, that scripture—that is, the small-s kind—derives not from inherent technical qualities so much as socially determined ones. In both cases, the task of interpretation takes on a material component, as Hayles describes: "The implication for studies of technology and literature is that the materiality of inscription thoroughly interpenetrates the represented world. Even when technology does not appear as a theme, it is woven into the fictional world through the processes that produce the literary work as a material artifact."[27] This is not to deny that technologies function in determinable ways whether people understand them or not, nor to deny that capital-S Scripture may have an origin independent from human beliefs about it. Rather, the social focus of both definitions simply means that to the extent we can know about such things at all, we know them through interpretation—that is, through representations whose imaginative power we share (or do not share) with others, and whose meaning depends in no small part on how those representations work. Like data, inscriptions do not speak for themselves; someone always speaks for them, whether a Moses, a Hamlet, or a Steve Jobs.

Whether or not capital-S Scripture speaks for itself is a matter of faith, but there is no question that the written nature of Biblical Scripture influences how we think about the written and the writable. As Cantwell Smith notes, "the matter of writing [is] something that our word 'scripture' quietly posits, or presumes," a fact borne out by *scripture*'s cognates in other European languages and in its antecedents in Greek ("*he graphe, hai graphai*") and Hebrew ("*ketuvim*").[28] Yet the division between written and oral texts is not always absolute. Even in Shakespeare's time the textual identity of Scripture was a hybrid one, split between the Bible Shakespeare likely read (the Geneva) and the Bible he likely heard from the pulpit (the Bishops').[29] Multiple texts open the question of competing textual authority, and the scenario of competing Scriptures goes right back to the two sets of Mosaic tablets. Though we have no way of knowing whether the texts of the two sets of tablets were identical or revised—one imagines an exasperated God moving the commandment against idolatry to the top of the list—the account in Exodus does make clear that the form of textual transmission changes, as mentioned above. With the first set of tablets, God writes (Exodus 32:16); with the second, He dictates to Moses, who writes (34:1).

A traditional interpretation would emphasize the sameness of the text in both versions, since the Hebrew and Christian God is one who renews covenants throughout the Bible (renewal being a trope distinct from repetition). But the idea of a divine power that guarantees this sameness between versions casts the idea of human inscription in a new light. Bruno Latour, for example, emphasizes the sameness and permanence of inscriptions in scientific contexts, particularly in his notion of science as a social field enabled by the circulation of "immutable mobiles."[30] Latour has been challenged on the "immutable" part of his theory by book historian Adrian Johns.[31] His study *The Nature of the Book* advances a thesis much like Hayles's and Gitelman's, that the trustworthiness of inscriptions—printed ones specifically, in Johns's study—is an evolving and socialized process that is intertwined with, rather than driven by, the nature of the technologies. As Johns puts it, fixity is not so much an "inherent" property as a "transitive" one, created and changed in part by social perceptions.[32] One consequence of Johns's argument is that representations of inscription, like those in Exodus and *Hamlet*, take on a role largely omitted in Latour's account of inscription. In that sense, how writing technologies are thought to work, and how they are depicted as working, are at least as important as how they actually work.

What then makes a writing technology scriptural, then, as distinct from merely inscriptional? One factor I will discuss in relation to *Hamlet* is a cultural investment in, and struggle to reckon with, the mysterious aspects of inscription. As the cultural reception of the iPad reminds us, digital technologies in particular expose these unknowable—or at least generally unknown— qualities due to their relatively recent entry into the cultural imagination. As Gitelman points out, "Digital media inscribe too, and they do so in what are mysterious new ways. (Mysterious to me, at least, and anyone else without an engineering background.) [...] I execute commands to save my data files—texts, graphics, sounds—but in saving them, I have no absolute sense of digital savability as a quality that is familiarly material."[33] Derrida relates the same experience in an oft-quoted passage from *Archive Fever*:

> [W]hile tinkling away on my computer[,] I asked myself what is the moment *proper* to the archive, [...] the instant of archivization strictly speaking, which is not [...] so-called live or spontaneous memory (*mnēmē* [or] *anamnēsis*), but rather a certain hypomnesic and prosthetic experience of the technical substrate. Was it not at this very instant that, having written something or other on the screen, the letters remaining as if suspended and floating yet at the surface of a liquid element, I pushed a certain key to "save" a text undamaged, in a hard and lasting way, to protect marks from being erased, [...] to stock, to accumulate, and [...] to make the sentence available in this way for printing and reprinting, for reproduction?[34]

One can only imagine what Derrida would have made of an iPad, whose tablet design enhances the illusion of unity between screen and inscription-bearing substrate. In this light, the mundane reflex of hitting the keystroke Command- or CTRL-s while typing becomes a cultural investment, an act of trusting to an agency beyond oneself. Derrida's emphasis on the word *save*, echoed by Gitelman above, points to the theological connotations the word still carries. Scripture is that which transcends the vagaries of textual transmission, and whose meaning is underwritten by divine authority.

III   THE SCRIPTURAL FOLIO

The single most consequential act of saving Shakespeare's texts "undamaged, in a hard and lasting way," as Derrida describes inscription above, was the publishing of the book now known as the Shakespeare First Folio in 1623. Like the iPad, the Folio's physical design provoked conflicting responses in its own time. One of the most well known is William Prynne's *Histrio-Mastix* (1633), which condemned Jonson's and Shakespeare's folio collections for usurping what Prynne regarded as Biblical materiality:

> Some Play-books since I first undertooke this subject, are growne from *Quarto* into *Folio*; which yet beare so good a price and sale, that I cannot but with griefe relate it, they are now new-printed in farre better paper than most Octavo or Quarto *Bibles*, which hardly finde such vent as they [. . .].[35]

Following Prynne's identification of certain markers—the folio format; high-quality paper; ubiquity in the book market—it has become a critical commonplace to equate the 1623 Shakespeare First Folio with the Bible. Indeed Prynne complains of the Folio's excess in what may be the first shot in the debate over the materiality of Shakespeare's texts (a debate continued in Edward Pechter's chapter in this volume). As Prynne puts it in his printed marginalium to the quotation above, "Shackspeers Plaies are printed in the best Crowne paper, far better than most Bibles". Whatever we might make of Prynne's fears, he bases his own case on the ability of material substrates to affect the meaning and power of the inscriptions they carry.

There is some basis for the generalization that the folio format made Jonson's and Shakespeare's collected works seem somehow Biblical. The folio format was indeed used for important books thought to deserve a place in history, unlike the smaller and more ephemeral quarto and octavo formats. Although early modern Bibles were printed in nearly every format imaginable, from large folios to tiny thirty-twomos, the folio format regularly provided Bibles with the most monumental of book forms. According to A.S. Herbert, T.H. Darlow, and H.F. Moule's bibliography of printed English Bibles, folio was the standard format for every major translation in the sixteenth and early seventeenth centuries; that is, whatever additional small formats might have been used to give a particular Bible greater marketability or portability (such as the 1560 Geneva Bible in quarto), practically all translations were printed in folio at least once, and usually on their first appearance.[36]

However, while there is a clear connection between the 1623 Shakespeare Folio as an archival format and the reception of Shakespeare's texts, the relation between the Folio's form and content may be more complicated than an implicit analogue to folio Bibles. Charlton Hinman's monumental study of the 1623 Shakespeare Folio acknowledges the symbolism of the book's format, but asserts that the publishers' choice of format was also determined by practical considerations having to do with volume and encyclopedic scope—an ambition reflected in the Folio's (inaccurate) claim, in its prefatory materials, to be "absolute in its numbers." As Hinman describes,

> many factors must have been considered when the Folio was planned, but the format adopted was in large measure pre-determined by the number and length of the plays to be printed and by the desire to set them forth "all in one volume." Here, to be sure, were the collected *works* of Shakespeare; and it has been plausibly suggested that the publishers wished to confer upon these works the dignity customarily associated with reproduction "in folio." No doubt they did. Yet they can have had no real choice as to format—or at least [. . .] no choice that we can suppose based on the nature rather than on the extent of the material to be printed.[37]

Here Hinman offers an important and easily overlooked point about the Folio's symbolic status as an archive. As obvious as the Folio's symbolic link to the Bible and other books of cultural heritage may seem to be, that status is conferred upon the Folio not entirely by design, but also by the Folio's encyclopedic scope. Folio was a format for completists.

Hinman's points about the connection between the folio format, on one hand, and the information management problem presented by Shakespeare's texts, on the other, prompts us to see new implications in the Folio/Bible homology that seems so obvious in Prynne. His preoccupation throughout the part of *Histrio-Mastix* where he mentions Shakespeare is specifically the size of books and the scale of texts. Prynne's preface to his own book twice expresses anxiety about books impudently swelling from quarto format to folio, first in the passage quoted above mentioning the alarming growth of playbooks in size and number, and again when he excuses his own omission of some Scriptural and patristic quotations for fear of "augment[ing] this *Quarto* Treatise into many *Folio* Volumes."[38] Prynne's fears about his readers becoming lost among book-based navigational aids for Scripture are of a piece with the long history of bibliographical anxiety over the Shakespeare Folio as a textual archive—the specter of lostness haunts both. It is not the case, then, that Shakespeare's Folio simply appears Biblical, but rather that both books in folio format become scriptural technologies that restructure originary acts of writing within a new archival form.

The folio format thus raises and assuages anxieties about accuracy, completeness, memory, and substitution. All of these themes appear in Heminges and Condell's epistle to the Folio's readers, but they also return us to Hamlet's reference to writing tables and its connection to the Mosaic Tablets. For example, Marjorie Garber notes that the conjunction of "tables" and Hamlet's ghostly father's "commandment" evokes the parallel moment in Exodus, but the evocation unsettles rather than stabilizes the play's representation of memory and textual transmission. As Garber puts it, "we can see the operation of substitution here through erasure, the inscription on the tables of 'thy commandment,' which is—to revenge? to remember? to do the one through the agency of the other?"[39] Emphasizing the importance of the first and second sets of the tablets in Exodus, she sees erasure and substitution operating throughout *Hamlet* in other moments, such as Hamlet's unidentified revisions to *The Mousetrap* or his substitution of the forged commission that leads to Rosencrantz's and Guildenstern's deaths (in place of his own); of these examples she notes, "Hamlet's writing is [. . .] already a copy, a substitution, a revision of an original that does not show its face in the text."[40]

One could go further to link Garber's insights to what Paul Werstine aptly terms the textual mystery of *Hamlet*, since that mystery embodies the very ambivalence and disunity she describes in Hamlet's writing.[41] *Hamlet* stands on one hand as a literary inheritance, Shakespeare's greatest writing preserved by the archive, but on the other as a complex textual network of what may be substitutions, imperfect copies, and revisions. Even the staging of Hamlet as a writer and reviser of texts depends partly upon the interventions of others into Shakespeare's texts. For example, Hamlet's reference to writing tables points not just to technologies of prosthetic memory, but also to a "prosthesis of the inside," as Derrida calls the substrate in *Archive Fever*.[42] Derrida's phrase in part explains how Hamlet's speech can be performed without any actual writing tables present as a prop, with the result that Hamlet's reinscription of the Ghost's words becomes entirely psychological and apparently unmediated. The explicit stage direction in line 109 that Hamlet *"writes"* does not appear in any of the authoritative early editions (F, Q2, and Q1). It was added in 1709 by Nicholas Rowe, and subsequent editors have moved it around in the speech. (Harold Jenkins's collation, for example, notes that John Dover Wilson's edition inserts the stage direction after line 107, a placement that would make Hamlet's uttering of the commonplace idea "That one may smile, and smile, and be a villain" simultaneous with his writing of it.) Rowe's emendation makes this speech on writing and memory that much more the product of the inscription technology of the Shakespeare edition.[43]

Similarly, Leah Marcus's reading of Hamlet's speech shows that the play itself enacts the ambivalence that textual scholars collectively feel about the reliability of its texts. She brings up Hamlet's tables as a detail to support her larger thesis that F manages the text of Hamlet with an eye to its presentation in print, pointing out an apparently minor textual crux in Hamlet's speech regarding the number of ghostly *adieus* that may, depending on how an editor handles it, affect the interpretation of Hamlet's mnemonic efforts. In all three sources, Hamlet himself quotes the Ghost as saying "adieu" twice before "remember me," but in Q1 and Q2 the Ghost himself says "adieu" three times, rendering Hamlet a faulty remembrancer of the Ghost's words from only a moment before. Marcus notes the significance that F's Ghost says "adieu" only twice, which makes F-Hamlet's memory accurate, and which supplies a two-*adieu* reading for modern editors who wish memory to tally with experience, "so that Hamlet's writing has the precision we expect of a 'copy.'"[44] Jenkins, for example, does not emend from F, leaving his Ghost with three *adieus* and his Hamlet with an error.

The material mediations and editorial interventions possible in this speech, read in light of Garber's and Marcus's points, make it impossible to consider the representation of memory in this scene without facing the question of the presence or absence of Rowe's stage direction, or of the accuracy of Hamlet's quotation of the Ghost, and thus of the material mediation of Shakespeare's text.[45] Hamlet's speech thus serves as a test case for the representational stakes of inscriptive media, old and new. Those representational stakes are indivisible from the forms of imaginative engagement that scriptural technologies enable. Put simply, faith in the text begins with the form of the book.

IV: HAMLET'S iPAD (AND THE iPAD'S *HAMLET*)

> "Ah!" cried the old man, brightening up, "now I know. Look," turning the leaves forward and back, till all the Old Testament lay flat on one side, and all the New Testament flat on the other, while in his fingers he supported vertically the portion between, "look, sir, all this to the right is certain truth, and all this to the left is certain truth, but all I hold in my hand here is apocrypha."
>
> "Apocrypha?"
>
> "Yes; and there's the word in black and white," pointing to it. "And what says the word? It says as much as 'not warranted;' for what do college men say of anything of that sort? They say it is apocryphal. The word itself, I've heard from the pulpit, implies something of uncertain credit. So if your disturbance be raised from aught in this apocrypha," again taking up the pages, "in that case, think no more of it, for it's apocrypha."
>
> Herman Melville, *The Confidence-Man*[46]

Like the old man in Melville's novel, pinching the pages of the Biblical Apocrypha between his fingers and letting the "certain truth" of the Old and New Testaments fall to either side in the volume before him, readers of codex books may experience textual faith and material form in perfect alignment. The gesture transfers naturally to Shakespeare, and it is even possible to imitate Melville's bibliographic symbolism with the Shakespearean apocrypha added to the second impression of the 1664 Third Folio. Since the plays *Pericles, The London Prodigal, Thomas Cromwell, Sir John Oldcastle, The Puritan, A Yorkshire Tragedy,* and *Locrine* were bound in sequence at the end of the volume, following *Cymbeline,* a reader with a modern sense of Shakespeare's canon can physically isolate the plays that modern scholars deem "not warranted." (Now, of course, the reader would need to let the leaves of *Pericles* fall gently away to join the accepted canonical plays.)

The desire for a perfect textual archive has articulated itself through similar bibliographic metaphors based on what Gary Taylor calls the Folio's "massive authority," literally an authority derived from material properties of the Folio as a book. According to Taylor, this authority

> has tended to impose an autonomous model [of textual production]— despite overwhelming evidence to the contrary, both within the Shakespeare canon itself, and in literary history generally. Attempts to identify collaborators in the Shakespeare canon have been characterized as "disintegration"—another spatial metaphor, which takes the sheer physical oneness of the many bound copies of the 1623 volume as an accurate reification of an ideal authorial wholeness.[47]

A parallel explanation of the effect Taylor describes may be found by shifting contexts to Northrop Frye's discussion of the Bible in *The Great Code.* In what amounts to Frye's note on the texts, he begins by conceding that

> the Bible is more like a small library than a real book: it almost seems that it has come to be thought of as *a* book only because it is contained for convenience within two covers. In fact what the word "Bible" itself primarily means is *ta biblia,* the little books. Perhaps, then, there is no such entity as "the Bible," and what is called "the Bible" may be only a confused and inconsistent jumble of badly established texts.[48]

Frye immediatley answers his own objection: "However, all this, even if true, does not matter. What matters is that 'the Bible' has traditionally been read as a unity, and has influenced Western imagination as a unity. It exists if only because it has been compelled to exist." However, for Frye it is not so simple, and he makes room for the possibility of an aesthetic unity that transcends historical contingency: "Yet, whatever the external reasons, there has to be *some internal basis* even for a compulsory existence" (emphasis added). In this configuration of objections to and rationales for treating the Bible as a textual unity, Frye succinctly lays out the stakes of the same problem that Taylor identifies in Shakespeare's texts. Even when presented with bibliographical evidence about the far-from-ideal textual process that resulted in the Folio, many Shakespeareans would still give some version of Frye's answer. There can be little question of the book's role in compelling these kinds of textual unities to exist, as Frye notes, but the role of the e-book in this process is less certain.

With Taylor's and Frye's points about bibliographical and textual unity in mind, it is worth noting that the old man in Melville's story also employs the original form of digital reading, using his fingers to manipulate and mark divisions in the text he reads.[49] Scriptural writing tropes, along with the metaphor of the book as archive, have reentered the cultural imagination through hand-held, tablet-style reading devices, with consequences for how Shakespeare will be read and imagined in years to come. Amazon.com, for example, markets a "Kindle Edition" of *Hamlet* as it does for all its public domain texts, applying a label which conflates the bibliographical categories of edition and format, and which echoes the First Folio's enabling fiction of the unity of received text and material format. More than other e-reading devices, however, the iPad stands in direct connection to this symbolic tradition of reading and writing in its emphasis on human hands. Hamlet likely used a stylus with his writing tables, but the God of Exodus writes digitally, with divine finger on divine substrate (at least with the first set of tablets). Let us conclude, then, by taking Hamlet's speech as a test case for the symbolic and material stakes of reading Shakespeare on an iPad.

As of December 2010, nearly a year after Steve Jobs's iPad rollout, a search for "Shakespeare" in the Apple iPad App Store returns about 100 results, many of which are only tangentially related to Shakespeare by accidents of metadata. The most highly rated Shakespeare app, and the one appearing first in the order of results, is one simply titled *Shakespeare,* published by the company Readdle. The app offers a complete set of Shakespeare's plays and poems along with supplementary materials, such as several Shakespeare portraits, and tools such as a glossary and concordance, accessible through a straightforward and usable interface. Like Adams and Triplet's *Writing Tables,* the app bundles together tools and references in a package for a specific device, emphasizing their grouping as a single object in a way that a website cannot. The symbolic value of the concordance is especially worth noting, since it was the publication of that particular tool that famously prompted the *Saturday Review* in 1863 to call Shakespeare the "Englishman's secular Bible," now that both works had concordances of their own. Like the nineteenth-century Folio facsimile which David Scott Kastan calls "an edition proudly sounding the *sola scriptura* theme, like that which had marked the Protestantism of the time of its writing," the *Shakespeare* app also promises Shakespeare texts detached from the messy histories of their transmission.[50]

The source for the app's texts, a website called Playshakespeare.com, notes that its texts are not scholarly editions, but like many free Shakespeare sites it offers corrected texts derived primarily from those of the Folio and the 1866 Globe edition.[51] PlayShakespeare.com says more about its texts than most other free sites of its kind, but still remains part of a pseudo-editorial tradition that retreats to the authority of the Folio and the Globe edition instead of engaging with each of Shakespeare's texts case by case and working through the complex transmission questions that each one presents.[52] Oddly enough, the Shakespeare canon the app represents includes plays which did not appear in the Folio, and which have at various times been considered "not warranted": *Pericles*, *Edward III*, and *Sir Thomas More*—here they are symbolically restored to the archive which the iPad app takes the Folio to embody and authorize. This early and evidently successful app deals with Shakespeare's texts not as inscriptions—as material texts with histories—but rather as a unified and downloadable body of Shakespearean scripture, whose precise origins and chain of transmission remain mystified but nonetheless accessible to readers.

However, the text of *Hamlet* resists easy translation, which may explain why it is such a fascinating play to encounter in new media. What Gitelman calls the "savability" of written inscriptions and their counterparts in memory is precisely what *Hamlet* calls into question.[53] The scriptural authority of the Folio, even when translated to digital forms, must always exist in paradoxical tension with the erasability represented by Hamlet's writing tables. Reading *Hamlet* on the iPad, then, also means reading the iPad through *Hamlet*. As much as the iPad might seem like perfection of the wax writing tablets of antiquity—instantly and infinitely erasable and rewritable—our acts of reading and writing on the iPad are nonetheless regulated by the kind of authority that governs inscriptions. That authority manifests itself in Digital Rights Management systems and iTunes, the centralized approval and distribution system of Apple's App Store, Apple's refusal to support Firefox and Flash on the device, and the deliberate lack of direct access to a file system or command-line interface. What may or may not be inscribed in an iPad's local memory and screen is governed by rules nearly as complex and intractable as Mosaic law or the rules that seem to bind Old Hamlet's ghost. In this light, the device that Jobs presented to the world that morning was both a blank slate, ready to receive the future, and an inscribed list of rules constituting a social order.

Readdle's *Shakespeare* will certainly not be the only major Shakespeare app created for the iPad, but it provides a telling counterpoint to the imagery of the rollout event described in this chapter's introduction. Like Apple's ironic choice of a Moses image that stands for erasure, not permanence, the textual simplicity of this first major Shakespeare app forgets the nature of Shakespeare's texts in order to represent them. Using the app requires an act of faith in the noiseless transmission of texts, but it remains to be seen whether that faith will eventually be troubled by the kind of doubt that has made the print editing of Shakespeare so exciting and contentious in recent decades. Predictions about the liberating or disintegrating effects of hypertext on Shakespeare's corpus were rampant in the first decade of digital editions on the Web, but my purpose here has been to show that it is different with e-books for tablets. The old continuities of scriptural symbols are not so easy to escape. As those of us who study the history and materiality of literary texts become app designers ourselves, not merely the audiences of tech demos, we need to understand the symbolic as well as bibliographical implications of the stage direction that appears (without square brackets) in the Readdle *Shakespeare* app's version of Hamlet's speech, next to his reference to memory tables: "*He writes.*"

NOTES

1. Martin Peers, "Apple's Hard-to-Swallow Tablet," *Wall Street Journal*, 30 December 2009, Eastern edition, C12.
2. The rollout video may be viewed at http://www.apple.com/apple-events/january-2010/ and downloaded from the Apple Keynotes podcast on iTunes (accessed 31 July 2010).
3. See Douglas M. Lanier, "Shakescorp Noir," *Shakespeare Quarterly*, 2002, vol. 53, no. 2, 157–80.
4. *The Holy Bible, with Illustrations by Gustav Doré*, London: Cassell, Petter, and Galpin, ca. 1866.
5. Michael Joyce, *Othermindedness: The Emergence of Network Culture*, Ann Arbor: University of Michigan Press, 2001, p. 213.
6. Peter Stallybrass et al., "Hamlet's Tables and the Technologies of Writing in Renaissance England," *Shakespeare Quarterly*, 2004, vol. 55, no. 4, 379–419, p. 415. Just like the iPad, the Adams and Triplet writing tables (in sixteenmo format) were designed to be used in both landscape and portrait orientations; see Roger Chartier, *Inscription and Erasure: Literature and Written Culture from the Eleventh to the Eighteenth Century*, Philadelphia: University of Pennsylvania Press, 2007, pp. 23–5. On the history of wax tablets more broadly, see Richard H. Rouse and Mary A. Rouse, "Wax Tablets," *Language & Communication*, 1989, vol. 9, no. 2, 175–91.
7. William Powers, *Hamlet's BlackBerry: A Practical Philosophy for Building a Good Life in the Digital Age*, New York: HarperCollins, 2010.
8. Unless otherwise noted, all *Hamlet* quotations come from Harold Jenkins's Arden 2 edition; Walton-on-Thames, UK: Thomas Nelson, 1997.
9. Marjorie Garber, *Shakespeare's Ghost Writers: Literature as Uncanny Causality*, New York: Routledge, 1997, pp. 152–3; P.K. Ayers, "Reading, Writing, and Hamlet," *Shakespeare Quarterly*, 1993, vol. 44, no. 4, 423–39; Stallybrass et al., "Tables."
10. See Ann Blair, *Too Much to Know: Managing Scholarly Information Before the Information Age*, New Haven, CT: Yale University Press, 2010.
11. Stallybrass et al., "Tables," pp. 411–2.
12. Ibid., p. 415.
13. Ibid., p. 416.
14. Ibid., p. 417.
15. Frances A. Yates, *The Art of Memory*, Chicago: University of Chicago Press, 1966.
16. Gary Taylor, "The Renaissance and the End of Editing," in George Bornstein and Ralph G. Williams (eds) *Palimpsest: Editorial Theory in the Humanities*, Ann Arbor: University of Michigan Press, 1993, p. 135.
17. Wilfred Cantwell Smith, *What Is Scripture?: A Comparative Approach*, Minneapolis: Fortress Press, 1993, p. ix.
18. In William T. Liston (ed.) *Francis Quarles' Divine Fancies: A Critical Edition*, New York: Garland, 1992, p. 125.
19. All quotations are from Robert Carroll and Stephen Prickett (eds) *The Bible: Authorized King James Version with Apocrypha*, Oxford: Oxford University Press, 1997; original italics indicating non-Hebrew interpolations have been removed.

20. On the metaphor of blotting one's name from the book of life, see Schofield's chapter in this volume, pp. 49–53.
21. In the edition in which Doré's images appear, they illustrate the subsequent recounting of the story in Deuteronomy 9–10 (see Figure 5.1).
22. Stallybrass et al., "Tables," p. 415.
23. Jacques Derrida, *Archive Fever: A Freudian Impression*, trans. Eric Prenowitz, Chicago: University of Chicago Press, 1998, pp. 11–2; emphasis in original.
24. N. Katherine Hayles, *Writing Machines*, Cambridge, MA: MIT Press, 2002, p. 24.
25. Ibid.
26. Lisa Gitelman, *Always Already New: Media, History, and the Data of Culture*, Cambridge, MA: MIT Press, 2006, p. 6; cf. Bruno Latour's characterization of "inscription device[s]" in specifically scientific contexts in *Science in Action: How to Follow Scientists and Engineers Through Society*, Cambridge, MA: Harvard University Press, 1987, pp. 68–9.
27. Hayles, *Writing*, p. 130.
28. Cantwell Smith, *Scripture*, p. 7.
29. See Scott Schofield's chapter in this volume, pp. 50–1.
30. Bruno Latour, "Visualization and Cognition: Thinking with Eyes and Hands," *Knowledge and Society: Studies in the Sociology of Culture Past and Present*, 1986, vol. 6, 1–40.
31. Adrian Johns, *The Nature of the Book: Print and Knowledge in the Making*, Chicago: University of Chicago Press, 1998, pp. 11–19.
32. Ibid., pp. 19–20.
33. Gitelman, *Always*, pp. 19–20.
34. Derrida, *Archive*, pp. 25–6.
35. William Prynne, *Histrio-Mastix*, London, [1633], sig. **6ᵛ (emphasis in original).
36. Major folio Bibles include: the Coverdale Bible (1535, the first folio Bible in the English language; the 1537 edition was the first folio Bible printed in England), the Matthew Bible (1537), Taverner's Bible (1539), the Great Bible (1539, and especially frequently in folio thereafter), the Geneva Bible (1562), the Bishops' Bible (1568; folio editions were printed in 1584–5 specifically so that English churches would be equipped with their own Bibles), and the King James version (1611). The King James Bible was printed five times in folio between 1611 and 1623. See Arthur Sumner Herbert, *Historical Catalogue of Printed Editions of the English Bible, 1525–1961: Revised and Expanded from the Edition of T.H. Darlow and H.F. Moule, 1903*, New York: American Bible Society, 1968.
37. Charlton Hinman, *The Printing and Proof-Reading of the First Folio of Shakespeare*, vol. 1, Oxford: Clarendon Press, 1963, p. 48; emphasis in original.
38. Prynne, *Histrio-Mastix*, sig.***2ʳ.
39. Garber, *Ghost Writers*, p. 152.
40. Ibid., p. 153.
41. Paul Werstine, "The Textual Mystery of Hamlet," *Shakespeare Quarterly*, 1988, vol. 39, no. 1, 1–26. Emma Smith also depicts *Hamlet*'s textual condition in metaphorical terms drawn from the play itself in "Ghost Writing: *Hamlet* and the Ur-Hamlet," in Andrew Murphy (ed.) *The Renaissance Text: Theory, Editing, Textuality*, Manchester: Manchester University Press, 2000, pp. 177–90.
42. Derrida, *Archive*, p. 19.

43. For a different reading of this scene and Rowe's stage direction, see Charlotte Scott, *Shakespeare and the Idea of the Book*, Oxford: Oxford University Press, 2007, pp. 130–4.

44. Leah S. Marcus, *Unediting the Renaissance: Shakespeare, Marlowe, Milton*, New York: Routledge, 1996, p. 138.

45. The more recent Arden editions of *Hamlet* (edited by Ann Thompson and Neil Taylor), following a multiple-text approach with three different editions based on Q1, Q2, and F, are consequently more conservative in their stage directions than Jenkins and omit any stage direction that Hamlet writes. Their Q2 text's annotation to line 107, however, says in no uncertain terms that "Hamlet now produces a literal writing tablet or notebook," enabling the editors to intervene in the Q2 text without seeming to.

46. Herman Melville, *The Confidence-Man: His Masquerade*, New York: W.W. Norton, 2006, pp. 241–2.

47. Taylor, "Renaissance," p. 135.

48. Northrop Frye, *The Great Code: The Bible and Literature*, Toronto: Academic Press Canada, 1981, p. xii; emphasis in original; see also Travis DeCook's discussion in this volume of the history of the Biblical text as a unified corpus, p. 162.

49. See Peter Stallybrass, "Books and Scrolls: Navigating the Bible," in Jennifer Anderson and Elizabeth Sauer (eds) *Books and Readers in Early Modern England: Material Studies*, Philadelphia: University of Pennsylvania Press, 2002, pp. 42–79.

50. See David Scott Kastan, *Shakespeare and the Book*, Cambridge: Cambridge University Press, 2001, pp. 107–9.

51. http://www.playshakespeare.com/about-us (accessed 16 June 2011)

52. On the Globe edition and its ubiquity among free digital Shakespeare websites, see Andrew Murphy, "Shakespeare Goes Digital: Three Open Internet Editions," *Shakespeare Quarterly*, 2010, vol. 61, no. 3, 401–14.

53. Gitelman, *Always*, p. 19.

6 Shakespeare and the Bible
Against Textual Materialism[1]

Edward Pechter

Asked "to uncover the cultural *work* performed by the links between Shakespeare and the English Bible," we might start with the basis for the linkage itself. Interpretive traditions may "have yoked the Biblical and Shakespearean corpora together as mutually reinforcing sources of cultural authority," but Shakespeare does not emerge as a canonical scripture until 1623, acquiring fully canonical status only with the work of Edmund Malone and the Romantic critics roughly a millennium and a half after the Bible had achieved its own authority. Such a belated succession, while it may result in mutual reinforcement, is also likely to produce the jarring dissonances felt to exist between "contesting scriptures."[2] Does Shakespeare succeed the Bible as the night the day, or are the two yoked together by violence? From one angle, Shakespeare seems to reinforce an established authority, but the relation may also be construed as a "drastic swerve from the sacred to the secular," in which Shakespeare displaces the Bible from its privileged position.

I am quoting Stephen Greenblatt, for whom Shakespeare's "emptying out" of religious authority is only part of the story. Greenblatt's *Lear*, while exposing the comforting presence of religious ritual as a fraudulent "ideology," at the same time "intensifies" our "craving for such satisfaction." Although "drained of its institutional significance," the "forlorn hope of an impossible redemption persists" at the end of the action; and in this "process of evacuation and transformed reiteration," religious feeling is not so much eradicated as resituated in the context of imaginative engagement. Even as the play disaffects us from the kind of belief secured ultimately by Biblical authority, it produces a compensatory affection elsewhere, in the "force of *King Lear*" to "make us love the theater."[3]

If *Lear* is understood both to deplete and replenish religious tradition, the Shakespeare–Bible relationship can be represented in terms of continuity and discontinuity—of similarity and difference—at once; and not just can be, but has to be. Without similarity there would be no relationship to represent, but the absence of difference, adding up to identity, would again leave us with no relationship to represent. Similarity and difference are reciprocally constituting categories, and their interdependence extends to comparison and contrast, the analytical operations by which these categories are registered. Comparison and contrast, moreover, form the foundation for whatever understanding we can achieve (hence "compare and contrast" as the obligatory introduction to essay topics and exam questions). They may not exhaust our repertoire of interpretive actions, but they function together as the irreducible primitives on which all interpretations—not just Greenblatt's in "Shakespeare and the Exorcists"—are built.

The situation described here should not seem controversial (I'm doing basic deconstruction), but it has far-reaching implications for the assessment of critical practice, to which I will be turning at the end of things. For now, though, I am interested less in the structure of Greenblatt's analysis than in the objects to which he directs his attention. Or, rather, fails to direct it; for about the early publication history which makes "*King Lear*" a difficult phenomenon to fix, and about the various bibliographical incarnations going back to Tyndale (if not Wyclif) which make "*the* English Bible" a misleadingly definite designation, Greenblatt says nothing at all. If the Shakespeare–Bible link is his subject, its components function as synecdoches, standing in for general categories (religious conviction on the one hand; theatrical or, more broadly, aesthetic value on the other) rather than for any material entity (this book produced by that technology designed for reception within such and such a historical situation). In disregarding such matters, Greenblatt might be taken to view "the materiality of the text," the concept Margreta de Grazia and Peter Stallybrass installed at the cutting edge of Shakespeare studies in 1993, as without consequence for interpretive practice.[4]

"Shakespeare and the Exorcists" must look like an oddly idealist point of departure in a collection devoted to the material book, but something like Greenblatt's approach nonetheless determines my initial trajectory here. I am interested in the stakes, according to some of the many commentators who have taken up the question, when a reasonably continuous exchange is negotiated between religious conviction and aesthetic interest—when "the imagination" serves (in Ernest Tuveson's phrase) "as a means of grace."[5] I do not pursue this anomalous agenda to the edge of doom, but even when I shift over to reflect finally on the normative values of textual materialism, I have, as my saber-rattling title suggests, substantial reservations. Textual materialism has been used to identify a diverse body of material, including some of the most compelling productions in recent work critical work, so that claiming to be against (or for) it doesn't add up to a clearly meaningful position. But in what I take to be its dominant or default mode, the material book functions as a signal to align analysis with an historical particularism and a suspicion about literary power; and in this form its continued prominence on the current scene may be too much of a good thing. For all its striking achievements, the history of the material book, so I argue at the end, is not the place to invest so much of our critical resources at the present time.

I CONTINUITY

"The future of poetry," as Matthew Arnold saw it in 1880,

> is immense; in poetry, where it is worthy of its high destinies, our race, as time goes on, will find an ever surer and surer stay. There is not a creed which is not shaken, not an accredited dogma which is not shown to be questionable, not a received tradition which does not threaten to dissolve. Our religion has materialised itself in the fact; it has attached its emotion to the fact, and now the fact is failing it. But for poetry the idea is everything; the rest is a world of illusion, of divine illusion. Poetry attaches its emotion to the idea; the idea *is* the fact. The strongest part of our religion to-day is its unconscious poetry.[6]

With this pained sense of disenchantment ("Europe's dying hour," as he puts it in *Memorial Verses*), Arnold looks to poetry for the recuperation of an attenuated faith. His hopes, based on an impossibly elevated conception of poetry, were bound to be disappointed. When Arnold limits poetry to the conditions "where it is worthy of its high destinies," he requires us to exclude comedy (Chaucer) and satire (the eighteenth century) in favor of tragedy (Shakespeare), epic (Homer), and sacred subjects (Dante), to reduce as much as possible all elements of a strictly personal response and to consign historical analysis to a strictly subordinate position. The consequences—"high seriousness," and "criticism of life" are the relevant critical touchstones— virtually identify poetry with religion, so that claiming that poetry will recuperate religious value turns out to be something like a tautology.

The *OED* defines *recuperation* as "the recovery or regaining of something (material or immaterial)," and none of its definitions or examples entails any negative connotations. For these we can turn to Wikipedia, where *recuperation* is defined "in the sociological sense . . . first proposed" by "Guy Debord and the Situationists," as "the process by which socially and politically radical ideas and images are commodified and incorporated within a mainstream society."[7] When I characterized Arnold's project as recuperative, most readers probably understood the term in a Wikipedic context, because "the sociological sense" tends to be the default for textual materialism. But taken neutrally, as establishing connections between past practice and current use, recuperation is not necessarily wrong-headed (or, for that matter, right-minded). Such assessments derive from the value conferred on these practices, past and present, and on the processes by which they are recovered from or assimilated back into tradition. The problem I was pointing to in Arnold lay in the latter area. The lines connecting residual and emergent beliefs are drawn with a solidity that obscures significant differences between the old religion and the new aesthetics, overinvesting in continuity at the expense of difference. There are some recuperative projects, however, where the process, though inevitably still beset with complications, is nonetheless treated with more nuance and finesse, nowhere more so than in the reflections of Johann Gottfried von Herder who, since he wrote on both Biblical and Shakespearean interpretation, may be said to illustrate the Shakespeare–Bible link in more than just a metaphorical sense.

According to Herder, an engagement with Shakespeare requires first of all an unconstrained abandonment to the spirit of the text. As he puts it in *Shakespeare* (1773), "if then, my dear reader, you were too timid to give yourself over to the feeling of setting and place in any scene, then woe betide Shakespeare and the withered page in your hand."[8] This idea of imaginative sympathy is central to Herder: *Einfühlung*, his term for it, is, according to Hans Frei in *The Eclipse of Biblical Narrative*, Herder's invention.[9] Failing to extend it, we deprive not only Shakespeare of its vital energy but ourselves of the power it might communicate to us. (The page is withered, but as Herder's metaphor suggests, so is the hand holding the page.) In *The Spirit of Hebrew Poetry* (1782), Herder puts us into the same interpretive relation with the Bible as with Shakespeare—a kind of feedback loop co-activated by the text and our identification with it. To a skeptical interlocutor, baffled by the cultural and linguistic remoteness of the Hebrew Bible, Herder prescribes *Einfühlung* again: "if you place yourself in the circumstances of the ancient herdsmen, in their wandering unsettled mode of life, the most distant derivative will still give back something of the original sounds of the words, and of the original feeling."[10] The advice resonates with a "famous passage about the Old Testament" quoted by Frei: "Become with shepherds a shepherd, with a people of the sod a man of the land, with the ancients of the Orient an Easterner, if you wish to relish these writings in the atmosphere of their origin."[11]

The striking coincidence between Herder's treatments of Shakespeare and the Bible prompts David Norton, reflecting on "the relationship between religion and literature," to characterize "Herder's theological aesthetic" as "one of the most thorough discussions of the connections, even the identity, between the two." The moment we try to fill in the details, however, these connections unravel and the identity breaks down. According to Norton, anyone "who would read the Bible as literature . . . must willingly suspend his disbelief."[12] But the words elided from Coleridge's *Biographia*, "that willing suspension of disbelief *for the moment*, which constitutes poetic faith,"[13] insist on the provisionality of aesthetic engagement, and provisionality as an approach to the Bible seems problematic. As Auerbach says in *Mimesis*, Homeric effects, by contrast with Scripture, works "merely to make us forget our own reality *for a few hours*."[14]

As Frei remarks, the "total surrender" Herder requires of us to "the spirit of any specific past" is at the same time "necessarily accompanied by an equally pervasive detachment at every other level." The *Einfühlung* is thus "confined solely to the aesthetic mode. No particular past manifestation had any more normative claim on one's own religious, philosophical, moral, or even aesthetic positioning of oneself than any other."[15] The effect is similar to Keats's negative capability, taking "as much delight in conceiving an Iago or an Imogen,"[16] and Keats in turn is of a piece with Norton's other requirement for anyone who would read the Bible as literature, that he "must give as much credence to God as he would to a successful character in literature."[17] But the God of the Bible is a jealous God, demanding something more than the conditional assent accorded to a well-rounded literary character. The Book of God, moreover (as Gabriel Josipovici calls it),[18] is a jealous book, asking us not merely to "relish the atmosphere" of its origin in the moment of our engagement ("fancy dies/ In the cradle where it lies"), but submit once and for all to its revelation of truth (*"tolle, lege"*— "pick it up, read it").[19]

Herder has no hesitation in acknowledging Scripture as the revealed word of God, but he seems to have no great investment in doing so either. As Frei puts it, his affirmations of the "historical factuality of the stories of the Bible" are accorded "no ultimate explanatory status in their own right"; the "essential thing" is rather "the spirit that led to this kind of realistic writing," and communicating with the spirit requires the empathy of an aesthetic sensibility more than it does archival research or religious faith, and from this angle, if Herder "failed to distinguish between factuality and fact-likeness,"[20] he doesn't have to. Fact-likeness effectively absorbs factuality by virtue of its higher position in the hierarchy of Herder's interpretive interests. "Realistic writing"—*"l'effet de réel"*— constitutes what we take to be the reality behind the text. Salvation, it seems, is an effect of Biblical discourse.

At other times, however, it is truth itself that matters most to Herder, independently of the script through which it is mediated. "Whoever turns a gospel of Christ into a novel has wounded my heart," he writes to the "imaginary correspondent" addressed in his *Letters Concerning the Study of Theology*, "even though he had done so with the most beautiful novel in the world."[21] Such a passionate commitment to the primacy of Biblical truth does not square with the priority Herder elsewhere accords to a strictly aesthetic engagement with Scripture, but in *The Spirit of Hebrew Poetry* Herder focuses on the relationship between the Hebrew and Christian Bibles in a way that at least gestures toward reconciliation.

> The basis of theology is the Bible, and that of the New Testament is the Old. It is impossible to understand the former [i.e., New Testament] aright without a previous understanding of the latter [i.e., Old Testament]; for Christianity proceeded from Judaism . . . Let the scholar then study the Old Testament, even if it be only as a human book full of ancient poetry, with kindred feeling and affection, and thus will the New come forth to us of itself in its purity, its sublime glory, and more than earthly beauty.[22]

In the standard view Herder inherited, the Old Law depends on the fulfillment provided retrospectively by the New. In this passage, though, Herder effectively reverses the relationship. The Hebrew Bible is not just chronologically but ontologically prior; it is not superseded by but is rather the foundation for whatever theological understanding might be communicated by the Christian Bible. Having choreographed this daring reversal, however, Herder then restores the traditional order, or at least the conclusion to which it had led. The transcendent revelation of the Gospels is now seen to emerge as the crowning realization of an imaginative engagement with the poetry of the Hebrew Bible. "Poetic faith," as Coleridge designated our willing and temporary suspension of disbelief, morphs somehow into the stability of religious conviction.

"Somehow" is the key term here. If "Poetry reveals the God-given oneness of life," as Norton sums up Herder's "theological aesthetic,"[23] the revelation "comes forth of itself," independently of any antecedent circumstances. Herder never explains how an investment of "kindred feeling and affection" in a "human book" develops into the "more than earthly beauty" of divine revelation—still less why it has to. If Herder's "basic position" is that we "may believe in the oneness of life without believing it is God-given," then the "necessary connection between poetry and religion" does not seem necessary at all.[24] Disconnection seems a more likely consequence, as in Lessing's *Education of the Human Race* (1780), where a secular consciousness shows no tendency to proceed upward toward transcendent purity but remains steadfastly rooted in the worldly interests of its origins—where the imagination does *not* become a means of grace.

Herder might look to be caught in the recuperative predicament I described in Arnold, but far from glossing over the contradictions of his position, Herder is at once conscious of the differences between religious conviction and aesthetic experience and eager to thrust them on to the consciousness of his readers. Hence his regular use of a dialogical mode. When he addresses an "imaginary correspondent," as in his remark that novelizing the Gospel "wounds my heart," the effect is to enlarge the discursive space to accommodate a different point of view; but since Herder elsewhere expresses this point of view *in propria persona*, the difference cannot be taken as absolute. Like the "skeptical interlocutor" mentioned earlier, the antagonists who swell the scene of Herder's writing function as not-so-secret sharers, giving voice to different aspects of Herder's own contradictory beliefs. Herder explains that *The Spirit of Hebrew Poetry* is written as a series of dialogues in order to "escape" the "necessity of contradictions, of strife, and of numberless citations."[25] But it cannot be the mere fact of contradiction he would escape (dialogue, of course, foregrounds the fact) but rather the felt need to decide among contradictory beliefs—the commitment of disputatious rhetoric to win the argument at all costs—he wishes to avoid.

Herder was committed to the distinct advantages of specific formations—national and ethnic identities, historical epochs, cultural institutions and expressions. He understood that these did not exclude other formations from which different advantages might be claimed, and he was unwilling to sacrifice the various benefits available from any or all sides. When it came to religious and aesthetic experience, Herder saw no reason to favor either one decisively. He would have understood Northrop Frye's point that "Ultimately, as we should expect, the Bible evades all literary criteria"[26]—he himself sometimes occupies the position from which Frye's claim emerges; but he resists the all-or-nothing consequences that Frye's "ultimately" demands. As Frei says, Herder accords "no ultimate explanatory status" to the "factuality" of Scripture. But then he accords no such status to its literary effects either. To claim that "*in the long run*," the "spirit or outlook" is "more important" for Herder than "the factual truth" of Scripture,[27] attributes a desire for finality that is alien to his principles and temperament.

Herder's respect for contingent differences and his resistance to synthesizing metanarratives have allowed him to be incorporated smoothly into the routines of postmodern thought, but perhaps too smoothly. If he insisted on the distinctions among historical periods, he did not conceive of historical process as a radically discontinuous series of ruptures. He had an unshakable conviction in the unfolding meaning of history—the "oneness of life," as Norton describes it, God-given or not. In the same way, his respect for distinct identities should not be confused with cultural relativism. Like most participants in the European Enlightenment, Herder supposed that we meet each other across our differences—historical, geographical, cultural—on the ground of a shared humanity. In this sense, Herder is indeed committed to "the necessary connection between poetry and religion," since both, whatever their irreconcilable modes of sensibility and belief, answer to the same fundamentally human need.

II   DISCONTINUITY

Reading Herder is an extraordinarily dramatic experience. Religious conviction and aesthetic interest are necessarily connected, he tells us—and essentially different from one other. Their relationship illustrates at once a continuity in historical process—and a decisive break from the past. But however peculiar Herder's instinct to foreground the volatile admixture of beliefs that constitute his thought, the same general structure typically sustains the work of other commentators for whom the religion–aesthetics link is similarly rendered at once secure by fundamental similarity and precarious by undeniable difference. I am thinking of Frank Kermode, who explores the complex relation between Biblical and literary hermeneutics in a contrast between myths and fictions: "Myths call for absolute, fictions for conditional assent." Northrop Frye develops the same point in terms of two different functions of myth, "the poetic and the concerned": "as a story, it is poetic and is recreated in literature; as a story with specific social function, it is a program of action for a specific society."[28] To these we might add the commentators Tuveson describes, going back from the Romantics through Montagu and Akenside and Hutcheon and Shaftesbury et al., at least as far as to Addison. The list could be greatly expanded.

But how, in any case, is textual materialism is related to all this? David Scott Kastan's *Shakespeare and the Book* can get us moving toward an answer. Although "the material form and location in which we encounter the written word are active contributors to the meaning of what is read," Kastan argues that in "literary studies there has long been a tendency to act as if the works we read have a reality independent of the physical texts in which we engage them." Kastan is "deeply suspicious" of this tendency and proposes a corrective "focus on the physical forms in which literature circulates and on the conditions that govern both its production and consumption." This "does not in any way," he assures us, "deny the importance of [the text's] symbolic patterning, somehow refusing its 'literariness' in favor of its social existence." Rather, "such attention seeks" a "more comprehensive conception" of critical practice that "should expand, not in any way limit, our understanding of the text."[29]

Bill Brown, introducing a "cluster" of essays on "Textual Materialism" solicited for a 2010 issue of *PMLA*, takes a similarly reassuring line. A materialist "book history," while it "draws attention to those determinants (from questions of layout to questions of law) that worked to stabilize the semantic experience for a specific readership in a specific time and place," does not deny that "the literary work" can "be said to 'transcend' the object (Genette)." Although the "experience of *Great Expectations* is a different experience" in its different material forms, "we're still generally willing to say that each experience is the experience of *Great Expectations*. Across those very different mediations, the novel in some sense remains the same." The "experience of texts," Brown concludes, "amounts to a dialectical drama of opacity and transparency, physical support and cognitive transport, representation as object and as act."[30]

Brown's "dialectical drama" coincides nicely with Kastan's claim for a "more comprehensive" approach, "expanded" to include the material and historical specificity of books along with the "'literariness'" of the texts they inscribe. "Dialectical," moreover, as long as we jettison the idea of a synthesis that often comes with it, seems to fit across the whole range of both Scriptural and literary analysis. According to Frei, "Biblical interpretation since the eighteenth century has always proceeded in two directions," one following a tradition of "figural reading," the "chief use" of which was "for unifying the canon" across "differing cultural levels and conditions" as a way "of learning what abiding meanings or values these writings might have," the other focused on the "specific historical circumstances" surrounding the early inscriptions of the text as a way of determining "the origin and, in some respects, the reliability of biblical writings."[31] Marjorie Garber describes a similar situation for Shakespeare. "Shakespeare is in a way always two playwrights, not one: the playwright of *his* time, the late sixteenth and early seventeenth centuries in England, and the playwright of *our* time, whatever time that is."[32]

It should come as no surprise that Biblical and Shakespearean interpretation may each be described as dialectical. If (as I argued at the beginning) interpretation develops perforce from a sense of both continuity and discontinuity, every critical analysis can be called dialectical. The problem with this bird's eye view, however, is that it doesn't leave us with much to do beyond saluting the dialectical dramas as they march by our reviewing stand. For more leverage, we need to reflect on the different emphases and particular configurations of this universal structure, and here a closer look at Brown and Kastan will help.

Brown's "dialectical drama" is notably lopsided. Opacity and physical support dominate transparency and cognitive transport. Textual Materialism is drawn chiefly to those particular and peculiar circumstances— the "specific readership" and "specific time and place"—for and out of which this or that book has been produced. Textual materialism is much less interested in continuity, those "abiding meanings and values" that (in Frei) allow "the literary work" to appeal across "differing cultural levels and conditions" as far as to the here and now (in Garber) of "*our* time, whatever time that is." The inverted commas in Brown's "'transcend' the object" work to contain literary power within the space of what "might be said" by other people. The idea of transcendence has long been in general circulation, so attributing it to Genette seems gratuitous, but the citation has a pointed effect: reduced to the formalist excesses of an outworn buried narratology, the literary tends to be stripped of its residual legitimacy (who wants yesterday's papers?).

Kastan, too, places inverted commas around a key concept in his critical apparatus, and with similar effects. "Literariness," to be sure, might be justified, in that there is no solid consensus about the term. But if literariness is subject to dispute, so too is its opposing term, "social existence," which Kastan nonetheless transcribes without punctuational hedging. Clarity may not be the issue here. With "symbolic patterning," Kastan has no trouble specifying a clear association between literariness and formalism, and this reductive identification works (as in Brown) to produce a diminished phenomenon, the more so in contrast to the putatively robust solidity of social existence. The inverted commas, then, do not so much acknowledge uncertainty as imply triviality.

If this implication tends to raise doubts about Kastan's commitment to a "comprehensive" approach, his treatment later of Lewis Theobald reinforces skepticism. Theobald made significant advances in the historical recovery of early Shakespearean texts, while at the same time (or in close temporal proximity) freely adapting the plays to serve current interests.

This inclusive approach to the abiding meanings of the literary text and the original inscriptions of the material book might seem to embody the "expanded" and "in no way limited" approach Kastan claims to want. Yet by characterizing Theobald's attitude as an "amphibian contentment," Kastan seems rather to disparage ignorant complacency than appreciate large-mindedness; his representation of Theobald's procedure, "in one mode, presumptuously altering his plays for success on the stage, while, in another, determinedly seeking the authentic text in the succession of scholarly editions that followed Rowe's," suggests not so much a normative value as a pathological self-contradiction. A "schizophrenic relation to Shakespeare," Kastan calls it. "It must seem odd."[33]

As the adverbs suggest, Kastan prefers the determination of a materialist historicism to the presumption of appropriative pragmatism (another lopsided dialectic), and the same preference motivates "Shakespeare and the 'Element' He Lived in," written two years earlier to introduce his *Companion to Shakespeare Studies*. Following "the most familiar of the clichés of Shakespeare studies," that "he is our contemporary," we are said to "drag him forward into our present, ignoring how much he is a stranger in it," when it is rather "the differences" that "must be insisted on." To justify this claim, Kastan expands on the passage from *Antony and Cleopatra* alluded to in his title.

> The riches of [Shakespeare's] artistic achievement, like Antony's "delights," may well raise themselves "dolphin-like . . . above/ The element they lived in," but they can never fully escape it; even the acrobatic dolphin is dependent upon its natural element for life and can never safely be removed from it for any length of time.[34]

Transcendence is diminished here to an appealing fantasy. Though it's "pretty to think so," as Jake Barnes says to Lady Brett in *The Sun Also Rises*, the dolphin Shakespeare can no more than Jake raise himself above his cultural and material constraints.

Strictly speaking, the figure doesn't work; Shakespeare has managed to survive "safely," even flourish for centuries, among audiences and readers largely indifferent to the element he lived it. But it's the tone, rather than facts or logic, that matters—a disarming combination of hard-headed realism and good-natured sympathy, as in the "Gentle madam, no" with which Dolabella declines to credit Cleopatra's vision. *Antony and Cleopatra* includes other voices in which Dolabella's Roman values sound more patronizing, even dismissive. So here: putting Shakespeare back into his proper place—the material book in which he was first read, the theatrical space where his plays were first performed, the social existence of his earliest readers and audiences—is hard to distinguish from cutting Shakespeare down to size, downgrading the literary power by which the plays transcend the conditions of their original production. He was not

for all time but of an age. As in *Shakespeare and the Book*, Kastan denies
any such intention.

> This is not, *of course*, to suggest that the proper goal of our engage-
> ment with Shakespeare is to sequester him safely back in his own time
> . . . Art is not, *of course,* reducible to its historical determinants . . . It
> should *go without saying* that to focus on the enabling conditions of
> Shakespeare's art is not to detract from the plays they enable.[35]

These reiterated protestations are, again, not fully reassuring. After so
much *occupatio*, what forgiveness?

By now it should be clear how textual materialism fits in with the other
critical approaches reviewed earlier. It belongs at the opposite end of the
spectrum from the recuperative project from which we began. Where
Arnold downplays difference, difference is what textual materialism is all
about.

In this respect, textual materialism exhibits a deep family resemblance
to recent work emphasizing the disparity between Renaissance interpretive practices and our own. Historical scholars have for some years been
amassing evidence to suggest that Renaissance readers typically extracted
nourishing tidbits from texts without much regard for the ideas of textual
coherence or authorial intention which tend to guide modern interpretation. They had, as Marion Trousdale argued in 1973, "a different sense of
meaning and a different value placed on form."[36] John Wallace develops the
point a year later: the Renaissance reader "was involved for his own good,
and it was immaterial (or only occasionally material) whether one reader's
interpretations were the same as another's, or identical with the author's."[37]
More recently, John Kerrigan, citing Thomas Lodge's advice "'What a Sto-
icke hath written, Reade thou like a Christian,'" comments that the text is
the reader's "to use, to modify and select from."[38]

Trousdale, Wallace, and Kerrigan all emphasize that this readerly freedom was subject to practical constraints. As Kerrigan puts it, although "the
means of extracting" significance "were particular, indeed personal," the
extracted significances themselves inclined to uniformity, the established
"truths accessible (and for the most part already familiar) to all."[39] (Just
"being a Christian," a notably inclusive category for a post-Reformation
Englishman, is enough.) Recent historians of Renaissance reading practice,
working in a more self-consciously materialist mode, have downplayed the
stabilizing pieties of a shared religious conviction. As a result, Renaissance
interpreters, disconnected from text and author and now from a community of believers, seem to have nothing but their own "particular, indeed
personal" needs to direct response.

Charles Whitney, for example, rejecting as unhistorical "all the scholarly attention given to collective response," devotes *Early Responses to
Renaissance Drama* to "demonstrating the actual diversity and creativity

of early reception." Simon Forman, Whitney's primary exhibit to illustrate "the early modern fashion," was "drawn to plays featuring specialties of his own, prognostication, magic, and medicine," forming his judgment in ways "directly related to his identity and experience."[40] It's not just that Forman was "involved for his own good"; his capacity to register value is peculiarly limited to the eccentricities of his own self-centered sensibility. He "was offended by the treacherous murder of a fellow oracle," Whitney claims of one response[41]; but professional/craft solidarity or any other form of fellow feeling was not in Forman's nature. As Barbara Traister points out, "Forman cut his own route, setting up as a medical and astrological practitioner outside the system, claiming God-given powers as his justification." His "sense of being set apart," she adds ("always 'mistrustful,'" "[o]ver and over" expressing "fear of being cheated, robbed, jailed, fined, gulled, or even murdered"), "led to loneliness and a degree of paranoia."[42] Small wonder he is claimed as a source for Jonson's Alchemist.

The same bizarrely obsessive egotism would seem to make Forman a poor candidate for the role of exemplary figure, but Whitney's point is that eccentricity is the norm for the "diversity" and "pluralism" of early modern response. From this perspective, the Renaissance reading practices represented in the current critical mode may be said to aspire to the condition of marginalia—those often illegible marks made by usually anonymous readers for "peculiar, even personal" reasons we lack the context to determine. As William Sherman puts it in a symposium on "Material Culture," "a significant proportion of the notes in books have more to do with the life of the reader than the content of the text."[43] Developing the point in his monograph for the University of Pennsylvania Press series on "Material Texts," Sherman alters "a significant proportion" to "a large proportion" and confronts directly the implicit issue of whether Renaissance practice is so remote from us as to be not merely different from but radically discontinuous with what we understand. Because the implications of *reading* "do not fit well with the evidence that survives from the pre-modern archive," Sherman "(somewhat perversely) avoid[s]" the word in favor of "the language of 'use.'"[44] Renaissance engagements with texts are (*pace* Monty Python) something completely different.

Between the extreme difference of textual materialism, then, and the virtual identity of recuperation, where should we want to position ourselves? The obvious answer, that we should occupy the middle, registering both the continuities and discontinuities, turns out to be unhelpfully general. If every textual and historical interpretation proceeds perforce from an interplay of similarity and difference, the middle, after all, is not just the right place but the only place to be. But the same deconstructive principle that stipulates all interpretation to be dialectical declares that all dialectics are lopsided (every binary is a hierarchy). The question, then, remains: should our position in the middle be closer to the recuperative or the materialist pole?

The case against recuperation is forcefully represented in current work. By emphasizing continuity, recuperation tends to produce an uncritical inflation of the values found in a reified tradition, ignoring the manifold ways in which traditions are constructively contested to serve particular interests. Stephen Greenblatt, describing his professional formation at Yale during the 1960s, identifies the problem: "one of the more irritating qualities of my own literary training" was "its relentlessly celebratory character" as "a kind of secular theodicy. Every decision made by a great artist could be shown to be a brilliant one; works that had seemed flawed and uneven ... were now revealed to be organic masterpieces," the "triumphant expression of a healthy, integrated community."[45] Greenblatt was bidding an unfond farewell to all that, and most practitioners of academic literary criticism have endorsed his valediction.

The case against discontinuity is less prominently represented at present, but Northrop Frye is a notable exception. In *The Great Code*, Frye (like Frei) distinguishes between a "critical approach" to the Bible, which "establishes the text and studies the historical and cultural background," and a "traditional" approach, which interprets Scripture "in accordance with what a consensus of theological and ecclesiastical authorities have declared the meaning to be." As Frye sees it, the critical approach, which has "dominated Biblical criticism for over a century," is focused so intently on the material genesis of the text that it effectively precludes other kinds of engagement. The Bible is "certainly the end product of a long and complex editorial process," but the "end product needs to be examined in its own right," and once "disintegrating the text became an end in itself," this examination becomes virtually impossible. While "any number of books" demonstrate that the creation story derives from "the latest of the four or five documents that make up" Genesis, there is little speculation along the line that "creation stands at the beginning of Genesis, despite its date, because it belongs at the beginning of Genesis."[46] As Frye sums up the argument in an address to the English Institute a few years earlier, what we need, instead of the "narrowly historical obsession" of a "retreat into some hypothetical embryonic stage of textual development," is a criticism that can "tell us something about why the books of the Bible exist as they now do in their present form."[47]

Greenblatt's description suggests why we might keep some distance from Frye's position. Frye's argument against disintegrating the text invests questionably in the value of textual unity. He "would lead us to an integrated study of the Book of Genesis, and eventually of the whole Bible, as it now stands,"[48] and, once we "accept the whole Bible as an imaginative unity of myth and metaphor," to a revelation of "the entire structure of post-Classical European literature, for which the Bible provided a mythical and metaphorical framework."[49] But since this enterprise admittedly depends on our participation in a hermeneutic "tradition" in "accordance with a consensus of theological and ecclesiastical authorities," you can see why Greenblatt might be irritated.

Still, irritation by itself doesn't take us very far. Tzachi Zamir may be right to suggest that the current focus "on past-present discontinuities" derives from the sense that "continuities tend to attach themselves to an oppressive interpretation of human nature"[50]; but what alternative interpretations are proposed? Textual materialism can be appreciated simply as an antidote to Frye's vast glomming (my enemy's enemy is my friend), but sooner or later those who want "to stabilize the semantic experience for a specific readership in a specific time and place" have to answer the question Shylock is asked about his pound of flesh: "what's that good for?"[51]; or, more specifically, to take on Frye's claim that "the procedure is futile," because

> there is, quite simply, no end to it. If we start to "demythologize" the Gospels . . . in quest of some historical core of events of which we can say "this at least must have happened," we shall find that we have thrown out so much of the Gospels that not one syllable of any of the four of them is left.[52]

You throw the sand against the wind, and the wind blows it back again.

This might be dismissed as the grumbling of a superannuated idealism, but a toned-down version of Frye's skepticism is audible within materialist precincts themselves. Robert Weimann, citing the promise of a "'revolution in Shakespeare studies,' as Margreta de Grazia and Peter Stallybrass term it" (in their piece on "The Materiality of the Shakespearean Text" mentioned earlier), wonders why the revolution "has not provided us with satisfying answers yet": "it is one thing to acknowledge . . . that bibliographic standards often reflected 'personal taste rather than textual corruption,'" but "quite another question to define and clarify the new premises" on which a more secure critical practice might be built.[53] Exposing the sutures that confer a retrospective cohesion onto Shakespeare and the Bible and the relation between them does little to clarify the felt need for continuity addressed by these compelling representations of unity in the first place. It is one thing to disassemble the Frankenstein creature, quite another to eradicate the desire to bring the dead back to life.

If all this makes it hard to choose a position on the spectrum I described earlier, the choice may be unnecessary after all, at least as an absolute and binding commitment. In 2001, Greenblatt's *Hamlet in Purgatory* predicated its whole endeavor on a passionate engagement with textual energy:

> My only goal was to immerse myself in the tragedy's magical intensity. It seems a bit absurd to bear witness to the intensity of *Hamlet*; but my profession has become so oddly diffident and even phobic about literary power, so suspicious and tense, that it risks losing sight of—or at least failing to articulate—the whole reason anyone bothers with the enterprise in the first place.[54]

In effect, Greenblatt reverses his position of eleven years earlier. Faced with the skeptical detachment dominating current work, he is drawn now to something like the "secular theodicy" he found so "irritating" then. There is no scandal here. Circumstances change, and unless we are gods or Jonsonian humors, we change with them. Meaning and value are context-specific. "To all things *there is* an appointed time, and a time to euerie purpose vnder the heauen"; "Nothing is good . . . without respect. . . . / How many things by season season'd are/ To their right praise and true perfection!"[55]

From this angle, the question becomes where we want to position ourselves *now*. The answer requires a complex judgment about (in Arnold's phrase) "the function of criticism at the present time," and readers will disagree with one another and probably with themselves from time to time. As I see it, Greenblatt's view of the situation looks about right. This is not necessarily to be against textual materialism, because textual materialism is not necessarily phobic about literary power. When Sherman tells us he has "been astonished by the sheer volume of notes produced by early readers" and "equally astonished by the variety of techniques, habits, and interests they document,"[56] his astonishment echoes the estrangement of Russian Formalism, with its High Modernist agenda of making it new. But the potential for innovation has not figured prominently in most materialist projects, which tend to prefer eliminating "literariness" to renewing it. (After communicating his astonishment, Sherman quotes appreciatively from an essay called "Literary History without Literature," objecting to "the destructive poverty of the category of 'literature'" and the "various exclusions" associated with the "establishment of the literary," whose effect "twists the connection between [literary] texts and the culture in which and for which they were produced.")[57]

The future of poetry is not immense, but it will be more secure if we create a larger space within the disciplinary discourse to accommodate literary and theatrical power. Those of us whose business is poetry—workers in song—can only profit from such an enterprise. The literary traditions we have inherited from Arnold and the Romantics may include nightmarish elements from which we want to escape, and some textual materialist projects will continue to produce knowledge of compelling interest; but the prospect of another twenty years dominated by the dismissals of "'literariness'" for the presumed ideology of its hypothetical cultural work is not encouraging. "War wearied hath perform'd what War can do." It's time to move on.

NOTES

1. Thanks to Gordon Fulton and Paul Stevens, for encouragement and advice, to Gary Kuchar, for sharing his much more substantial knowledge of this material with me, and to Alan Galey and Travis DeCook, for editorial intelligence and forbearance beyond any reasonable expectation.
2. For these quotations, see the Introduction to this volume, pp. 1 and 2.
3. Stephen Greenblatt, *Shakespearean Negotiations: The Circulation of Social Energy in Renaissance England*, Berkeley and Los Angeles: University of California Press, 1988, pp. 125–7.

4. Margreta de Grazia and Peter Stallybrass, "The Materiality of the Shake-spearean Text," *Shakespeare Quarterly*, 1993, vol. 44, no. 3, 255–83.
5. Ernest Lee Tuveson, *The Imagination as a Means of Grace: Locke and the Aesthetics of Romanticism*, Berkeley and Los Angeles: University of California Press, 1960.
6. Matthew Arnold, "The Study of Poetry," in R.H. Super (ed.) *English Literature and Irish Politics: Complete Prose Works of Matthew Arnold*, Ann Arbor: University of Michigan Press, 1973, vol. 9, p. 161.
7. Wikipedia, <http://en.wikipedia.org/wiki/Recuperation_%28sociology%29>, accessed May 4, 2 011.
8. Johann Gottfried von Herder, *Shakespeare*, edited and translated by Gregory Moore. Princeton University Press, 2008, p. 42.
9. Hans W. Frei, *The Eclipse of Biblical Narrative: A Study in Eighteenth and Nineteenth Century Hermeneutics*, New Haven and London: Yale University Press, 1974, p. 184.
10. Johann Gottfried von Herder, *The Spirit of Hebrew Poetry*, trans. James Marsh, vol 1, Burlington, VT: Edward Smith, 1833, p. 36. <http://www.archive.org/stream/thespiritofhebre01herduoft#page/n311/mode/2up>, accessed May 4, 2011.
11. Frei, *Eclipse*, p. 185.
12. David Norton, *A History of the Bible as Literature*, Cambridge: Cambridge University Press, 1993, p. 198.
13. Samuel Taylor Coleridge, *Biographia Literaria or Biographical Sketches of My Literary Life and Opinions*, edited by James Engell and Walter Jackson Bate. London: Routledge, and Princeton, NJ: Princeton University Press, 1983, part 2, p. 6.
14. Erich Auerbach, *Mimesis: The Representation of Reality in Western Literature*, Princeton, NJ: Princeton University Press, 1953, p. 15 (emphasis mine).
15. Frei, *Eclipse*, p. 185 (emphasis mine).
16. John Keats, *Selected Letters*, edited by Grant F. Scott. Cambridge, MA: Harvard University Press, 2002, p. 195.
17. Norton, *History*, p. 198.
18. Gabriel Josipovici, *The Book of God: A Response to the Bible*, New Haven, CT: Yale University Press, 1988.
19. Shakespeare, *Merchant of Venice*, 3.2.68–9; Saint Augustine, *Confessions*, newly translated and edited by Albert C. Outler. Philadelphia: Westminster Press, 1955.
20. Frei, *Eclipse*, p. 186.
21. Quoted in Frei, *Eclipse*, p. 187.
22. Herder, *Spirit*, vol 1, pp. 22–3.
23. Norton, *History*, p. 199.
24. Ibid., pp. 199, 201.
24. Herder, *Spirit*, vol 1, pp. 20–21.
26. Northrop Frye, *The Great Code: The Bible and Literature*. In Alvin A. Lee (ed.) (2006). *The Collected Works of Northrop Frye*. Toronto, Buffalo, and London: University of Toronto Press, vol. 19.
27. Frei, *Eclipse*, p. 191, my emphasis.
28. Frank Kermode, *The Sense of an Ending: Studies in the Theory of Fiction*, London, Oxford, and New York: Oxford University Press, 1966, p. 39; and Northrop Frye, *The Great Code*, p. 10. Kermode develops the idea most fully in *The Genesis of Secrecy: On the Interpretation of Narrative*, Cambridge MA: Harvard University Press, 1979. Frye devotes an entire chapter to the similarities and differences between "the poetic and the concerned"

in *Words with Power: Being a Second Study of "The Bible and Literature,"* in Michael Dolzani (ed.). (2008). *The Collected Works of Northrop Frye,* Toronto, Buffalo, and London: University of Toronto Press, vol. 26.

29. David Scott Kastan, *Shakespeare and the Book*, Cambridge: Cambridge University Press, pp. 3–5.
30. Bill Brown, "Introduction: Textual Materialism," *PMLA,* 2010, vol. 125, no. 1, 24–28, pp. 24–26.
31. Frei, *Eclipse*, pp. 7, 17.
32. Marjorie Garber, *Shakespeare After All*, New York: Pantheon Books, 2004, p. 28.
33. Kastan, *Shakespeare and the Book*, p. 93.
34. David Scott Kastan, Introduction: "Shakespeare and the 'Element' He Lived in," in *Companion to Shakespeare Studies*, Oxford and Malden, MA: Blackwell, 1999, p. 4.
35. Ibid., pp. 3, 5, my emphases.
36. Marion Trousdale, "A Possible Renaissance View of Form," *English Literary History*, 1973, vol. 40, no. 2, 179–204, p. 201.
37. John M. Wallace, "'Examples are Best Precepts': Readers and Meanings in Seventeenth-Century Poetry," *Critical Inquiry*, 1974, vol. 1, no. 2, 273–90, p. 275.
38. John Kerrigan, "The Editor as Reader: Constructing Renaissance Texts," in James Raven, Helen Small and Naomi Tadmore (eds) *The Practice and Representation of Reading in England*, Cambridge: Cambridge University Press, 1996, pp. 102–24, p. 117.
39. Ibid., p. 128.
40. Charles Whitney, *Early Responses to Renaissance Drama*, Cambridge: Cambridge University Press, 2006, pp. 2, 147, 149, and 155.
41. Ibid., p.155.
42. Barbara Howard Traister, *The Notorious Astrological Physician of London: Works and Days of Simon Forman*, Chicago: University of Chicago Press, 2001, pp. 27, 6, and 27.
43. William Sherman, "Used Books," *Shakespeare Studies XXVIII*, Cranbury, NJ, London, and Mississauga, Ontario: Associated University Presses, 2000, pp. 145–8.
44. William Sherman, *Used Books: Marking Readers in Renaissance England*, Philadelphia: University of Pennsylvania Press, 2008, p. xiii.
45. Stephen Greenblatt, *Learning to Curse: Essays in Early Modern Culture*, New York and London: Routledge, 1990, p. 168.
46. Frye, *Great Code*, p. 11.
47. Ibid., p. 18.
48. Ibid., p. 11.
49. Frye, "History," p. 18.
50. Tzachi Zamir, *Double Vision: Moral Philosophy and Shakespearean Drama*, Princeton, NJ: Princeton University Press, 2007, p. 57.
51. Shakespeare, *Merchant*, 3.1.52.
52. Frye, "History," p. 18.
53. Robert Weimann, *Author's Pen and Actor's Voice: Playing and Writing in Shakespeare's Theatre*, Cambridge: Cambridge University Press, 2000, pp. 40, 41.
54. Stephen Greenblatt, *Hamlet in Purgatory*, Princeton: Princeton University Press, 2001, p. 4.
55. Ecclesiastes 3.1, Geneva Bible; *Merchant*, 5.1.99 and 107–8.
56. Sherman, *Used Books*, p. xii.
57. Ibid., p. xv.

7 Going Professional
William Aldis Wright on Shakespeare and the English Bible[1]

Paul Werstine

In 1884 the Shakespearean and Biblical scholar William Aldis Wright published *The Bible Word-Book: A Glossary of Archaic Words and Phrases in the Authorised Version of the Bible and the Book of Common Prayer.*[2] The pages of this glossary represent the entanglement of not only the text of the English Bible with the English literary canon, but also the various strands of knowledge and collaboration that ran through the professional life of a late Victorian philologist, bibliographer, editor. Most striking in *The Bible Word-Book* and elsewhere in Wright's work is the contrast between his generally rigorous devotion to history in his philology and his relaxation of that rigor in bringing into philological conjunction the King James Version of the Bible and the Shakespeare canon, neither of which in history could have exercised any influence on each other.

Let us begin by examining a curious entry in this glossary, for the word *cherubins*, and consider the implications it holds for a reader of the King James Bible in 1884 (see Figure 7.1 the following page).

As an entry in a glossary, the text would be expected to contain an explanatory equivalent to or *gloss* on the headword *cherubins*, as do almost all the other entries in this particular glossary. The word in question seems to cry out for such explanation because, as *OED* notes under *cherub*, Biblical "accounts [of cherubins] . . . are not consistent": sometimes the reference is to "living creatures" and sometimes to "images," as in the passage that Wright quotes from Exodus 25.18, 19. Later Christian mysticism includes cherubins among angels. It is puzzling that Wright fails to include any such comparable information about the headword in this entry.

Instead, he gives his readers his knowledge of historical philology (including etymology and morphology) and textual criticism (including the genealogy of the reading "cherubims" in the Authorized Version [AV] and the Prayer Book), the disciplines of Wright's scholarly expertise. While we are not told what *cherubins* means, we are told by Wright the philologist the languages from which it was borrowed and given several examples of its usage prior to the AV, with deference to Shakespeare in the entry's three citations from his plays, which appear emphatically at·

Cherubins, *sb.* (Ps. xviii. 10, Pr.-Bk.). This form of the word, which has been retained from the Wicliffite and Coverdale's versions, came into the language through the French *cherubin*, and Italian *cherubino.* Cotgrave (*Fr. Dict.* s.v.) has,

Cherubin : m. A *cherubin.*

Rouge comme vn cherubin.   Red-faced, *Cherubin*-faced, hauing a fierie facies like a *Cherubin.*

In the earlier Wicliffite version, Exodus xxv. 18, 19 is thus rendered :

And two goldun *cherubyns* and forgid with hamers, thow shalt make on either party of the preiyng place; that o *cherubyn* be in the o syde of Goddis answeryng place, and that othere in that othere.

See also Chaucer, *Canterbury Tales*, prol. 626 :

A Sompnour was ther with us in that place,
That hadde a fyr-reed *cherubynes* face.

'Cherubin' being once admitted into the language as a singular noun, the plural 'cherubins' is regularly formed.   Our translators have followed the Geneva Version in using the hybrid form 'cherubims,' in which the sign of the English plural is added to a word which is already plural in Hebrew.   Misled by this some editors of Shakespeare print 'cherubim' as if it were singular in *The Tempest*, I. 2. 152 :

O, a *cherubin*
Thou wast that did preserve me.

Shakespeare always uses 'cherubin' and never 'cherubim;' as for instance in *Othello*, IV. 2. 62 :

Patience, thou young and rose-lipp'd *cherubin.*

In one case (*Macbeth*, I. 7. 22) 'cherubin' is plural as in the Te Deum, 'To thee cherubin and seraphin continually do cry.' It is therefore, perhaps, not necessary to change it to 'cherubim,' although everywhere else in Shakespeare the plural is 'cherubins.'

Figure 7.1   Entry for "Cherubins" in *The Bible Word-Book* (London, 1884). Image courtesy of the Caven Library, Knox College, University of Toronto.

the end. On the whole Wright appears to privilege Shakespeare's customary forms—*cherubin* in the singular and *cherubins* in the plural. It is also noteworthy that although Wright is composing a glossary to the AV, he chooses as his headword a word that, he says, does not appear in that translation of the Bible, but is instead drawn from Shakespeare. That playwright's usage seems to function as a standard of philological value, as is widely the case in Wright's *Word-Book* and as is consistent with Wright's explicit judgments of Shakespeare as a writer: "the greatest of merely human men . . . the subtlest of thinkers," whose "language" is that of "the most eloquent of poets."[3] Nonetheless, as a professional philologist, Wright at the same time tolerates wide variety in the word's morphology. He recognizes *cherubims* as a "hybrid form," rather than condemning it as an error arising from a failure to understand *cherubim* as a Hebrew plural. Later he allows the early printed *Macbeth* text the use of the singular *cherubin* as a plural, in accord with the usage of the English translators of the ancient Latin hymn "Te Deum." As a textual critic, he notes that AV translators were influenced by the creators of the 1560 Geneva Bible in printing *cherubims*. These purely scholarly issues elbow out of the entry any practical considerations of *cherubins'* multiple meanings or references that might enable a user of Wright's glossary to get on with reading the AV or the Prayer Book, the purpose for which one would buy his book in the first place.

Wright acknowledges in his preface to the *Word-Book* that the work was originally designed by Jonathan Eastwood to serve just this purpose specifically for Sunday School children who were being taught to read by reading the AV, but that he turned Eastwood's work in a different but much more scholarly direction:

> A portion of [what became the *Word-Book*] was published some years ago [by Eastwood] in a periodical for Sunday Schools called 'The Monthly Paper.' . . . With his consent I modified the treatment of the words, in which he aimed more especially at the instruction of Sunday School children, and endeavoured, in most instances by recasting each article, to render the work a contribution to English lexicography. Besides this, I added a large quantity of examples from my own reading, arranging them in chronological order, and more than trebled the number of words in Mr Eastwood's original list. For such etymological notes as occur in the course of the volume I am alone responsible.[4]

While Wright felt sufficiently indebted to Eastwood to publish the first edition of *Word-Book* in 1866, two years after Eastwood's death, as their jointly authored work, by the time he published the second edition in 1884, he had so transformed the book in the direction of an authoritatively comprehensive work of scholarship that he listed himself as its single author. To this second edition, Wright brought his experience as "Secretary to the Company appointed for the Revision of the Authorised Version of the Old Testament,"[5] a group of first twenty-five, then twenty-seven Biblical scholars, who would meet almost eight hundred times over the course of sixteen years (1870–85) to consult about their revision. [6] "In the course of the Revision work," he observed, "my attention has been called to the language of the Authorised Version, sentence by sentence, phrase by phrase, and word by word, in such a way that I trust nothing of importance has escaped my notice. In this second edition therefore will be found many archaisms of language and usage which were not recorded in the former, and many additional illustrations which I have gathered in the course of eighteen years' reading."[7] The entry "Cherubins"—with its illustrations of the word's etymology and usage, its careful attention to the forms of the word in particular translations of the Bible—is one of Wright's additions to the 1884 edition.

Wright's *Word-Book* in many ways typifies his scholarly publications on both the Bible and Shakespeare. Its conception, initial design, and early development is the work of another. Wright completes the work by bringing to it the learning and skills in philology, bibliography, and textual criticism of a professional scholar. In this way he adds considerable scholarly value to the design and the labor he receives from another, even if occasionally Wright's scholarship obscures the usefulness and accessibility of the publication to a larger readership, as is the case with the "Cherubins" entry from the *Word-Book*. This pattern in Wright's publishing career extends through his contributions to the Cambridge Shakespeare editions, the Clarendon Press Shakespeare series, and *A General View of the History of the English Bible*, publications from across most of his career. All in all the pattern informs Wright's published work on the Bible and Shakespeare until very near the end of his life, but not his other published work, which is rich and varied.[8] His individual scholarly habit was not then essentially collaborative, for he famously "said that an editor who knows his business is better without a colleague."[9] Where Shakespeare and the Bible are concerned, though, he was willing to constrain his evidently strong personality and to submit to the directions and purposes of others.

In another way, too, the *Bible Word-Book* and particularly the "Cherubins" entry exemplify Wright's peculiar treatment of Shakespeare, together with other canonical early modern literary figures, and the Bible. Even though Wright was an historical philologist who paid appropriate attention to the chronology of publication of works in assessing the possible influence of one work on another, as will be strikingly in view when this essay turns to his revision of *A General View of the History of the English Bible*, nonetheless when Wright was handling important literary figures, especially Shakespeare, and the AV, he seems to have set their historical relation—or rather lack of relation—aside. From a strictly historical point of view, it makes no sense to bring Shakespeare's usage to bear on the usage of the AV, as Wright does in the "Cherubins" entry and widely throughout the *Word-Book*, because most of Shakespeare's writing, including the three plays explicitly cited or quoted in the particular entry, had yet to see to print in 1611 when the AV was published, and what Shakespeare that was then published was scattered across separate quartos and the occasional octavo. No one then could have had any sense of what Shakespeare's usage was. No one could have any such sense until 1623 when thirty-six Shakespeare plays were published in folio, and no one would begin to assess Shakespeare's usage for yet another hundred years. Nor was Shakespeare's usage affected by that of the AV; his Bibles were the Geneva and the Bishops' of the sixteenth century. The same is largely true of Ben Jonson's usage, also occasionally cited by Wright in the *Word-Book*, for Jonson's works were not published in a collection until 1616 in a folio that included only the production of the first half of his career. The usage of, for example, George Herbert, Philip Massinger, and John Milton, whom Wright also quotes, has even less relevance to the AV, for these writers published only after 1611. When Wright brings the AV into relation with literature (usually in the form of Shakespeare), he is no longer writing as an historical philologist, but as a presentist. Only from his own historical perspective do these two texts, the AV and Shakespeare, rise up as the twin pillars of early modern usage.

This observation is not meant to detract from either the value or the significance of Wright's scholarly achievements. With his collaborators on the Cambridge Shakespeare, he produces an edition that will serve as the standard one for nearly a century—remarkable testimony to the quality of his work.[10] Just as Jonathan Eastwood's trial run on the *Bible Word-Book* is that of a highly educated man (with a MA from Cambridge) but nonetheless an amateur scholar whose profession was churchman, so the editing of Shakespeare before the first Cambridge Shakespeare (1863–6) is also the work of amateurs—no matter how gifted, learned, and dedicated they were—and, like the *Word-Book*, Shakespeare editing is ready in the 1860s for transformation by scholars. Among the Cambridge editors' nineteenth-century predecessors in the editing of Shakespeare, Edmond Malone and James Boswell the Younger, editors of the twenty-one volume 1821 Variorum, had trained as lawyers.[11] So had the American Richard Grant White, who had an undergraduate degree from the University of the City of New York and had also studied medicine; his first edition dates from 1857–66.[12] Both Charles Knight, with many editions beginning with the Pictorial Edition of 1838–43, and John Payne Collier, whose first edition of four appeared in 1842–4, were primarily journalists.[13] Samuel W. Singer, with two editions of 1826 and 1856, was a bookseller before he was an editor.[14] James Orchard Halliwell, whose edition appeared in 1853–65, and Alexander Dyce, the first of whose three editions was published in 1857, both devoted their lives to scholarship, but neither was associated with an academic institution after they ceased to be university students.[15] Before Howard Staunton turned to the editing of Shakespeare, at which he enjoyed some success, he was a chess master.[16] For a somewhat closer but still very distant match to the Cambridge editors, we must turn to the American Henry N. Hudson (whose first edition dates from 1851–6), who worked successively as a farmer, coachmaker, Shakespeare lecturer, and Boston clergyman, and who lectured on Shakespeare at Boston University.[17]

The editions published by these amateur editors vary a great deal. At one extreme there is the variorum style of the Boswell-Malone 1821 edition, which captures in its voluminous notes all the commentary then published on the Shakespeare texts. At the other extreme is Dyce's 1857 edition, with its brief introductions to the texts, which treat mainly their dates and sources, and its notes following each text that are confined to discussions of the readings that he prints. In spite of such variety in the editing, what all these editions share is an effort by their editors to provide a context for the Shakespeare texts that will render them accessible to readers and increase readers' chances of engaging with and appreciating Shakespeare. To some extent, all these editors (although Dyce least so) are moved by the spirit alive in Jonathan Eastwood as he is drafting his *Bible Word-Book*.

With the Cambridge editors, it is quite otherwise. The Cambridge Shakespeare differs from its predecessors in that it is devoted entirely to establishing a text of the plays and poems, and presenting the basis for that text, and not at all to contextualizing, commenting on, or explaining that text. Its introductions to the texts list only the sixteenth- and early seventeenth-century printings in octavo, quarto, and/or folio and discuss only issues of textual transmission. The initial co-editors—John Glover, Wright's immediate predecessor as Librarian at Trinity College, Cambridge, and William George Clark, a fellow and sometime tutor at the College and public orator of the University—present their narrowly defined scholarly goals at the beginning of their Preface to the first volume:

> The main rules which we proposed to ourselves in undertaking this Edition are as follows:
>
> 1. To base the text on a thorough collation of the four Folios and of all the Quarto editions of the separate plays, and of subsequent editions and commentaries.
> 2. To give all the results of this collation in notes at the foot of the page, and to add to these conjectural emendations collected and suggested by ourselves, or furnished to us by our correspondents, so as to give the reader in a compact form a complete view of the existing materials out of which the text has been constructed, or may be emended.[18]

These collation notes are the only notes on Cambridge Shakespeare pages. However inhospitable this edition is to lay readers, it was an enormous scholarly undertaking insofar as it obliged its editors to locate all extant early printings of the plays and poems and to compare to each other not only the different quartos and folios, but also the different copies of each of these printings. Just to access each of the early editions was a challenge in that for such a popular play as *Richard III*, there are editions in 1597, 1598, 1602, 1605, 1612, 1622, 1629, and 1634. Most of these are now held by public institutions, but in the Cambridge editors' day many were still in private hands and less accessible. However, it was not enough for the Cambridge editors to locate and collate single copies of the quartos, for they knew that copies of the same edition might well differ from each other:

> As is the case with most books of that time, different copies of the first Folio are found to vary here and there; generally, however, in a single letter only [This characterization has turned out to be a bit too restrictive]. It is probable that no one copy exactly corresponds with any other copy. We have indicated these variations, wherever they were known to us, in a note either at the foot of the page or at the end of each play.[19]

Such variation within a single edition arose from the cost of the paper on which the books were printed. The paper was expensive because virtually all of it had to be imported. Therefore, when a proofreader discovered what he took to be an error in a sheet being run off the press, he might well order the press stopped for as long as it took to correct the apparent error, but would not order destroyed the sheets that had already been printed with the error in them because paper was too valuable. Consequently, uncorrected sheets would be bound up at random with corrected sheets in the copies of books offered for sale on the bookstalls.

When Wright succeeded Glover both as Clark's co-editor on the Cambridge Shakespeare and as Librarian at Trinity College, he took up the laborious task of collating multiple copies of multiple quartos with no less vigor than if he had conceived of the plan for the edition himself—such apparently was the power that editorial service to Shakespeare could exert in the 1860s on the will of the individual scholar. Wright's correspondence often mentions trips he made to prominent centrally located libraries—the Bodleian and the British Museum, as well as the Duke of Devonshire's Library at Devonshire House in London—to consult or collect quartos for collation. His letter to Macmillan of 24 January 1864 advises of his plan to come to London to collect quartos of *Richard II* from the British Library and Devonshire House to collate and then to go to Oxford to collate more.[20] Wright's efforts in this regard did not cease with publication of the first Cambridge edition of 1863–6 but continued in the expectation of publication of the second edition that appeared in 1891–3. There are over a thousand letters in Wright's Shakespeariana in the Wren Library at Trinity College, Cambridge,[21] many of them responses to Wright's inquiries about particular copies of quartos of the plays and poems as to their dates of publication and particular readings—strong evidence of how he continued to bend himself to the task of making the Cambridge edition as complete as he could, according to Glover's original conception of its design.[22] From the very beginning of his work on the Cambridge Shakespeare, Wright had striven to make it as accurate as possible; writing to Macmillan very early in his work on the first edition on 23 September 1863, he vowed, "This volume will be the most perfect of any."[23]

The Cambridge edition was equally ambitious in offering to record in its footnotes, in the words of its original editors Glover and Clark, "all emendations suggested by commentators."[24] However, these editors later indicated some exceptions in this regard: "In recording conjectures, we have excepted only (1) those which were so near some other reading previously adopted or suggested, as to be undeserving of separate record, and (2) a few . . . which were palpably erroneous. Even of these we have given a sufficient number to serve as samples."[25] In preparing for his second edition, Wright was equally scrupulous, as his Shakespeariana indicates, in cataloguing every letter he received that contained an emendation, no matter how improbable, checking the proposed emendation against his record of the history of conjectural emendation by editors and others, and thereby distinguishing original conjectures from those proposed in ignorance of this history. This evidence testifies to the impressive extent to which Wright was willing throughout his scholarly career to expend every possible effort to execute a plan for an edition not of his own devising—as long as the edition was of Shakespeare and was relentlessly scholarly.

So strong was Wright's commitment to his collaboration on the Cambridge Shakespeare that he even defended, when required to do so, features of the edition with which, the historical record shows, he personally disagreed. One of these features is modernization of spelling and punctuation; it makes sense that Wright, in his total commitment to the scholarly, would prefer, as he did, old-spelling editions, no matter how forbidding to readers, to modern-spelling ones.[26] Nonetheless, when the controversialist C.M. Ingleby attacked the Cambridge Shakespeare for printing a particular modernization, Wright rose to the defense of this reading. The line at issue between Ingleby and Wright is from *Measure for Measure*—a play, it is to be noted, from the first volume of the first Cambridge edition, and therefore one on which Wright did not work, so that he is defending as if it were his own the work of Glover and Clark. In the Cambridge Shakespeare, the line reads "fond shekels of the tested gold" (2.2.149). The textual note at the bottom of the page indicates that "shekels" is Pope's emendation of the Shakespeare First Folio's reading, "sickles." In one of the very rare notes at the end of this play, its editors note that they have modernized the Folio's "sickles" to "shekels" in accord with their plan to produce a modernized edition.[27] Wright's ability to identify the two readings as forms of the same word with reference to his philological knowledge of Biblical translation is impressive:

'Sickles' and 'shekels' are . . . two different forms of the word which have come down to us from two different sources. 'Sicles' held its place from Wicliffe down to the Bishops' Bible. It was very likely what Shakespeare read in church. Wicliffe of course got it from the Vulgate. 'Shekels' comes from the Hebrew through the Geneva version.[28]

Besides demonstrating Wright's unflinching solidarity with his fellow editors, Wright's defense of this reading also provides a glimpse of the underpinning of the Cambridge Shakespeare in the same historical philology often in evidence in Wright's *Bible Word-Book*—underpinning that is seldom visible in the Cambridge Shakespeare itself, which reserves its notes entirely for reference to the establishment of its text.

However much Wright disliked editorial collaboration and modernized editions, nonetheless he continued to collaborate with Clark, after their completion of the first Cambridge Shakespeare, on the Clarendon Press Series of Shakespeare's plays in modern spelling. Together they edited only four plays, but after Clark's retirement from the Series, Wright continued with editions of thirteen more plays, all in modernized texts and in the same format as the first four collaborative volumes, again suppressing his own preferences to the design of the originally collaborative enterprise. The Clarendon Press Series brings us back around to Wright's interests in philology and the Authorized Version, despite the latter's irrelevance to Shakespeare. His impressive erudition is evident in his ability to cite a wide range of texts and dictionaries from Shakespeare's period in providing examples of comparable usages of the same word that Shakespeare uses. For the purposes of this essay, however, what is remarkable about Wright's notes on Shakespeare is his resort to the King James Bible (KJB), the so-called Authorized Version (AV). Commentators had long referred to the Bible to explain Shakespeare's allusions, as they still do, and when they do, they refer to the versions of the Bible to which Shakespeare's language seems closest, sometimes the Geneva Bible, sometimes the Bishops' Bible. However, as is evident from Wright's commentary on *The Tempest*, for example, the version of the Bible he has uppermost in mind and the one he thinks his reader too will know is the AV. When Prospero tells Miranda "in my false brother/ Awaked an evil nature" (1.2.93–4), Wright draws his readers' attention to the word *awaked*:

This form of the preterite [simple past tense, abbreviated "pret."] is always found in Shakespeare. Both 'awaked' and 'awoke' occur in the Authorised Version; as for instance Gen. xxviii.16, 'Jacob awaked out of his sleep'; and ix.24, 'And Noah awoke from his wine.' Again, Shakespeare always uses 'waked,' and never 'woke'; and in this his usage agrees with that of the Authorised Version. The two forms are perhaps due to the fact that our word 'wake' represents two A. S. [Anglo-Saxon] words, *wácian*, pret. *wácode* or *wácude*, and *wæcan*, pret.

wóc. But this will not explain the existence of the two forms 'shook' and 'shaked,' which are found in Shakespeare as well as in the Authorised Version.[29]

The note has strayed a long way from the text to which it refers; indeed the reader has no need for such a note in order to read Shakespeare's lines, an indication that again scholarly interests have elbowed out practical considerations, just as is the case sometimes in the *Bible Word-Book*. The pleasure of the note, to play on the title of the translation of the well-known Roland Barthes book, seems to lie for Wright and, he must suppose, for his readers in juxtaposing the language of Shakespeare and the AV.

> The same juxtaposition can be found in Wright's *Bible Word-Book*:
> **Awaked**, for *Awoke*, the past tense (Gen. xxviii. 16, &c.) and the past
> participle for *Awake*. It is the common form in Shakespeare.
>
> In which hurtling,
>
> From miserable slumber I *awaked*.
> *As You Like It*, IV. 3.133.
> Faith, none for me; except the north-east wind,
> Which then blew bitterly against our faces,
> *Awaked* the sleeping rheum.
> *Rich[ard] II*. I.4.8.
> Peace, ho! the moon sleeps with Endymion,
> And would not be *awaked*.
> *Mer[chant] of Ven[ice]* V.1.110.
> It occurs also in *Piers Plowman*, B text, XIV. 332:
> And wepte and weyled . and þere-with I *awaked*.[30]

One might infer from my own juxtaposition of these quotations from Wright's Clarendon edition of *The Tempest* and his *Bible Word-Book* that he as a scholar was a one-trick pony explaining Shakespeare in terms of the AV and vice versa. No wonder it was so easy for him to turn from his editing of Shakespeare to his philological work on the AV when the two endeavors were one and the same.[31] His letters record his rapid turning from the AV to Shakespeare and back again. Writing to Alexander Macmillan, then the intended publisher for his work-in-progress *The Bible Word-Book*, on 17 January 1864, Wright described his return to Shakespeare and the fourth volume of the Cambridge edition after finishing, at least for the time being, his work on the Bible: "We are hard at work at [Shakespeare's play] Richard ii. and awful work it is—the worst by far of any play we have yet had. After many false starts the Bible Wordbook is at length—off."[32] Near the end of the same year on the 21st of November, Wright told Macmillan of his plans to reverse this transition now that the single-volume Shakespeare edition, the 1864 Globe, was finished: "Now the Globe is off my hands I shall go on with the Bible Wordbook."[33]

However, such a view would unfairly diminish Wright's achievement. I have already referred to the wide range of texts and dictionaries of which Wright had an intimate philological knowledge that he could bring to bear with equally illuminating force on Shakespeare and the AV. He also very much appreciated that the AV, unlike Shakespeare, did not capture the language only as it existed at the moment of its own composition. In his *Bible Word-Book*, he gave a brief account of the history of the language of the AV:

> In considering the language of our English Bible, we must bear in mind that it has become what it is by a growth of eighty-six years, from the publication of Tyndale's New Testament in 1525 to that of the Authorised Version in 1611. Further, it must be remembered that our translators founded their work upon the previous versions, retaining whatever in them could be retained, and amending what was faulty. The result was therefore of necessity a kind of mosaic, and the English of the Authorised Version represents, not the language of 1611 in its integrity, but the language which prevailed from time to time during the previous century.[34]

Here Wright the philologist and textual scholar is careful to attend to the question of just which earlier published texts influenced with their usage the AV translators. One can only wonder that this same historical precision is not brought to bear on the appropriateness of including in his *Bible Word-Book* illustrations from Shakespeare, whose usage, as noted above, could not have directly influenced the translators.

Such historical precision is brought by Wright rigorously to bear on his revision late in his career of Bishop Brooke Foss Westcott's *A General View of the History of the English Bible*. Again, as he did in his work on the *Bible Word-Book* and Cambridge Shakespeare, he is happy to accommodate himself to the conception and initial design of the work's original creator: "Bishop Westcott's History of the English Bible is in hand. I shall make no change in his plan which is admirable, but I shall verify every statement and follow up some lines of investigation which he has suggested in the versions of the Old Testament."[35] When Wright publishes his revision, he notes in detail that his verification has revealed a persistent shortcoming in the work: Westcott's presentism in using modern editions of Luther and Erasmus's Bible translations, whose language cannot have influenced the sixteenth-century English Bible, rather than editions of these translations that had been published in time to be available to Tindale and Coverdale:

> In estimating, for instance, the influence of Luther upon Tindale it is useless to quote the modern editions. Luther's New Testament as contained in his Bible of 1534 could have had no influence upon Tindale's version of 1525, and Luther's final edition of 1541 could not have affected Tindale's of 1534 and 1535. In like manner, Tindale in 1525 could only have

known of the New Testament of Erasmus as it appeared in the first three editions of 1516, 1519, and 1522, and it was not till 1534 that he could have used the edition of 1527. Similar remarks apply to Coverdale.[36]

There appear to coexist in Wright the historical bibliographer, textual critic, and philologist (so much in evidence in this quotation) and the avid reader of literature, particularly Shakespeare, who will not deprive his *Bible Word-Book* readers of the pleasure of the dramatist's words on the narrow scholarly grounds that apply, for example, to Westcott's book.

On the whole, this essay reflects on paradoxes evident in some of Wright's work on the English Bible and Shakespeare in the 1860s and after. In her study of *Shakespeare and the Politics of Culture in Late Victorian England*, Linda Rozmovits points to "the extraordinary production of writings about Shakespeare, religion, and the Bible" in precisely this period.[37] She goes on then to justify her claim with considerable reference to the works of the "flamboyant and literal-minded."[38] As this essay has been intent on showing, the voracious market for books on Shakespeare and the Bible also afforded an opportunity, previously unavailable, for the publication of scholarship on Shakespeare and the Bible of a very high order. At the same time, though, the power exerted on late Victorian culture by these texts, either separately or in conjunction, was such that it could enforce tremendous exertions on the part of a scholar as talented, energetic, and learned as Wright in the service of several projects that were not even of his own design. The Cambridge Shakespeare was even of a design different from the one he would have preferred. Indeed the power of Shakespeare and the Bible was such that on occasion each was able to shove its way into Wright's work on the other even when, according to the exacting standards of strictly historical scholarship, it did not properly belong.

NOTES

1. I would like especially to thank both Adam C. Green, Assistant Archivist and Manuscript Cataloguer at Trinity College Library, Cambridge, and the staff of the BL Manuscript Room for essential help with this paper.
2. Second Edition Revised and Enlarged, London: Macmillan, 1884, pp. 127–8. All references are to this edition.
3. John Glover, William George Clark, and William Aldis Wright (eds) *The Works of William Shakespeare*, 9 vols, Cambridge and London: Macmillan, 1863–6, vol. 9, p. xx.
4. *The Bible Word-Book*, pp. vii–viii.
5. *The Bible Word-Book*, p. x.
6. *Oxford Dictionary of National Biography*, Oxford: Oxford University Press, 2004–. Web. 24 July 2010.
7. *The Bible Word-Book*, p. x.
8. As, for example, his edition of the *Letters & Literary Remains of Edward FitzGerald*, 7 vols, London: Macmillan, 1902, the culmination of more than a decade of his individual work. Only very near the end of his life did he publish

alone an edition of the Authorized Version of the Bible as printed in the original two issues in 1909 and his Hexaplar English Psalter in 1911 (*ODNB*).

9. *ODNB*.
10. Andrew Murphy, *Shakespeare in Print: A History and Chronology of Shakespeare Publishing*, Cambridge: Cambridge University Press, 2003, pp. 205–6.
11. *ODNB*.
12. "Richard Grant White," *Classical Encyclopedia*. Available at http://www.1911encyclopedia.org/Richard_Grant_White (accessed 24 July 2010).
13. *ODNB*.
14. *ODNB*.
15. *ODNB*.
16. *ODNB*.
17. New York Shakespeare Society, *Shakespeariana*, New York: L. Scott, 1890, vol. 7, pp. 248–50. Academic editing of Shakespeare, though, began outside the English-speaking world with Nikolaus Delius, who "studied Romance and English philology and Sanskrit at the universities of Bonn and Berlin" and, holding a doctorate, was associate professor of English at Bonn when his first edition of 1854–61 saw print (Walther Killy and Rudolf Vierhaus [eds in chief], *Dictionary of German Biography*, trans. Christiane Banerji et al., Munich: K.G. Saur, 2001–6).
18. *Works of William Shakespeare*, 1863–6, vol. 1, p. ix.
19. Ibid., p. xxvi.
20. BL Add. MS 55015 f. 13.
21. Add. MS. b. 58.1–217; 59.1–376; 60.1–258; 61.1–138; 62.1–47.
22. It might seem from this description that Wright was parasitical on the larger community of librarians, scholars, and literati in drawing out this information. Nothing could be further from the case. From Wright's own letters in the BL we find he served other scholars the same way, responding to their queries about particular books and manuscripts held by the Cambridge libraries, especially Trinity College's, of which he was librarian (1863–70). For example, writing to W. Carew Hazlitt and referring to the copy of *Coryates crambe* at Trinity, Wright says on 28 August 1866, "it differs so much from the copy of which the collation is given in Lowndes that I have sent you a list of the contents with the signatures of each leaf. The copy you have seen appears to contain the same number of leaves as that in Lowndes" (BL Add. MS 38899, f. 107). Wright even offers to check for Hazlitt the rightness of the catchwords throughout (f. 119, 9 Sept. 1866). On 18 June 1867, Wright offers Hazlitt "a catalogue of books printed in England before 1600 which are in our Library" (f. 400).
23. BL Add. 55015 f. 6.
24. *Works*, vol. 1, p. xx.
25. Ibid., p. xxi.
26. *ODNB*.
27. *Works*, vol. 1, p. 392.
28. Trinity College, Cambridge, Add. MS b. 61. 54.
29. William Aldis Wright (ed.), *The Tempest*, Clarendon Press Series, Oxford: Clarendon, 1876, p. 78.
30. *The Bible Word-Book*, p. 63.
31. In his *Bible Word-Book*, Wright used the Globe Shakespeare for his references, even though he had never liked the name *Globe Shakespeare*. Writing to Macmillan on 8 July 1864, he says he and Clark think the title "Globe" to be "claptrappy" and would prefer "Hand Shakespeare" (BL Add. MS 55015 f. 18).

32. BL Add. MS 55015, f. 11.
33. Ibid., f. 22v.
34. *The Bible Word-Book*, p. vi.
35. BL Add. 55015 ff. 154v–5.
36. Brooke Foss Westcott, *A General View of the History of the English Bible*, William Aldis Wright (ed.) 3rd ed., London: Macmillan, 1905, pp. xi–xii.
37. Linda Rozmovits, *Shakespeare and the Politics of Culture in Late Victorian England*, Baltimore, MD: Johns Hopkins University Press, p. 22.
38. Ibid., p. 25.

8 "Stick to Shakespeare and the Bible. They're the roots of civilisation"

Nineteenth-Century Readers in Context

Andrew Murphy

[E]very year sees now three or four fresh impressions of [Shakespeare's] works. They are of all sorts and sizes and prices . . . reproductions of old and scarce copies for the luxurious student, penny a week issues for the apprentice or artisan. And they all sell. No book that ever was printed—save one—has had a circulation so enormous, so increasing, so real.[1]

So declared the *Daily News* on 26 April 1864, three days after the tercentenary anniversary of Shakespeare's birth. What is the book mentioned here that is the only one to rival Shakespeare for circulation? Well, the Bible, of course: it, quite literally, goes without saying. The linking of the two books is naturalized and deep-rooted and, from precisely around the period of the tercentenary, the relationship between the two texts became ever tighter and more complex. Linda Rozmovits has very interestingly speculated as to why this intensification should have happened specifically in this period, arguing that developments in theological thinking led to a "secularizing" of the Bible, so that it ceased "to be a record of divine revelation and was becoming, instead, a work of literature."[2] Seeing the Bible as literature facilitated a form of thinking in which literature itself might, in its turn, be conceived of as a kind of sacred cultural text, with the result that, in a parallel movement, Shakespeare was elevated to the status of a kind of "secular scripture." For Rozmovits, the two books existed in a dynamic balance in the period, such that "the relative position of each derived from the energy of the other,"[3] with Shakespeare gaining a decided ascendancy by the beginning of the twentieth century.

In this essay, I wish to map out a narrative that might be seen as running in parallel to that established by Rozmovits in her study. Her analysis is, necessarily, predicated on a relatively elite readership: those who would have been aware of the challenges to literalist readings of the Bible advanced by, for example, the 1860 *Essays and Reviews* collection or William Colenso's *The Pentateuch and the Book of Joshua Critically Examined* (1862), both of which publications in varying ways (and to varying degrees) sought to treat the Biblical texts as historical documents, rather than foregrounding the idea of divine inspiration. Josephine Guy has noted that, in fact, none of this work "had an immediately disruptive consequence for everyday church-going"[4] and, in a way, my own concern here is with this community of ordinary worshippers—or, to be more precise, with those *non-elite* readers for whom high level theological argument had relatively little purchase, but for whom, nevertheless, the Bible and Shakespeare *did* also hold a peculiar, interpenetrating force in the period. For these readers, too, the books existed in a dynamic relationship and the energies of that dynamic shifted noticeably at the beginning of the twentieth century. This shift is consonant with what Rozmovits maps out for her quite different reading community, but it also has its own particular valences.

My focus here, then, is on a cohort of nineteenth century readers whose literacy skills were hard earned, as, coming from impoverished backgrounds, they struggled to achieve a culturally enriched life. The linking of the Bible and Shakespeare is a persistent thread running through the autobiographies of these readers. To take three sample cases: John Harris (1820–84), the Cornish miner and poet, writes that "the first books I bought were a Bible and a hymn-book, and then Shakespere"[5]; Joseph Arch, born near Stratford-on-Avon in 1826, declares that "Shakespeare and the Bible were the two books I was brought up on"[6]; and Robert Smillie (1857–1940), who had spells working in a shipyard and as a coal miner, before becoming a trade unionist and then a politician, observes in *My Life for Labour*: "Outside the boards of the Bible I know of no greater mental stimulus than Shakespeare. If I were doomed to dwell on a desert island alone for the rest of my life, with two books, these are the two I would pack."[7]

That a connection between the Bible and Shakespeare *did* exist for this community of readers is, then, clear. But the question to be addressed here is what prompted that connection, beyond what we might style a kind of common bibliolatrous elevation of the two books? There are, I wish to suggest, effectively two related answers to this question: one connected with education, and the other having to do with language. To begin with the issue of education: the nineteenth century witnessed a massive expansion of educational provision throughout the United Kingdom. At the beginning of the century, the illiteracy rate was relatively high and, even by 1840, as much as a third of men and half of women were still making a mark in the official register when they got married, rather than signing their names.[8] This is a relatively crude measure, of course, as the ability to write is a wholly separate skill from the ability to read, but, nevertheless, it does give a rough indication of the level of general literacy in the period. By the end of the century, by contrast, the ability to read and write was almost universal throughout the United Kingdom. This great expansion of literacy was the product of the gradual emergence of a school system, initially established by the Christian churches but, ultimately (by the closing decades of the century), brought largely under the formal control of the government. With the emergence of a school network serving the poorest sectors of society a new readership emerged and, as we shall see, many of these new readers ultimately found their way to Shakespeare. But the central fact I wish to register here in the first instance is the extent to which a single text sat at the absolute center of the nineteenth century popular educational enterprise—that text being the Bible.

Francis Place, a tailor who amassed a personal library of some 1,000 volumes, provides a useful starting point for beginning to map out a little of the history of the expansion of educational provision in the nineteenth century. Place was born in 1771 and he observed of his early home life that "[e]xcepting an old bible there was not a book in my father's house belonging to him, and from him I never received any encouragement to read."[9] Place was almost entirely self-taught and, like many others in the eighteenth century, he struggled to gain the education he desired, as there were virtually no organized school facilities available to the poorest sectors of society during the course of his youth. As the eighteenth century drew to a close, however, opportunities for receiving basic formal education did begin—very slowly—to emerge, and the presence of the Bible as the only book in Place's childhood world anticipates much of what was to come. The first attempt to provide regular education to children of the poorest families on a more or less formalized and relatively extensive basis emerged in 1786, when William Fox, in consultation with Robert Raikes, founded the Sunday School Society (Raikes himself had set up a Sunday school at St Mary le Crypt in July 1780).[10] The Sunday school system was rapidly extended throughout the country and the historian John Burnett has observed that the expansion of the Sunday School movement was of great importance, bringing educational opportunities of a kind to millions who had to work on six days of the week. The Sunday Schools introduced into England the idea of universal, free education on which ultimately the system of day-schooling was built.[11] Joseph Barker, who was born in Bramley in Yorkshire in 1806, and who became himself a Methodist minister, attended his local Sunday school and observed of it that "Almost the only opportunity I had of learning anything, except what I might learn at home, was by attending the Sunday-school."[12] Education both in and out of the home was, for Barker, dominated by the Bible: "I recollect my eldest sister and my elder brothers teaching me my letters from a large family Bible that we had, and I also recollect teaching my younger brothers their letters afterwards from the same great book."[13]

The teaching provided at the Sunday schools was generally rather circumscribed. For example, George Jacob Holyoake (1817–1906), a whitesmith turned journalist and publisher, observes somewhat coldly in his autobiography that "For five years I was a scholar in the Carr's Lane Sunday Schools, yet save Watts's hymns and reading in the Bible, I learned nothing."[14] Holyoake clearly wished for an education that encompassed more than just the religious instruction provided by his church school. But the only alternative to the Sunday schools available at the turn of the century were the so-called dame schools (where the teachers were, in fact, as often men as women): small-scale operations, generally run by just one person and often providing little more than cheap childcare. Thomas Wyse's summary description of these schools (in a report written for the Central Society of Education)—"the simplicity of childhood is taught by ignorance, and often by imbecility"[15]—is perhaps a little harsh, if wholly accurate where at least some of the dame schools were concerned.[16]

Whatever their faults, at the dame schools, too, religious instruction tended to dominate class time. Indeed, a comment by the Chartist Robert Lowery (1809–63) indicates that attendance at a dame school may almost have been seen as synonymous with acquiring the ability to read the Scriptural text, as he writes: "I had been at a Dame's school at North Shields and could read the Bible."[17] Likewise, Thomas Wood (b. 1822) noted of his experience at a dame school:

> I was sent to a school taught by a man called Jim Lister. The mode of education was singular. I only remember one book in the room, which was his living-room. It was a big Bible, bound in leather. The little ones learnt letters out of it. Bigger ones learnt to read. I am not quite sure we ever read anything but the first chapter of St. John.[18]

Again, Scriptural reading was, essentially, what defined education within this community, as Wood notes: "To read a chapter in the Bible was deemed a respectable attainment and to write a letter a scholarly acquisition, and persons who would perform these exploits were deemed fortunate."[19]

By the opening decades of the nineteenth century, the British churches started to move into the territory occupied by the dame schools, as they began to expand beyond the provision of Sunday teaching to offer low-cost (or free) weekday education as well. In 1808, the dissenting churches established the British and Foreign School Society (BFSS), with (in England) the national church responding by setting up the National Society for the Education of the Poor in the Principles of the Established Church (1811). An element of competitive rivalry existed between the two bodies right from the start and this competitiveness had the beneficial effect of greatly multiplying the number of schools available to the children of the poor in a relatively short space of time, making affordable education far more accessible than it had ever been before.

Once again—and unsurprisingly, given the context—religious instruction dominated the curricula of both BFSS and National Society schools. Thomas Cooper (1805–92), the shoemaker and political activist, observed of the church school he attended that "the course of instruction was limited to reading the Scriptures, writing, and the first four rules of arithmetic, simple and compound."[20] James Bonwick (1817–1906), who became himself a teacher within the church school system and, ultimately, a writer of educational textbooks, noted that the "only reading was from the *Scripture Lessons*, that is, *selections* from the Bible."[21] Even history was taught in the first instance using the Bible, with predictably eccentric results: "Our History was at first only confined to the Bible. We learned what happened to a small and but partially civilized nation two or three thousand years ago. Of Egypt, Assyria, India, Greece, Rome, or even England, we knew nothing."[22]

If those educated within the church system read almost exclusively in the Bible during the course of their school days, they often quickly enough found their way to a broader range of texts when they were outside the classroom. The route which led onwards from the Bible often took a predictable course, generally involving what David Vincent has identified as "the classics of religious imagination"—in particular, Bunyan's *Pilgrim's Progress* and Milton's *Paradise Lost*.[23] These texts might be seen as occupying a kind of liminal ground between the sacred and the secular and, indeed, one autobiographer tellingly describes *Paradise Lost* as "being partly fiction and partly truth."[24] References to the two works are numerous throughout the autobiographical materials. With regard to *Pilgrim's Progress*, William Heaton, handloom weaver and poet, recalls being sent to the local Methodist Sunday school, where he was "put in the first bible class, where I progressed pretty well."[25] Once he had mastered the basics of reading, his "kind and indulgent mother borrowed 'Bunyan's Pilgrim's Progress' for my perusal, which delighted me very much. I rambled with Christian from his home in the wilderness to the Celestial City; mused over his hair-breadth escapes, and his conflict with the giant Despair. I was very much delighted with it."[26] Joseph Lawson (b. 1821) notes, of the community of Pudsey in West Yorkshire, that "the house that had a family Bible, hymn-book, prayer-book, or catechism, the Pilgrim's Progress, or News from the Invisible World, together with a sheet almanack nailed against the wall, was considered well furnished with literature."[27] Likewise, for Thomas Cooper, "the immortal 'Pilgrim's Progress' was my book of books. What hours of wonder and rapture I passed with Bunyan when a boy!"[28]

Milton too was much read within this community. Samuel Bamford positively eulogizes the poet: "Oh! John Milton! John Milton! of all the poetry ever read, or ever heard recited by me, none has so fully spoken out the whole feelings of my heart—the whole scope of my imaginings—as have certain passages of thy divine minstrelsy."[29] The emphasis on "*divine* minstrelsy" here is again noteworthy—an encomiastic extravagance, of course, but it also has a kind of notional truth to it, if one takes seriously Milton's own claim that the poem is divinely inspired, a kind of seventeenth-century scripture. Thomas Cooper, too, had an abiding love for the poet's work, declaring that "Milton's verse seemed to overawe me, as I committed it to memory, and repeated it daily; and the perfection of his music, as well as the gigantic stature of his intellect, were fully perceived by my mind."[30] Cooper attempted to memorize *Paradise Lost* in its entirety. His project was part of an extraordinary larger program of self-education, which included learning Hebrew (to facilitate his Bible studies) and attempting to memorize in their entirety seven of Shakespeare's plays. The strain of his absurdly ambitious educational enterprise led to a complete physical and mental collapse, but not before Cooper had managed to memorize all of *Hamlet* and the first four books of Milton's poem. When, later in life, he was incarcerated for his political activities, he drew sustenance from reciting these memorized texts to himself in his prison cell.[31]

Cooper, as we can see, made the transition from the wholly sacred (in his Sunday school texts) through the liminally sacred (Bunyan and Milton), before finally arriving at Shakespeare's plays. Of his study of Shakespeare, he observes: "the sweetness, the marvellous power of expression and grandeur of his poetry seemed to transport me, at times, out of the vulgar world of circumstances in which I lived bodily."[32] The route taken by Cooper is one that is much travelled in the period. There is, of course, nothing *inevitable* about this course; certainly, many readers never progressed beyond the Bible, resting content simply to read their Scripture; and many who *did* progress were diverted to reading destinations other than Shakespeare. But William St Clair has usefully indicated, in *The Reading Nation and the Romantic Period*, that there was, in fact, a certain kind of *structural* predictability to what people at the lower end of the economic spectrum read in the period. As St Clair explains, this was a function of how copyright law changed over time. The 1774 House of Lords decision confirming copyright as being vested (in the first instance) in the author, and as being time-limited, had the effect of creating a relatively expansive public domain of texts. But subsequent copyright acts, which progressively lengthened the terms of *new* copyrights, increasingly caused that domain to shrink. This effected something of a bifurcation of the market: the retail price of new, or recently produced, work remained high, as publishers, holding exclusive access to it, faced no competition; public domain texts were, by contrast, necessarily offered at much reduced prices, as these were being sold in a competitive marketplace. The ultimate result of this bifurcation was, St Clair has argued, to create a relatively constrained, but affordable, "old canon," which dominated the reading of those at the lower end of the economic spectrum. This canon, he observes, "entered the long frozen culture of the English-language Bible, the ancient ballad and chapbook, and the magical or astrological almanac, within which the reading of the poor had been constituted since the early seventeenth century."[33]

Shakespeare was central to the "old canon" identified by St Clair and editions of the playwright's works proliferated over the course of the century. From the 1840s, publishers began experimenting with producing the plays by number and by part, in an effort to reach the newly emergent readers of the lowest economic sectors of society. In June of 1845, for example, J.C. Moore advertised "The Penny Shakspere. Plays and poems of Shakspere. No. 1, to be continued weekly, and completed in sixty numbers, 8vo. (pp. 16), beautifully printed, one penny."[34] The edition was also to be issued in monthly parts, at 4 1/2d in a wrapper. As the *Daily News* quotation with which I began indicates, the tercentenary celebrations of 1864 intensified this process of Shakespearean dissemination. A great many publishers issued new editions in the tercentenary year, in an attempt to cash in on the heightened levels of interest in all things Shakespearean. To take the case of John Dicks, for example: he began issuing complete plays at the rate of two for a penny in April of 1864; he then gathered the plays into a cloth-bound volume, which he offered for sale at 2s, subsequently reissuing the collection in paper covers for just 1s. In all, he claimed to have sold almost a million copies of the edition.[35]

What we witness across the nineteenth century, then, is the emergence of a new reading community. The capacity to read is gained in a popular school system which, in all its manifestations, privileges the Bible over all other texts. The products of this system frequently pass through a phase of reading "transitional" texts—imaginative reworkings of sacred narratives—before advancing to more fully secular literature. The range of secular reading matter available to them is relatively circumscribed, as a result of developments in copyright legislation. Within the available pool of texts, Shakespeare serves as the dominant author, his position as the "National Poet"—which, as Michael Dobson has demonstrated, had been gathering momentum since Garrick's day—cementing itself with the 1864 tercentenary, which prompted a proliferation of cheap editions. The strong link between the Bible and Shakespeare for this particular community of readers may thus seem clear and may help us to understand how J.R. Clynes, the mill worker turned trade unionist and politician born in 1869, found himself being told, as he sat in the library of the Oldham Equitable Co-operative Society: "Stick to Shakespeare and the Bible. They're the roots of civilisation."[36] But there is also one further issue that I would like to take up here and it relates, specifically, to the question of language.

In exploring this question, I would like to return to Thomas Cooper's extravagant autodidactic program. A striking feature of his project is its heavy emphasis on memorization. The intended objective of memorizing all of *Paradise Lost* and seven of Shakespeare's plays is undoubtedly likely to seem absurd to us now. But while it may be wholly predictable that Cooper failed to meet his greater target, it is striking just how much text he *did* manage to commit to memory: four books of Milton's poem and *all* of *Hamlet*—indeed, he took the leading role in a production of the play staged in Leicester (to raise funds for his own defense when his Chartist activities led to his being tried for inciting a riot) on the grounds that he already knew his lines. Memorization was, in fact, an important component of education generally in the period and, again and again, autobiographers indicate that they learned whole sections of texts by heart—particularly passages from the Bible. The printer Robert Skeen (b. 1797) observes of his childhood that "The *Bible* was the great school-book; and the portions I committed to memory (as extra lessons) were considered proof of unusual ability by the seniors of the village."[37] Joseph Skipsey (1832–1903), the coalminer poet, who served for a spell as caretaker of the Shakespeare Birthplace (until an endless stream of American anti-Stratfordians drove him to doubt and despair),[38] once set himself the task of memorizing the Bible in its entirety, but his biographer, Robert Spence Watson, notes that "before he had got very far with the painful and somewhat unnecessary task, some good friend discovered what he was about and succeeded in persuading him from going any further with its commitment to memory."[39]

The fact that studying the Bible often went hand-in-hand with memorizing passages from the sacred text had, I would argue, an important consequence for those who subsequently came on to read Shakespeare, in that it had the effect of essentially "preloading" familiarity with early modern English in this cohort of readers, since, in the vast majority of cases, the particular text of the Bible they were memorizing from was the King James Version, which had, of course, been translated into the idiom of Shakespeare's own time. Mary Anne Hearn (1834–1909), a school teacher who wrote under the pseudonym "Marianne Farningham," serves as a useful case study here. For Hearn, the Bible served as a center point, not just for her education, but for her family life as well. "The Bible," she writes, "was in our home the children's library," and she relates:

> We had a beautiful old family Bible with pictures, and this was always brought out on Sunday evenings, and we used to sit and stand around our mother while she told us stories. It seemed that every Sunday evening, before bedtime, we went to Bethlehem. Every little touch and incident was so dwelt upon that the Holy Birth became part of our life. All the words of Jesus grew so familiar to us that we were never able to forget them after.[40]

This general familiarity was reinforced by specific acts of memorization, as Hearn indicates:

> It was a happy thing, for which I have been thankful all my life, that I was made to learn by heart long passages of Scripture. Let no one think that this was ever a hardship. The grand themes, and the stately, beautiful language in which they were told, fed my very life. I think the first I learned was the twenty-third psalm, and there has never been any time when every sentence has not appealed to me.[41]

Like many of her fellow autobiographers, Hearn came, later in life, to an acquaintance with, and appreciation of, Shakespeare's plays. Interestingly, it was her local clergyman who gave her a copy of the playwright's works, inscribing in it the dedication: "From her affectionate pastor."[42] Hearn cherished the book, feeling that it brought her "into a new world, and filled [her] with wonder and admiration."[43] And it is, in fact, the language of the plays and the linguistic connections between Shakespeare and the Bible that she specifically registers: "One thing surprised me very much; it was to find some expressions [in Shakespeare] which I had quite thought were only to be found in the Bible!"[44]

The connections linking the Bible and Shakespeare for this cohort of readers are, then, more than simply educational. Elementary training in reading the Bible made it possible for some of those from the lower economic segments of society to progress to reading Shakespeare, but the contemporary vogue for memorization also meant that, when these readers *did* arrive at Shakespeare, they were particularly well equipped to cope with what otherwise might have been challenging—even alienating—forms of language and usage. The King James Version had, effectively, *naturalized* early modern English for these readers—and, indeed, though written in a somewhat later period, *Pilgrim's Progress* and *Paradise Lost* would undoubtedly have helped as well.

As we progress into the later decades of the nineteenth century and beyond, the associations I have been tracking here begin to fragment. Again, Mary Anne Hearn serves as something of a useful case study. In her autobiography Hearn looks back over a long life that had mostly been dedicated to teaching and to service in education. At one point, she evokes an idealized image of a teacher motivated by religious impulses—in fact, probably a vision of her own younger self as she worked in the classroom.[45] "Somehow," she writes, "there was another look on her face and there were other tones in her voice when she talked to us about our Saviour. I am sure that her pleading words and Christian life had a great influence on the elder girls."[46] However, she concludes the passage by asking: "But what would school managers say to such a teacher now?"[47] Earlier in this passage, Hearn had logged the extent to which education had changed between the days of her childhood and her time of writing, at the beginning of the twentieth century:

> Sixty years ago the elementary education of the British schools was carried on by very different methods from those of the Council schools of the present day. The great book of the school was the Bible. The teachers were not obliged to pass government examinations, but they were required to be members of some Christian Church, and to love, revere, and teach the Book of books.[48]

What Hearn registers here is the fact that, as the final decades of the nineteenth century unfolded, education came more and more under government control. As funding for schools increased, Whitehall sought to impose regulations on the sector, demanding that pupils should pass standardized tests and instituting a regime in which funding was contingent on the pupils' success rate. By 1870, the state, as John Burnett notes, "hesitantly became a provider of elementary education" as "local School Boards were to be established to 'fill in gaps' left by the Church Societies, and charged with providing sufficient places for all children."[49] Over time, many of the church schools switched over to local board control and, gradually, the great church-led educational initiative of the earlier part of the century was wound down, as more and more schools came directly under state management. Other significant measures were also introduced: attendance at school became compulsory up to age 10 in 1876, extending to 11 in 1893 and to 12 in 1899.

Hearn, as we can see, viewed many of these developments with something of a jaundiced eye. But what she specifically objects to is a drift towards secularization in the school system, figured as what she sees as the suppression of that look of awe that had appeared on the face of her own younger self when she "talked . . . about our Saviour."[50] And she also deeply regrets, of course, the abandonment of dedication to the "Book of books."[51] The process of secularization was immediate and real for Hearn and she strongly opposed it. When the first School Board was formed in Northampton, Hearn (who had, by then, retired from teaching) was approached to stand for election to it, but she discovered that "some, at least, of the Radicals in our town were for having the Bible left out of the curriculum."[52] Since those who approached her included members of this group, she refused to stand as their candidate, declaring that "under no circumstances would I vote for religious instruction to be abolished."[53]

Hearn's fears notwithstanding, state control of the school system did not mean immediate and total secularization. Some late nineteenth-century autobiographers continue to make reference to reading the Bible in a classroom context, even when they attended state-controlled schools. Thus, Harry Alfred West, for example, born in 1880—a decade, of course, after the epochal 1870 Education Act—attended the Anvil Street Board School in Upper Stanton, North Somerset, and he recalled in his (unpublished) autobiography that "The school commenced each day with a formal service, which contained easily memorised moral extracts from the Bible."[54] And, even at the turn of the century, a thriving culture of Sunday school attendance still persisted, and the Bible—and, indeed, *Pilgrim's Progress*—remained central in the lives of many families. Thus, Daisy Cowper, born in Liverpool in 1890, fondly recalls attending Sunday school and notes that the Sabbath

> was more delightful than ever at tea-time, with a cosy fire and the prospect of reading, or crayoning or painting. Our favourite "Pilgrim's Progress" was laid on the table—not to be taken off—the "Sunday at Home" gave stories, and puzzles to solve requiring us to look up texts in the Bible.[55]

But in Cowper's account of her formal schooling, we find something new. Of her time in "Standard IV" at her local board school, she writes:

We learned about the Plantagenets, and extracts from Richard II was our recitation. I still recall the pleasure in rolling out, "Go, tie up yon dangling apricocks", "Dig me a grave upon the King's highway—a little grave, a narrow, . . . etc.", "With mine own hands I give away my crown," etc. for many lines, but, most appealing of all,
"Down, down, I fall, like glistering Phaeton,
Whose unruly and unprofitable jades . . . " etc.[56]

By Standard VI, Cowper was reading *The Merchant of Venice* and, staying on in school longer than most of her classmates (to the level of "ex Standard VII," beyond the normal range of most children), she studied *As You Like It* and came to know the play well enough that, three years later, she played the part of Rosalind in a local three-night production, "for at the try-out I already knew the words."[57]

Cowper's school experience serves to indicate nicely some of the significant changes that occurred in education once management of the system began to shift from church to state control. The churches had a simple agenda: the function of literacy was to facilitate Bible reading and, therefore, moral instruction. The fact that those who attended the church schools may subsequently have found their way to other reading matter was, essentially, incidental. The state's objectives were rather different. The aim now was something like the creation of useful citizens—and for this a broader range of knowledge than just Bible reading was required. As government control extended within the system, so the curriculum expanded beyond the elementary basics of Scriptural reading, writing, and perhaps a little arithmetic. At the same time, however, there was still a sense that education should not simply be limited to the purely functional and utilitarian. Children had to learn to read—this was a core skill, after all—but there was some debate as to what texts should be used to teach this skill, especially as the Bible did, in time, become less and less central within the increasingly secularized government-run school system. The answer, of course, was literature and, as Jonathan Rose has noted of the government-funded Board schools, "English literature became their most widely taught subject, especially after 1882, when readings from Shakespeare, Milton, Defoe, and other 'standard authors' were mandated for the higher grades."[58] Rose goes on to sum up the situation rather neatly by logging "a transference of reverence from the Good Book to the Great Books."[59]

The rise of English as a school subject resonated (at least in principle) with the program famously mapped out by that high priest of Victorian cultural theory, Matthew Arnold, in *Culture and Anarchy*. The function of culture for Arnold was, of course, to save society from the worst effects of Philistinism—that mindset that, at its best, gave us "[d]oors that open, windows that shut, locks that turn, razors that shave, coats that wear, watches that go, and a thousand more such good things"[60]—but that, at its worst, was crudely utilitarian and commercialist. For Arnold, the saving effects of culture should be distributed democratically, its benefits being carried down to the lowest levels of society:

> Plenty of people will try to indoctrinate the masses with the set of ideas and judgments constituting the creed of their own profession or party. Our religious and political organisations give an example of this way of working on the masses. I condemn neither way; but culture works differently. It does not try to teach down to the level of inferior classes; it does not try to win them for this or that sect of its own, with ready-made judgments and watchwords. It seeks to do away with classes; to make all live in an atmosphere of sweetness and light, and use ideas, as it uses them itself, freely,—to be nourished and not bound by them.[61]

We have seen that the roots of popular education in Britain had effectively been sectarian, with the BFSS and National Society competing to draw students to the religious orientation of the dissenters or the national church respectively. To this extent, the shift away from the sacred Scripture of the Bible towards the secular scripture of Shakespeare from the closing decades of the nineteenth century resonates with Arnold's call for a non-sectarian and non-*parti-pris* form of culture to be promulgated down to the lowest levels of society. Shakespeare was to be democratized. In the process, the Shakespeare text was expected to serve, in effect, as a cultural substitute for the Bible.

The history of Shakespeare and the Bible within general culture thus nicely maps on to that set out by Rozmovits for the higher levels of society: "It was as if God and Shakespeare occupied either end of a seesaw, the one falling as the other rose, the relative position of each derived from the energy of the other."[62] But we should note that the elevation of Shakespeare to occupy the ascendant position was not, however, without its own costs. As Bible reading declined with the general increase in secularism over the course of the twentieth century (and beyond), so the grounding that nineteenth-century readers enjoyed in early modern English faded, and Shakespeare's language began to seem increasingly alien to emerging new generations of readers. The plays became, as a consequence, more difficult to read. Likewise, where for many nineteenth-century readers Shakespeare was an exciting new discovery made outside the classroom, for pupils in the modern era Shakespeare has often been little more than a monotonous educational labor to be struggled through tediously. The shoemaker John Brown (1796–1859) writes of his first encounter with Shakespeare, reading a copy of *The Merchant of Venice* loaned to him by a roommate at a boarding house: "Never before had my senses been so completely captivated. I could have read all night."[63] This first reading experience leads him on to the rest of the plays, so that, he says, he frequently stayed up "till midnight reading Shakespeare,—when all around me was hushed in silence, save the distant rattle of some vehicle over the stones."[64] The possibility of a late-night, first-time encounter with Shakespeare such as Brown's was reduced almost to zero in the twentieth century, as virtually every child in the United Kingdom was introduced to Shakespeare for the first time in the classroom.

From the perspective of those in the lowest economic sectors of society, then, we might perhaps say that the triumph of Shakespeare as secular scripture also signals the death of Shakespeare as a genuinely popular author. Furthermore, as Patrick Joyce has observed of the nineteenth century, the "self-educated workingman . . . had literally nowhere to go but to the canon of 'high' culture, especially literature,"[65] whereas now, of course, the workingman (and woman) is spoiled for cultural choice. The signal characteristic of culture in the twentieth century and beyond has been its dispersal and fragmentation, through new forms, new media, new technologies. There are now, we might say, a great variety of wells from which one might choose to draw one's cultural waters.

There is, however, one further turn I would like to offer to my argument here. The history of the Shakespeare text can be said to be characterized generally by forms of parasitism. The texts themselves are parasitic, in the sense that Shakespeare, famously, virtually never offered wholly new narratives, relying instead on the work of others to provide him with plots and storylines. But other writers have, of course, produced work that can be said to be parasitic on Shakespeare—one thinks of the endless Restoration adaptations of the plays, for instance. And, perhaps, *symbiosis* might in fact be the better word here, since, by the Restoration, Shakespeare's plays had begun to feel old-fashioned and out-moded: Nicholas Rowe, in his 1709 edition of the plays declared that "there is not one Play . . . good enough to entitle it to an Appearance on the present Stage."[66] Adaptation thus helped Shakespeare to survive as a cultural force. It is often said that Nahum Tate's *Lear* kept Shakespeare's play off the stage for centuries, but another way of looking at it might be to say that it kept *Lear on* the stage at a time when Shakespeare's own version of the story had become unfashionable.

The relationship I have tracked between the Bible and Shakespeare in the nineteenth century is, perhaps, also parasitic/symbiotic. My argument has been that a particular fraction of the reading public was able to arrive at Shakespeare—and make sense of him when they got there—because of their experience of reading (and memorizing) the sacred text. And, as we have seen, for many among this group of readers, the two texts entered into a kind of compact, intertwining as "the roots of civilisation." In closing, I would like to suggest that the process of symbiosis continues into our own period. Though Shakespeare no longer holds the same cultural space as he did for the common reader in the nineteenth century, nevertheless the Shakespeare text still persists in new popular forms—one might think here, for instance, of commercial films based on the plays, whether closely (*Romeo + Juliet*) or very loosely (*She's the Man*). One might also consider the emergence of new hybrid cultural forms, such as "Manga Shakespeare," where abridged versions of the originals are restyled as comic books, or, again, the "Shakespeare in Asia" website, which provides access to videos and performance materials relating to Shakespeare and Shakespeare-inspired performances in China, Japan, and India.[67] It is this characteristic of adaptation, of symbiosis, that has allowed the Shakespeare text—now aligned with the Bible, now with emergent cultural forms, now with new technologies—to survive, century after century.

NOTES

1. Article on Shakespeare Tercentenary, *Daily News*, 26 April 1864; included in Stratford-on-Avon Records Office file ER1/58, vol. 1.
2. Linda Rozmovits, *Shakespeare and the Politics of Culture in Late Victorian England*, Baltimore, MD: Johns Hopkins University Press, 1998, p. 19.
3. Rozmovits, *Politics of Culture*, p. 20.
4. Josephine Guy (ed.) *The Victorian Age: An Anthology of Sources and Documents*, London: Routledge, 2001, pp. 210–11.
5. John Harris, *My Autobiography*, London: Hamilton, Adams, & Co., 1882, p. 59.
6. Joseph Arch, *The Autobiography of Joseph Arch*, London: MacGibbon & Kee, 1966, p. 22; originally published London: Hutchinson, 1898.
7. Robert Smillie, *My Life for Labour*, London: Mills & Boon, 1924, pp. 50–52.
8. For a comprehensive account of the expansion of literacy in the period, see David Vincent, *Literacy and Popular Culture: England 1750–1914*, Cambridge: Cambridge University Press, 1989.
9. Francis Place, *The Autobiography of Francis Place*, Cambridge: Cambridge University Press, 1972, pp. 46–7.
10. See Robert Raikes's entry in *ODNB*: http://www.oxforddnb.com/view/article/23016?docPos=2 (accessed 3 May 2011).
11. John Burnett (ed. & intro.), *Destiny Obscure: Autobiographies of Childhood, Education and Family from the 1820s to the 1920s*, London: Allen Lane, 1982, p. 140.
12. Joseph Barker, *The Life of Joseph Barker*, London: Hodder & Stoughton, 1880, p. 34.
13. Ibid., p. 35.
14. George Jacob Holyoake, *Sixty Years of an Agitator's Life*, 2 vols, London: T. Fisher Unwin, 1892, vol. 1, p. 33.
15. Thomas Wyse, "Education in the United Kingdom,—its Progress and Prospects," in Central Society of Education, *Papers*, vol. 1, London: Taylor and Walton, 1837, p. 58.
16. Wyse was an MP and served as "Chairman of the Committees" of CSE.
17. Robert Lowery, *Robert Lowery: Radical and Chartist*, London: Europa, 1979, p. 41; originally published serially in the *Weekly Record of the Temperance Movement*, 15 April 1856 to 23 May 1857.
18. Thomas Wood, autobiography published serially March–April 1956 in *Keighley News*, 10 March 1956, p. 5.
19. Wood, *Keighley News*, 3 March 1956, p. 3.
20. Thomas Cooper, *The Life of Thomas Cooper*, Leicester: Leicester University Press, 1971, pp. 13–14; originally published London: Hodder & Stoughton, 1872.

21. James Bonwick, *An Octogenarian's Reminiscences*, London: James Nichols, 1902, p. 12.
22. Ibid., pp.17–18.
23. David Vincent, *Bread, Knowledge and Freedom: A Study of Nineteenth-Century Working Class Autobiography*, London: Methuen, 1981, p. 110.
24. Barker, *Life*, p. 53.
25. William Heaton, *The Old Soldier; The Wandering Lover: and Other Poems; Together with a Sketch of the Author's Life*, London: Simpkin, Marshall & Co.;, and Halifax: T. & W. Birtwhistle, 1857, p. xvii.
26. Heaton, *Old Soldier*, p. xvii.
27. Joseph Lawson, *Letters to the Young on Progress in Pudsey during the Last Sixty Years*, Firle, Sussex: Caliban, 1978, p. 61; originally published Stanningley, West Yorks: J.W. Birdsall, 1887.
28. Cooper, *Life*, p. 22.
29. Samuel Bamford, *The Autobiography of Samuel Bamford*, 2 vols, London: Frank Cass, 1967, vol. 1, p. 194.
30. Cooper, *Life*, pp. 63–4.
31. See Thomas Cooper, letter to the *Northern Star*, 3 September 1842, vol. 5, no. 251, 6.
32. Cooper, *Life*, p. 146.
33. William St. Clair, *The Reading Nation in the Romantic Period*, Cambridge: Cambridge University Press, 2004, p. 139.
34. Advert (no. 670) for J.C. Moore edition of Shakespeare, *Publishers' Circular*, 16 June 1845, vol. 8, no. 186, 181.
35. "The Shilling Shakespeares," *The Bookseller*, 1 July 1868, p. 451.
36. John Robert Clynes, *Memoirs, 1869–1924*, London: Hutchinson, 1937, p. 50.
37. Robert Skeen, *Autobiography of Mr. Robert Skeen, Printer*, London: Wyman, & Sons, for private circulation, 1876, p. 2.
38. See Robert Spence Watson, *Joseph Skipsey: His Life and Work*, London: T. Fisher Unwin, 1909, pp. 74–5.
39. Watson, *Skipsey*, p. 20.
40. Marianne Farningham (pseud. of Mary Anne Hearn), *A Working Woman's Life: An Autobiography*, London: James Clarke, 1907, p. 19.
41. Ibid., p. 28.
42. Ibid., p. 71.
43. Ibid.
44. Ibid.
45. The teacher is referred to in the text as "Miss Hearn."
46. Farningham, *Working*, p. 46.
47. Ibid.
48. Ibid., p. 45.
49. Burnett, *Destiny*, p. 135.
50. Farningham, *Working*, p. 96.
51. Ibid.
52. Ibid.
53. Ibid. She did, in fact, subsequently come to an understanding with those who wished to support her and served two three-year terms on the board.
54. Harry Alfred West, "The Autobiography of Harry Alfred West: Facts and Comments," TS, Brunel University Library, Uxbridge, UK, n.d., vol. 1, no. 745, p. 9.
55. Daisy Cowper, "De Nobis," TS, Brunel University Library, Uxbridge, UK, n.d., vol. 1, no. 182, p. [50].

56. Ibid., p. [80]. The final lines here are, of course, a partial misremembering of: "Down, down I come like glist'ring Phaeton,/ Wanting the manage of unruly jades."
57. Cowper, "De Nobis," p. [87].
58. Jonathan Rose, *The Intellectual Life of the British Working Classes*, New Haven, CT: Yale University Press, 2002, p. 33.
59. Ibid., p. 34.
60. Matthew Arnold, *On the Study of Celtic Literature*, in *The Works of Matthew Arnold*, 15 vols, London: Macmillan, 1903, vol. 5, p. 92.
61. Matthew Arnold, *Culture and Anarchy*, Oxford: Oxford University Press, 2006, p. 52.
62. Rozmovits, *Politics of Culture*, p. 20.
63. John Brown, *Sixty Years' Gleanings from Life's Harvest. A Genuine Autobiography*, New York: Appleton & Co, 1859, p. 35.
64. Ibid., p. 45.
65. Patrick Joyce, *Visions of the People: Industrial England and the Question of Class 1848–1914*, Cambridge: Cambridge University Press, 1991, p. 38.
66. Nicholas Rowe (ed.), *The Works of Mr. William Shakespear*, London: Jacob Tonson, 1709, vol. 1, p. xxvii.
67. With regard to Manga, see in particular the Shakespeare titles published by Self Made Hero, available at http://www.selfmadehero.com/books.php?imprint=1 (website accessed 3 May 2011). For the "Shakespeare in Asia" website, see http://sia.stanford.edu/home.html (website accessed 3 May 2011); see also MIT's "Shakespeare Performance in Asia" website, at http://web.mit.edu/shakespeare/asia/ (website accessed 3 May 2011).

9   The Devotional Texts of Victorian Bardolatry[1]

Charles LaPorte

I

Among the most significant differences between today's Shakespeare criticism and that of the nineteenth century may be found in that former era's theological preoccupations. Take, for instance, two unrelated studies entitled *Shakespeare and the Bible*: one by Steven Marx (2000) and one by T.R. Eaton (1858).[2] These two works share a great deal. Both draw up extensive and (it should be acknowledged) highly compelling evidence for Shakespeare's wide-ranging acquaintance with Scriptures. But whereas the twenty-first-century scholar here treats Shakespeare's personal religious views as unknowable and in most senses irrelevant to the broader question of Biblical influence, the nineteenth-century one insists that the Bible must have brought Shakespeare to appreciate God's "Divine will so far as regards mankind," "the mystery of the redemption by the blood of the Saviour," and "the change wrought in human nature by original sin."[3] Now, Marx might (for all we know) be as religious as Eaton, but it would be hard to imagine him making claims like these, even if his editors in the Oxford Shakespeare Topics Series would allow him to do so. According to the secular logic of today's literary scholarship, a scholar's private views remain irrelevant to the question—and for the same reasons Shakespeare's own views now do. Nowadays, we can speak with great confidence and authority on the ways that Shakespearean drama reflects Scriptural tradition, reifies its claims, and relies upon it more generally. But we do not, as Eaton does, see all such matters as subordinate to the overarching question of whether these also express a divinely ordained revelation.

To make a comparison between a Victorian and a twenty-first-century study of *Shakespeare and the Bible*, then, is to hold in a nutshell the ways in which the establishment of English as an academic discipline has tended to steer literary studies away from questions of "Divine will," *per se*. To be sure, most of Eaton's conclusions will lend themselves to secular literary scholarship. The 165 pages between his introductory essay and brief conclusion serve to enumerate and to contextualize Shakespeare's Scriptural allusions with minimal interpolations or commentary. Here in the nineteenth century, we see a dramatic augmenting and professionalizing of the great scholarly tradition of "reference hunting and enumeration" mentioned by DeCook and Galey in their introduction to this collection.[4] The Oxford journal *Notes & Queries*, for instance, was founded in 1849 to facilitate just this kind of scholarly practice; it still mostly consists of demonstrating overlooked links between independent literary works. And Eaton shows himself to be a careful literary scholar of the *Notes & Queries* variety: he cites the Geneva version as that most frequently used by Shakespeare and he remains cautious about extrapolating too much from his parallels. These, indeed, he often lists without comment. At Bolingbroke's claim in *Richard II* that Gloucester's blood, "like sacrificing Abel's, cries / Even from the tongueless caverns of the earth" (1.1), Eaton points us to the Lord's rebuke of Cain in Genesis 4. At Celia's exclamation in *As You Like It* that Orlando's "kisses are Judas' own children" (3.4), he points us to Judas's kiss from the passion of St. Matthew (26.49). His unobjectionable and highly practical model of Shakespeare scholarship will culminate 140 years later in Naseeb Shaheen's comprehensive *Biblical Reference in Shakespeare's Plays* (1999), which does much the same thing. Only rarely does Eaton rise to a more developed reading of Shakespeare's plots and structures, such as when he depicts the character of Macbeth as a sort of latter-day King Ahab from the first Book of Kings (though the Macbeth/Ahab analysis, it is worth noting, anticipates by 142 years Marx's quite similar proposal that we view *The Tempest*'s Prospero as a latter-day Joseph.)

Significantly, however, the very organizational structures that attest to the kinship between Eaton's work and today's scholarship also bespeak a different genealogy and sensibility. The central feature of the 1858 *Shakespeare and the Bible*, its long list of "parallel" passages, actually serves to position the book within two somewhat antithetical mid-Victorian genres. On the one hand, Eaton signals the emergence of professional literary scholarship on English poetry, yet, on the other hand, his organization derives from a popular tradition of quotation books. More specifically, it belongs to a tradition of Shakespearean quotation books inaugurated by William Dodd's wonderfully successful *The beauties of Shakespear, regularly selected from each play: with a general index, digesting them under proper heads: illustrated with explanatory notes, and similar passages from ancient and modern authors* (1752). The popularity of such works exploded in the Romantic and Victorian eras, producing numbers of popular titles like *The Morality of Shakespeare's Drama Illustrated* (1775), *Shakespeare's Genius* (1821), *The Mind of Shakespeare As Exhibited in his Works* (1876), and *The Wisdom of Shakespeare* (1909). Seen from this newer (or, rather, older) vantage, Eaton's goal seems more religious than scholarly in our literary-critical sense: his work seems designed to establish and to disseminate Shakespeare's theological "beauties" with a religious nineteenth-century readership. And this alternative genealogy marks a key difference because the function of the quotation book is not to contextualize its *sententiae* and collected bits of wisdom, but simply to propagate them.

As Margreta de Grazia points out, the eighteenth- and nineteenth-century genre of Shakespearean quotation books derives from a premodern tradition of commonplace books, and this has dramatic consequences for the ways that we understand Shakespearean quotation in the modern era:

> Dodd's original edition is clearly an extension of the commonplace tradition; the principles governing his selection and organization of quotations derive from the topics or places of rhetoric and logic. When his compilation is reproduced at the end of the century, however, it loses this relation and becomes instead a register of Shakespeare's singular utterances.[5]

Traditionally, of course, commonplace books are compiled by their owners, who gather their own material. Many eighteenth- and nineteenth-century readers preferred prefabricated collections, though, which spared them the bother of actually identifying wisdom for themselves. No need to collect a resonant phrase from *The Winter's Tale* if Dodd has already gathered the wisdom of the Bard's whole corpus into one tidy catalogue. And while this phenomenon of prefabricated commonplace books never entirely displaces the homemade variety, it visibly serves to commodify and commercialize its contents in strategic ways. However distant it seems from the concerns of today's scholar, this commercial tradition has large repercussions for reading practices, which are strongly informed by anthologies, summaries, redactions, and collections, and are generally far less contextually oriented than we presume them to be.[6]

Given the apparent new commercial market for second-generation commonplace works and the financial opportunities for marketers of Shakespeare's "gems" and "beauties," it is no surprise that in the years following Eaton's theologically oriented study, we see emerge a whole set of popular titles that combine his religious preoccupations with Dodd's commercial genius. These include Frederic D. Huntington's *Religious and Moral Sentences culled from the Works of Shakespeare, compared with Sacred Passages drawn from Holy Writ* (1859), J.B. Selkirk's *Bible Truths with Shakespearean Parallels* (1862), W.H. Malcolm's *Shakspere and Holy Writ* (1881), J.F. Timmins's *The Poet-Priest: Shakespearian Sermons, Compiled for the Use of Students and Public Readers* (1884), Charles Alfred Swinburne's *Sacred and Shakespearean Affinities, being analogies between the writings of the Psalmists and of Shakespeare* (1890), and Charles Ellis's *Shakespeare and the Bible: Fifty Sonnets with their Scriptural Harmonies* (1896). As this list will suggest, the period witnesses the emergence of a veritable subgenre of commonplace book aimed specifically at celebrating the ways that Shakespeare and the Bible speak to one another.

II

I call works such as those above "devotional" Shakespeare texts. They borrow equally clearly from Dodd's aesthetic catalogues and from Eaton's scholarly charts of Biblical parallels. These prior authors organize Shakespeare's *œuvre* by dramatic work; Dodd also pioneers handy thematic rubrics to aid a reader's appreciation of each play and to facilitate easy reference: "Reflections on Gold," "The Baseness of Falsehood to a Wife," "On Commodity, or Self-Interest," and so forth. As Marjorie Garber remarks, "A reader in search of wise words about grief, politics, fatherhood, women, or any other conventional topic could consult Mr. Dodd's book with profit."[7] But Victorian devotional Shakespeare compilations take Dodd's rubricating practice to entirely new levels, using such thematic rubrics in lieu of (rather than in addition to) dividing a collection by dramatic work. That is, instead of collecting instances of the theme of, say, "Jealousy" in *Othello*, such volumes collect references to jealousy from Shakespeare's entire *œuvre*, pairing the famous "green-eyed monster" line from *Othello* (3.3) to a less well-known line from *The Comedy of Errors* and juxtaposing both of these with parallel sentiments from the Bible. This technique, as need hardly be pointed out, precludes any reader's potential interest in narrative, or in thematic developments within a given drama, or even in the differences between Shakespeare's comedies and tragedies.

The Victorian devotional Shakespeare genre is consistent enough in its methods and emphases that it will be helpful at this point to consider a representative sample such as that of Figure 9.1, from Malcolm's *Shakspere and Holy Writ*.[8] Malcolm, we see, uses the page openings themselves to organize Scriptural quotations, putting Shakespeare on the verso side and parallel quotations from the Bible directly across on the recto side. From Dodd, he takes a hermeneutic that divorces text from context; from Eaton he takes an intertextual focus that increases the spiritual edification on offer. The same can be said of devotional Shakespeare compilations as a body. Dodd affords beauties; Eaton, instruction. Combined, they join the highest of religious and literary authorities to the simplest and most expedient of organizational features. Even so small a sample as Figure 9.1 will reward exposition, so I will devote Section II of this essay to it.

Naturally, a text like that of Figure 9.1 solicits reading practices very different from those generally associated with Shakespeare in university English classrooms today—reading practices different even from those solicited by Dodd and Eaton. To appreciate this, it might be helpful to bring in the editorial theory of Jerome J. McGann, who urges scholars to differentiate between a given literary work's "linguistic codes" (its language) and its "bibliographic codes" (its formatting, fonts, spacing, margins, paper, etc.).[9] A work like Malcolm's shows how bibliographic and linguistic codes can shape meaning in very different ways. In Figure 9.1, we see that the very *mise-en-page*, the organization of the page, subordinates its quotations to

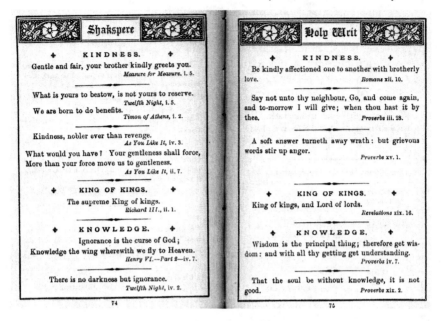

Figure 9.1 Malcolm's *Shakspeare and Holy Writ* (London and Belfast, 1881).

the prior idea that these can be matched to Biblical truths. This organization is reminiscent of a medieval breviary, down to the blackletter font in which "𝕾𝖍𝖆𝖐𝖘𝖕𝖊𝖗𝖊" and "𝕳𝖔𝖑𝖞 𝖂𝖗𝖎𝖙" are rendered at the top of the page with a trellised rambling rose design. Dodd-style rubrics—"Kindness," "King of Kings," "Knowledge"—serve to organize Shakespeare thematically and link these themes to equivalent-seeming Biblical expressions of the same idea. Malcolm's very use of type attests to the anachronistic influence of the Victorian Gothic Revival; sixteenth- and seventeenth-century printers invariably render Shakespeare's name in roman or italic fonts.[10]

Neither is directionality at issue here: English-language texts presume a left-to-right orientation, but here the source text appears on the recto, and the overall layout suggests a high degree of equivalence or interchangeability. Pride of place is apparently given to neither Shakespeare nor the Bible: indeed, Ellis's 1896 *Shakespeare and the Bible* puts texts from the Geneva Bible on the verso side, under the phrase "The Fountaine of Life" (again in a faux-antique blackletter), and Shakespeare on the recto.[11] The point lies rather in the manner that these two *œuvres* reflect one another: literarily, spiritually, and, finally, physically on the page. As DeCook and Galey mention, it was entirely unremarkable for the Victorians to associate the beauties and truths of Shakespeare with those of the Bible.[12] Nonetheless, McGann's distinction between linguistic and bibliographic codes calls our attention to the importance of bibliographical organization here, to the manner in which it promotes a notion of equivalency or mirroring between these texts. It is not just that these quotations are removed from their normal contexts more radically than either Dodd or Eaton had removed them. It is that they become enshrined here in a small, cloth-bound devotional book that validates its own hermeneutic practice on religious grounds.

Given all this heavy-handed bibliographical encoding, it may seem curious that only about half of the Biblical "harmonies" featured in Figure 9.1 actually correspond to what scholars generally understand by the Shakespearean lines in question. This, too, is wholly characteristic of the devotional Shakespeare genre. Parallel passages throughout the genre are least problematic where they suggest likely sources for Shakespeare's phraseology (on the *Notes & Queries* model of scholarship). Here, for instance, King Edward's citation of "the supreme King of kings" in *Richard III* unquestionably echoes the "King of kings, and Lord of lords" referenced in the seventeenth and nineteenth chapters of the Book of Revelation. In *Richard III*, the reference occurs where the dying King Edward IV asks Rivers and Hastings to embrace peace and reminds them of their accountability not only to himself, the king, but also to God. The formulation, at all events, receives frequent iteration in contemporary religious writings and sermons.

Less straightforward but still credible harmonies in Figure 9.1 include those from *As You Like It* and possibly *Henry VI, Part 2*. Both quotations from *As You Like It* lend themselves to the overall spirit of their designated harmony in the Book of Proverbs: "A soft answer turneth away wrath: but grievous words stir up anger" (15.1). In the first of these, the antagonist Oliver acknowledges toward the end of the play that his brother Orlando has won him over and "turne[d] away [his] wrath." Orlando has put himself into excessive physical danger on Oliver's behalf, it is true, but the play marks this self-sacrifice as of a piece with his courtly manners and overall chivalry. In the second quotation, which occurs earlier in the same play, the exiled Duke urges Orlando to demonstrate the chivalrous manners for which Oliver will later commend him. This second passage, indeed, nicely answers to the proverb, since the Duke's own "soft answer" actually performs the action that the proverb recommends: it turns Orlando from his wrath and calls him to himself, averting "grievous words" and "anger." Finally, the lines cited here from *Henry VI, Part 2* might seem in keeping with the general sense of the proverb classed by Malcolm under the rubric "Knowledge." The lines are delivered by Lord Saye during Jack Cade's Rebellion. Like Proverbs, they praise wisdom. Granted, they do nothing to forestall Saye's immediate political execution in *Henry VI*, but as wisdom has generally been found compatible with political martyrdom, this should probably not be held against their pairing.

By contrast with all of the above, however, the remaining quotations from Figure 9.1 will seem curiously at odds with their Biblical parallels to any twenty-first-century Shakespeare scholar. Take the remaining

three examples under Malcolm's rubric "Kindness." First among these is
Claudio's greeting to his sister Isabella in *Measure for Measure*: "Gentle
and fair, your brother kindly greets you" (1.5), which Malcolm pairs with
Apostle Paul's injunction to the Romans to "[b]e kindly affectioned one to
another with brotherly love" (12.10). Even laying aside the matter that Paul
seems not to have had biological siblings in mind when writing his Epistle
to the Romans, it must be acknowledged that this line in *Measure for Measure* looks nothing like the sort of charitable goodwill that the epistle recommends. Claudio seeks out his sister to save himself from execution by
the wicked despot, Angelo. And although this circumstance does not itself
preclude fraternal affection on the Pauline model, by Act 3, Claudio will
positively ask Isabella to prostitute herself to Angelo in order to save him.
One need not enter into the question of how far siblings ought to sacrifice
for one another to see that Paul could hardly be recommending such measures to the Christian community in Rome, and moreover that Claudio's
proposal deeply offends the religious sensibilities of his sister.

Following Claudio's greeting in *Measure for Measure*, we see a line from
Viola's well-known verbal duel with Olivia in the first act of *Twelfth Night*—
"[W]hat is yours to bestow is not yours to reserve"—harmonized with a
passage from Proverbs extolling neighborly generosity: "Say not unto thy
neighbour, Go, and come again, and to-morrow I will give; when thou hast
it by thee" (3.28). Briefly, the *Twelfth Night* quotation expresses Viola's
irritation with a veiled Olivia for rebuffing the advances of Viola's master,
Orsino. In *Twelfth Night*, "what is [Olivia's] to bestow" is her beauty and,
by analogy, her hand to a suitable lover. But the dramatic interest of the
exchange lies in its ironic play: Viola faults Olivia for her veiled "reserve"
while herself masquerading as a gentleman emissary called Cesario. This
being a Shakespearean comedy, Olivia completes the irony by falling in love
with Cesario, Viola's alter ego, at which point Cesario begins to reserve
the romantic favors that would be, in turn, his to bestow. Neither bestowal
falls easily under the rubric of Biblical charity. And either would violate
the logic of Shakespearean comedy, which ought to (and does) culminate
in the reciprocation of the heroine Viola's love for Orsino. It is hard to see
how any of this might count as "Kindness" in the manner of Orlando's
chivalry in *As You Like It*, or even Claudio's desperate overtures to Isabella
in *Measure for Measure*. And it is hard to see how such sexual claims can
elicit comparison to the comforts imagined in the "parallel" verses. No
Victorian exegete would extend the injunction of Proverbs 3.28 to sexual
favors, however needy one's neighbors might be in that regard.

The subsequent quotation from *Timon of Athens*, also harmonized with
Proverbs 3.28, still more openly flouts its context. "We are born to do
benefits," claims Timon early in the play to defend himself against charges
of extravagance. Under normal circumstances, this line might introduce a
thoughtful defense of altruism. Its pithiness and proverbial air appealed
to more than one devotional Shakespeare editor: before Malcolm, Selkirk

had selected it for juxtaposition with Deuteronomy 15.7–8 and Matthew 5.42, and so would Timmins after him. But context, again, is crucial. At the beginning of *Timon of Athens*, the title character is a reckless prodigal tumbling headlong into financial ruin: Timon's own steward describes him (correctly, to all appearances) as "[s]o senseless of expense / That he will neither know how to maintain it / Nor cease his flow of riot" (2.2.1–3). And Timon delivers this bit of wisdom in the midst of "riot," while hosting sycophants, hangers-on, and Amazonian dancers at a lavish banquet. Timon's extravagance thus has little obvious kinship with Deuteronomy's instruction that one must lend a poor brother "sufficient for his need" (as Selkirk and Timmins do) or Proverbs' suggestion that one be conscientious and generous with neighbors.

Finally, we see that Figure 9.1 concludes with Malcolm's citation of *Twelfth Night* under the rubric "Knowledge." Next to Proverbs' injunction that it is not good for "the soul to be without knowledge" (19.2), Malcolm places Feste the clown's instruction to Malvolio that "there is no darkness but ignorance" (4.2). The line sounds proverbial, truly, because Feste at this point in the play is pretending to be Sir Topas the curate and spouting all the proverbial-sounding nonsense that comes into his head: "Madman, thou errest. I say there is no darkness but ignorance, in which thou art more puzzled than the Egyptians in their fog." But Malvolio does not err in citing the darkness of the lumber room where he lies, unjustly incarcerated. And Feste, indeed, delivers his *bons mots* and bits of twisted wisdom for the amusement of Sir Toby and Maria, lookers-on who enjoy the spectacle of Malvolio's pain and humiliation. Most of what Feste says under the guise of Sir Topas goes too far afield to be mistaken for religious wisdom by even a quixotic Victorian collector such as Malcolm. In the remainder of their conversation, Feste positively chastises Malvolio for not subscribing to Pythagoras's views on the transmigration of souls:

FESTE: What is the opinion of Pythagoras concerning wildfowl?
MALVOLIO: That the soul of our grandam might haply inhabit a bird.
FESTE: What think'st thou of his opinion?
MALVOLIO: I think nobly of the soul, and in no way approve his opinion.
FESTE: Fare thee well. Remain thou still in darkness. Thou shalt hold th'opinion of Pythagoras ere I will allow of thy wits, and fear to kill a woodcock lest thou dispossess the soul of thy grandam. (4.2.50–60)

Here we see "darkness" as ignorance once again, but this time applied to Malvolio's rejection of the distinctly unchristian doctrine of the transmigration of souls. To crown the irony, Feste, Maria, Sir Toby, and Fabian have themselves devised this "common recreation" (2.3) to punish Malvolio for his religious airs (and, it should be allowed, his general priggishness). As

Olivia will later describe it, he is "most notoriously abused" at their hands. As in the majority of the instances above, then, to take the Shakespearean line at face value is to show a bewildering disregard for the irony of its context. To reproduce Sir Topas's words as proverbial in any Biblical sense is to produce a parody nearly as gross as the one performed by the false Sir Topas on the Shakespearean stage.

Once we begin to question the logic of the devotional Shakespeare genre, in fact, we quickly come to realize its astonishing, even glorious, perverseness. It testifies both to the power of Shakespeare's name and (albeit inadvertently) to the unruliness of Shakespeare's dramatic form—or perhaps of anyone's dramatic form—which can be atomized and picked apart for its constituent bits of wisdom in this way only if one ignores its dramatic context and narrative trajectory. These, by contrast, will usually complicate the meaning of even the most felicitous or the most gnomic of expressions. Small wonder that Victorian devotional editors (as in Figure 9.1) gravitate towards texts like Proverbs, Psalms, the epistles, and the like: texts that often feature admonitions and apothegms untethered to narrative trajectory or dramatic context. And small wonder that they give equally disproportionate representation to Shakespeare's fools and tricksters, whose quips and one-liners likewise lend themselves especially well to the devotional genre's editorial principles. For that matter, this point could be expanded to much Shakespearean quotation, including the secular and political quotation treated by Marjorie Garber in her engaging chapter on "*Bartlett's* Familiar Shakespeare."[13] But works in the Victorian devotional Shakespeare genre distinguish themselves from collections in the *Bartlett's* mode by tethering themselves uniquely to the Bible. They pursue a different and more elevated model of cultural authority, however awkwardly they lean upon the divine status of either text.

III

It will already be apparent to the twenty-first century scholar that nineteenth-century devotional Shakespeare editors can disregard the context of Shakespeare's actual plots and characters so regularly and with such apparent serenity because their reliance upon Shakespeare's literary cachet ultimately has little to do with the strictly literary elements of his work. That is, these texts seek to honor (or perhaps merely to exploit) Shakespearean expressions without actually showing much interest in the literary structures that for today's scholars give them meaning. As Garber would put it, they invoke "Shakespeare" instead of invoking Shakespeare because "quoting—or misquoting—Shakespeare's words is not the same as quoting 'Shakespeare.'"[14] Taken in isolation, a line like "There is no darkness but ignorance" represents "Shakspere" in a way that it may not represent Shakespeare—or, at least, in a way that jars against Shakespeare's dramatic rendering of Feste's impersonation of Sir Topas. Some volumes in the devotional Shakespeare genre disregard even the titles of Shakespeare's dramatic works. Timmins, for instance, withholds these when pairing Shakespeare and the Bible in his harmonies: in Timmins, a line like "It droppeth as the gentle rain from heaven" is linked to Deuteronomy but never to *The Merchant of Venice*, let alone to Portia, the line's speaker.[15] The "*Shakespearean Sermons*" of Timmins's subtitle consist entirely of lines collected from the master's *œuvre* and then combined into a kind of hodge-podge conduct book addressed to the edification of "Men of Business," "Young Men," and "Women." The resulting compilation, arch-Victorian in its sensibilities yet winningly postmodern in its approach, manages to offend against modern scholarly instincts in so many differing ways as to give it (for the connoisseur) a sort of outrageous sublimity. Only true faith in Shakespeare's divine unity could produce such glorious twaddle.

Such faith should give us pause, perhaps, committed as we are to a rather different understanding of Shakespeare. For our Enlightenment models of history might normally be thought to militate against such liberties, and scholars tracing the emergence of our modern literary perspective on Shakespeare's work point to the impact of Edmond Malone's 1790 edition as particularly influential in this regard. As de Grazia puts it,

> Malone's overwhelming preoccupation with objectivity marks a significant shift in the focus of Shakespeare studies from what might be termed the discursively acceptable to the factually verifiable, from accounts whose validity was assured by continued circulation to information whose accuracy was tested by documents and records.[16]

Without a doubt, Malone's legacy continues to shape our modern scholarly perspective on Shakespeare. But de Grazia's sense of a historical rupture between "discursively acceptable" (pre-Enlightenment) and "factually verifiable" (post-Enlightenment) ways of knowing Shakespeare seems problematic in its absoluteness:

> There can, then, be no desire to recover Shakespeare in his own terms, Shakespeare as he was before the late eighteenth-century intervention . . . for this desire belongs to the very apparatus that is under investigation; before it, or beyond its pale, it cannot even be contemplated, much less retrieved.[17]

It is fair enough to say with de Grazia that our very modern concern with the limits of knowledge about Shakespeare itself marks us as a product of the Enlightenment perspective governing Malone's appendices. The Enlightenment, that is, produces a number of expectations about textual fidelity, repetition, and verbatim-ness that give us more in common with Malone than Malone shares with Shakespeare (or earlier authors). As scholars, we cannot easily inhabit a perspective in which these things do not yet matter.

At the same time, Victorian devotional Shakespeare texts unquestionably show us how "acceptable" discursive practices can evolve in unexpected and unruly ways. Victorian devotional authors lean upon a Bard whom they presume to be "factually verifiable" even as they create an ever-more-discursively unpredictable one. Nor should this be dismissed as a popular phenomenon tangential to a "real" tradition of literary studies (which might stretch from the First Folio to Malone to the modern English department). Such trajectories habitually oversimplify the messy complexity of culture. English poetic study was by no means thoroughly professionalized or institutionalized when Eaton, Malcolm, or even Timmins were writing. When we reassign a position of significance to these popular devotional works, then, we see that the quasi-religious strain that we find perpetuated into so much twentieth-century English poetic study really belongs as much to Malone or to Timmins or to Eaton as it does to Matthew Arnold (who promoted the sacred English canon of poets with particular gusto and success).

In brief, bardolatry helped give rise to English departments long before English departments could help perpetuate bardolatry. When, at the beginning of the twentieth century, George Bernard Shaw coined the term "bardolater" to describe Shakespeare's most enthusiastic devotees, he was thinking not of then-emerging university English departments but of lay scholars such as those at F.J. Furnivall's New Shakspeare Society. But if these Victorian lay scholars are now chiefly remembered for their over-the-top expressions of reverence, they must also be given credit for advancing our understanding of the shape and evolution of the Shakespearean canon, of multiple authorship, of Renaissance literary culture. Furnivall himself—who wrote the introduction to Selkirk's *Bible Truths with Shakespearean Parallels*—was a major scholar of early English poetry: he argued strongly and persuasively (and undoubtedly correctly) for the multiple authorship of plays like *Henry VIII* and *Timon of Athens* when such views were still fiercely contested. But Furnivall seems to have found no contradiction between these two avocations. For that matter, Arnold himself gives implicit sanction to this kind of work in his "The Study of Poetry" (1880), which ends up at several points sounding like a more articulate version of Timmins.

IV

The Enlightenment shift towards a more "authentic" Shakespeare might seem to have little kinship with the devotional view, but perhaps they are two sides of the same coin. A religiously inflected canonization of Shakespeare occurred as it did because the Bible was at the center of a hermeneutic and religious crisis in which the Scriptures were being broadly reconceived of as inspired in a literary way—not as a divine catalogue of historical events, but as a human catalogue of poetic intimations about the nature of the divine.[18] Both de Grazia's "authentic" post-Enlightenment Shakespeare and my devotional one correspond to the contemporary emergence of modern Biblical criticism in the latter half of the eighteenth century. At the historical moment that Malone was applying an Enlightenment critique to premodern records in service of a more "authentic" Shakespeare, a whole host of German critics were applying a similar critique in service of a more "authentic" Scripture. No one familiar with the history of modern Biblical criticism, indeed, could miss the analogy to Malone's then-revolutionary attention to comparing the various early textual incarnations of Shakespeare's work, or to his edition's proud announcement that it was "collated *verbatim* with the most authentick copies."[19] Malone's impossible aspiration to achieve a perfect text, of course, itself makes inevitable his frustration with the less precise notions of faithfulness in quotation that prevailed in the sixteenth and seventeenth centuries and that were evidenced by Shakespeare himself on occasions where he fails to anticipate our modern standards of *verbatim*-ness (or, as Malone puts it, where he "had occasion to quote the same paper twice [but] from negligence he does not always attend to the words on the paper which he has occasion to quote").[20] Malone's pride in an "authentick" text and his corollary distress over the more freewheeling aspects of the early modern textual economy have clear analogues in nineteenth-century English Biblical criticism, where the desirability of establishing a single inspired text was, if anything, still more keenly felt.

By the time Malone was compiling his authoritative Shakespeare, both the progress of textual scholarship and the explosion of Evangelical religion had (somewhat independently) raised a number of questions about the reliability of the King James translation, for instance. Eventually, these concerns would prompt the publication of the next Authorized Version, the New Revised Version of the Bible that would appear in 1881 (O.T.) and 1885 (N.T.). But over the course of the nineteenth century, conservative believers had committed themselves increasingly often to the Inspirationist perspective that the divine Scriptures were dictated verbatim by God— especially when retrenching themselves in response to the twofold threat of modern textual criticism and earth science. As Dean (and future Bishop) John William Burgon preached in Oxford during the *Essays and Reviews* controversy of 1860 and the mid-century furor surrounding Darwin's *Origin of Species* (1859), "Every book of it, every chapter of it, every verse of it, every word of it, every syllable of it, (*where* are we to *stop?*) every letter of it, is the direct utterance of the Most High."[21] The NRV naturally disappointed such religious conservatives when it appeared not to offer anything like a conclusive rebuttal to recurring problems of translation and manuscript variation, let alone to the natural sciences. Burgon was among the quickest and loudest of its Victorian detractors when it appeared, finally, two decades after the sermon cited here. Devotional Shakespeare volumes are not pitched to an evangelical audience, who did not always approve of secular reading, yet they attest equally to what Doreen Rosman calls "the vigour of Victorian Christianity."[22] And once we acknowledge the parallels between the rise of modern Shakespeare criticism and modern Biblical scholarship, between the evangelical revival and devotional views of Shakespeare, we can come to appreciate how difficult it can be to draw strict lines between Shakspere and Shakespeare's literary achievement.

Even the most jarring and bewildering aspects of the devotional volumes here considered have enduring historical and religious precedents. Nineteenth-century commonplaces about Shakespeare will appear capricious and arbitrary to the modern Shakespeare scholar concerned with context or with the actual shape and texture of Shakespearean drama. Nonetheless, the Shakespearean devotional editors' manner of stringing together unrelated quotations has ample precedent in the Bible itself. Consider Paul's Letter to the Romans, cited in Figure 9.1, which cobbles together diverse books and verses from the Hebrew Bible in the very manner that appears so strange to us in Timmins. At one point in this letter (3.10–18), Paul cites in unbroken succession Psalms 14.1–2, Psalms 53.1–2, Psalms 5.9, Psalms 140.3, Psalms 10.7, Proverbs 1.16, Isaiah 59.7–8, and Psalms 36.1. Modern Biblical editions of course add quotation marks to help the puzzled believer sort out the verses that Paul lays down with machine gun-like rapidity, but quotation marks are a modern practice (only becoming a widespread convention in the eighteenth century) and they were unavailable to earlier readers of Pauline Scriptures. Most importantly, Paul pays no more attention to the individual character of Psalms or of Isaiah than Timmins and Malcolm do to that of *Twelfth Night*. As in the Pauline epistles, so in devotional Shakespeare texts, where lines are lifted from their previous context by sole merit of their Scriptural status.

One does not need an extensive acquaintance with the Bible to know that such liberal use of Scriptural quotations forms a crucial strategy of Scripture itself. The Christian Scriptures in particular regularly cite the Hebrew Bible in ways that the modern post-Enlightenment scholar must consider capricious if it is not somehow inspired. To adopt Garber's formulation for Shakespeare (cited above) would be to argue that "quoting—or misquoting—the Psalmist's words is not the same as quoting 'the Psalmist.'" But then, can we say that Paul in Romans quotes "the Psalmist" but not the real words of the Psalm? For Paul, one presumes, such a distinction would make no sense. His letters cite the text because they are a part of the sacred Bible, and the very preservation of Scripture attests to its sacredness: "as it is written," goes the Pauline phrase. For Paul, indeed, the whole value of such passages comes to depend upon their lending themselves to the greater glory of Christ. He does not remotely concern himself with the possibility that the Psalmist might not be David, who might not be Jesus's ancestor. These concerns would bedevil modern Biblical critics (who would also come to worry that the author of Romans might not be Paul), but here they seem very distant from the picture. My point is that for many of those who read Romans itself as a sacred text, the Shakespearean interpretation practiced by Timmins to such comical effect really has the highest and most significant of hermeneutic precedents and authorities.

The question for Eaton, for Malcolm, for Timmins, and for writers like them, then, remains one of religious truth. They cite Shakespeare in the way that Paul cites David (or in the way that the author whom we presume to be Paul cites the psalmist whom we might possibly presume to be David). It is instructive that Garber's characteristically generous and broad-minded consideration of popular Shakespeare quotation still falls far shy of recognizing or reflecting the truly foreign religious hermeneutic that we find in the devotional Shakespeare volumes. Garber celebrates the freely circulating discourse of "Shakespeare" as a means of perpetuating our discussion of Shakespeare's dramatic form.[23] But Victorian devotional authors deeply value Shakespearean expressions without demonstrating any interest in the dramatic form in which Shakespeare has wrought them. They celebrate the greatness of his dramas without acknowledging the greatness of drama, just as believers might revere, say, the Parable of the Good Samaritan without showing much interest in the parable as an art form. The point is never merely that the Parable of the Good Samaritan is a compelling story, but that it is a compelling story *as told by Christ* in the Gospels. Even for the nonbeliever, really, it is impossible to imagine this story as first told by anyone else: merely *a* parable of *a* good Samaritan. At just this point, it becomes impossible to distinguish the compelling aspects of the story from its position in the canonical Scriptures. This circumstance becomes increasingly true during the nineteenth century of the Shakespearean canon as well.

V

Really, then, it is the way that the Victorian devotional Shakespeare genre offends against modern scholarly instincts that suggests its usefulness for rethinking key aspects of our overall sense of literary history in Shakespeare's regard. Graham Holderness, Stanley E. Porter, and Carol Banks rightly urge that our inherited notions of works like *The Complete Works of Shakespeare* and the King James Bible owe a great deal to their editors' efforts to achieve "a common discourse, a uniformity of contents, and a particular significant structure."[24] But we can go further: the Victorian devotional Shakespeare collections remind us that once a common discourse and perceived uniformity of contents come to be taken for granted by a given reading community, the "significant structure" itself can be freely ignored. In such cases, it is not so much that differing early versions of a work like *Hamlet* or *King Lear* can be collapsed into one authoritative text through deft editorial management, it is that once that something authoritative can be taken for granted, suddenly any part of any version can be used as a synechdoche for the genius of the canon. *Hamlet* and *Lear* exist less powerfully as definitive texts passed down by any given set of Shakepearean editors (say, those of the First Folio) than they exist as abstractions loosely agreed upon by a reading community. Only as an idea can Shakespeare function as a freewheeling authority in the manner that the Bible (another idea) does.

Eaton's *Shakespeare and the Bible*, with which we began, captures beautifully how easily a text can remain recognizable as a work of literary criticism in the twenty-first-century sense of the term while still belonging to devotional genres that have since become culturally foreign. His ground-breaking methodology, once more, anticipates a secular logic only intermittent in Victorian criticism and to which his heirs in the devotional line remain marvelously immune. Yet even Eaton's study culminates in the strenuous claim that Shakespeare's genius expresses the course of Providence in much the way the Bible itself does: Shakespeare "does literally follow the order of God and of nature."[25] Such studies help pave the way for the establishment of English as an academic discipline not least of all by diminishing the gap between sacred and secular literatures, between literary and religious notions of inspiration itself in the post-Romantic era:

> It is pleasant to fancy the delight with which young Shakespeare must have feasted upon these and like divine lessons, unconscious, the while, that he was strengthening his pinions for loftier flights than had ever been attained by uninspired man.[26]

While Eaton's passage testifies strongly to an older, exclusively religious model of inspiration, in which sacred (i.e., Biblical) writers are "inspired" and profane writers "uninspired" by definition, still his expressions equally attest to a still-emerging Romantic meaning of "inspiration": to a concept of literary inspiration that pertains not to religious truth but to genius and originality. This latter meaning has entirely eclipsed the former meaning in most contexts: for us, an uninspired author is one with nothing original to say. But what is interesting here is to see how Eaton, an ordained churchman, also begins to contemplate inspiration as a question of degree. To read the above lines with an emphasis upon "uninspired" (rather than "ever") is to place Shakespeare in the vicinity of the Biblical authors.

It is easy to smile at the devotional texts of Victorian bardolatry. Or, rather, hard not to smile at them. Eighteenth- and nineteenth-century citation of Shakespeare offers a startling example of what Leah Price calls, in a pleasing phrase, "genius trumping genre."[27] But this expression is altogether too pleasing if it leads us to forget that literary genres never exist in a pure state, and that the "trumping" influence of genius is, in a certain sense, a *sine qua non* of the religiously inflected literary culture that we have inherited from Shakespeare's Romantic and Victorian heirs.

NOTES

1. I am grateful to Colette Moore, Alan Galey, and Travis DeCook for helpful suggestions on a draft of this essay, and to Erica Brunner for tracking down for me extra copies of Malcolm's *Shakespeare and Holy Writ*.
2. Steven Marx, *Shakespeare and the Bible*, Oxford: Oxford University Press, 2000; T.R. Eaton, *Shakespeare and the Bible*, London: James Blackwood, 1858.
3. Eaton, *Shakespeare*, p. 3.
4. DeCook and Galey, Introduction, p. 9. On the Victorian professionalization of Shakespeare editing, see Paul Werstine's contribution to this volume, "Going Professional: William Aldis Wright on Shakespeare and the English Bible."
5. Margreta de Grazia, "Shakespeare in Quotation Marks," in Jean I. Marsden (ed.) *The Appropriation of Shakespeare: Post-Renaissance Reconstructions of the Works and the Myth*, New York: Harvester Wheatsheaf, 1991, p. 61.
6. See Leah Price, *The Anthology and the Rise of the Novel*, Cambridge: Cambridge University Press, 2003.
7. Marjorie Garber, *Profiling Shakespeare*, London: Routledge, 2008, p. 289.
8. W.H. Malcolm, *Shakspere and Holy Writ*, London and Belfast: Marcus Ward & Co, 1881.
9. Jerome J. McGann, *The Textual Condition*, Princeton, NJ: Princeton University Press, 1991, p. 60.
10. I have scoured the British Library Shakespeare holdings and the Chadwyk-Healey EEBO database (Early English Books Online) for blackletter renderings of Shakespeare's name printed in his own lifetime but have found none. Victorian Bibles, by contrast, rely heavily upon blackletter. I am grateful to Alan Galey for pointing out this anachronism.
11. C[harles] E[llis], *Shakespeare and the Bible*, London: Samuel Bagster & Sons, 1896, pp. 28ff.
12. See pp. 1 and 12 in this volume's Introduction.
13. Garber, *Profiling*, pp. 278–301.
14. Ibid., p. 285.
15. J.F. Timmins, *The Poet-Priest: Shakespearean Sermons, Compiled for the Use of Students and Public Readers*, London: James Blackwood, 1884, p. 42.
16. Margreta de Grazia, *Shakespeare Verbatim*, Oxford: Oxford University Press, 1991, p. 5.
17. Ibid., p. 13.
18. For more on this topic, see Charles LaPorte, *Victorian Poets and the Changing Bible*, Charlottesville: University of Virginia Press, 2011; and Stephen Prickett, *Words and the Word: Language, Poetics, and Biblical Interpretation*, Cambridge: Cambridge University Press, 1986; *Origins of Narrative: The Romantic Appropriation of the Bible*, Cambridge: Cambridge University Press, 1996.
19. Malone qtd. in de Grazia, *Shakespeare*, p. 223.
20. Ibid., p. 222. Galey and DeCook nod to Enlightenment problems with variants in their introduction to this volume, p. 15. On the historical evolution of *verbatim*-ness in English, see Colette Moore, *Quoting Speech in Early English*, Cambridge: Cambridge University Press, 2011.
21. John W. Burgon, *Inspiration and Interpretation: Seven Sermons by the Rev. John W. Burgon*, London: Marshall Brothers, 1905.
22. Doreen Rosman, *The Evolution of the English Churches 1500–2000*, Cambridge: Cambridge University Press, 2003.

23. Garber, *Profiling*, p. 301.
24. Graham Holderness, Stanley E. Porter, and Carol Banks, "Biblebable," in Andrew Murphy (ed.) *The Renaissance Text: Theory, Editing, Textuality*, Manchester: Manchester University Press, 2000, p. 172.
25. Eaton, *Shakespeare*, p. 187.
26. Ibid., p. 12.
27. Price, *Anthology*, p. 78.

REFERENCES

Dodd, William, ed. *The Beauties of Shakespear: regularly selected from each play. With a general index digesting them under proper heads. Illustrated with explanatory notes, and similar passages from ancient and modern authors.* (London: Walter, 1752).

Shaheen, Naseeb. *Biblical Reference in Shakespeare's Plays* (Newark: University of Delaware Press, 1999).

Twelfth Night. 4.2.50–60. Eds. Roger Warren and Stanley Wells. (Oxford, Oxford University Press, 1994).

10 Apocalyptic Archives
The Reformation Bible, Secularity, and the Text of Shakespearean Scripture

Travis DeCook

Over the last centuries, the Shakespearean text has often been imagined in ways that exhibit parallels with an important construction of the Bible that arose during the Protestant Reformation, a construction that paradoxically exemplifies a logic which contributes to secular modernity. Secularity is defined by belief in a realm or realms fully separable from the divine; it follows that even religious discourse exemplifies secularity if it concedes a sphere that can be understood independently of God. As we shall see, when the Bible was accorded a newly autonomous status in the Reformation, it coincided with crucial intellectual shifts at the heart of what Charles Taylor calls secularity's "great disembedding."[1] This new framing of the Bible provides an example of how many aspects of secularity initially emerge from changes within religion itself, thereby undercutting the notion that the secular represents the subtraction of religion from neutral, universal rationality. [2]

The refashioning of the Bible has ramifications for the reception of the "cultural Shakespeare"—that is, for Shakespeare constructed according to the terms emergent with the modern category of culture, beginning in the eighteenth century. The text of Shakespeare becomes imagined in many ways parallel to the construction of the Bible, with both construed in strikingly similar ways as ideal archives. "Ideal archive" here entails notions of complete preservation, transhistoricity, and a conception of ontological and semantic self-grounding, all of which, as will be discussed, came to underpin the emergence of secularity.

The archival stories centered on Shakespeare and the Bible simultaneously rely on, reimagine, and disavow the materiality of the texts through which these monuments are transmitted. Perhaps the most conventional version of this ideal archive at present is implicit in BBC's *Desert Island Discs*, in which Shakespeare and the Bible are portrayed together as our "guarantee of civilisation and humanity."[3] While the hegemonic assumptions about Western culture underwriting the desert island scenario have received comment,[4] less attention has been given to the way it imagines a scene of loss and deprivation ameliorated by books, where books are imagined possessing a self-sufficient completeness mirroring that paragon of modern individualism,

Robinson Crusoe. Just as the desert island survivor is an isolated individual whose books substitute for society, so too are these books idealized as singular, absolutely bounded objects set off from social relationships, historical contexts, and material contingency.

This chapter examines a recurring precursor to the desert island motif: the homologous imagining of the Bible and Shakespeare as ideal archives pitted against the loss of civilization or the end of the world. Even when these imaginings are explicitly secular, they typically employ a set of desires and demands resembling those traditionally associated with religion, and portray the archive in apocalyptic terms. The archive here exemplifies both major meanings of *apocalyptic*: its original sense of unveiling a previously hidden fullness of meaning, and its derived sense of the catastrophic end of days. The ideal archive is emphatically imagined as a book or other singular material object, but also as a stable, unchanging origin, fully differentiated from the ravages of history outside its bounds. Accessing this archive requires no interpretation or attention to historicity—neither to the historical framework of the archive's emergence nor to the changing contexts of the reader. It is comprehensive, unified, and self-grounding; despite its supreme value, it is, at least to an elect readership, fully knowable. Despite this apparent religious coloring, these apocalyptic archives are symptomatic of central features of secular modernity, particularly in their textual ontology and epistemology.

With the advent of modern notions of culture, Shakespeare and the Bible have been called upon to perform this archival function in similar ways. But this function has important roots in the conception of the Bible taking shape in the Reformation. This chapter will begin with a discussion of the early English reformer and Bible translator William Tyndale and his construction of the Bible as an ideal archive. It will proceed to examine how Shakespeare and the Bible—the latter refashioned in cultural instead of theological terms—have been invoked alongside one another in homologous ways to this ideal Bible of the reformers' *sola scriptura* doctrine. The chapter will conclude with a discussion of cryptographic analysis of Shakespeare's writings. This marginalized but extensive (and thoroughly debunked) tradition is in many respects antagonistic to valuations of Shakespeare in cultural terms, replacing aesthetic and humanistic criteria with pseudo-scientific data analysis. At the same time, like the mutually reinforcing construction of Shakespeare and the Bible as the chief monuments of Western culture, the cryptographic analysts examined here call upon the text of Shakespeare—especially the monumental First Folio of 1623—to perform functions and fulfill desires similar to those the reformist Bible was called upon to fulfill. Revealing assumptions about the ontology of texts, meaning, and epistemology definitive of secular modernity, these ideal archives embody an aspiration towards absolute permanence in the face of future catastrophic loss whose particular form exemplifies a "secular religiosity."

I   "TILL THE DAY OF DOOM"

Before examining the ways the Bible and Shakespeare, when reproduced as ideal archives of Western culture, exemplify a secular apocalypticism, it is helpful to situate the concept of the ideal archive in terms of a crucial historical antecedent: the Reformation Bible. While the Bible for Christians has always been divinely inspired and therefore distinct from other books, strands of Reformation polemic emphasized this difference in a particularly absolute way, emphasizing the self-sufficiency of the Bible and its self-interpreting nature as a way of battling the hegemony of the Roman Catholic Church.

In many respects, this doctrine is tied to the history of media shift. The term "the Bible" in the singular ultimately derives from the plural Greek *ta biblia*, and this reconception of the Bible as a single entity owes something to the movement in material form from many scrolls to one codex.[5] However, this shift is taken to a whole new level with the Reformation: the separation of Biblical passages into discrete texts, frequent in medieval book production, was replaced with an emphasis on the Bible as a single book absolutely separate from all others.[6] James Kearney points out that "this vision of the Bible as a single text, complete and self-sufficient, would have been alien to most Christians prior to the Reformation."[7] John Milbank contends that the Biblical ontology that prevailed in the early modern period was the result of specific historical circumstances, including printing:

> the Bible as one continuous, primarily *written,* and initially naked, uncommentated-upon text was invented by printing, humanism, and the Reformation. Previously, the Bible was often apprehended in discrete manuscript scrolls adorned with surrounding glosses (like Jewish Bibles to this day), and illuminated pictures. Moreover, liturgically performed scripture and graphically depicted scripture (for example, on church walls) were regarded as equally "original" with the written text in a culture with continuing "oral" characteristics. The Reformation did not, therefore, make more widely available something which had previously existed; it disseminated something new.[8]

Milbank's comments about the Reformation Bible illuminate Tyndale's construction of the archival Bible as fully complete repository of transhistorical divine revelation, and as transparent and therefore fully knowable by the reader.

In his vehement early-Reformation debates with Tyndale, Thomas More frequently relies on arguments about the material and historical situatedness of Scripture and its consequent vulnerability to loss and corruption, in order to oppose the reformers' *sola scriptura* doctrine.[9] For More, divine revelation is continually clarified through temporal process occurring under the auspices of the Church, and is mediated through the consensus of Christendom.[10] By contrast, for Tyndale all revelation is already completely expressed in the Bible. Tyndale's defense of the singular importance of Scripture is frequently articulated in ways which place emphasis on a stark, unmediated binary separating the Bible from the rest of the world. It is true that, for the reformer, readers of Scripture imbued with the Holy Spirit are transformed by what they encounter and filled with new life. Yet, as Kearney puts it, for Tyndale "scripture is at odds with all that is other than scripture."[11] As we shall see, Tyndale presents the revelation contained in the Bible as fully knowable, self-sufficient fact, which undergirds his powerfully articulated logic of the Bible as complete archive of revelation. Tyndale's understanding is fundamentally dualistic, opposing Scripture against the chaos and loss characterizing the fallen world. As will be evident later in this chapter, modern celebrators of Shakespeare have presented the latter's texts in homologous terms.

Tyndale's defense of *sola scriptura* is fundamentally dependent on establishing Scripture as a full record of necessary doctrine. In his *Answer to Sir Thomas More's Dialogue*, he writes, "the pith and substance in general of everything necessary unto our soul's health, both of what we ought to believe and what we ought to do, was written [. . .] For if I were bound to do or believe, under pain of the loss of my soul, anything that were not written, nor depended of that which is written, what helps me the Scripture that is written?"[12] Tyndale requires a Bible which is fully complete, that can secure belief in unchanging, determinate meaning. In his *Obedience of a Christian Man*, Tyndale states that Christ "desired [. . .] no faith to be given either unto his doctrine or unto his miracles, without record of the Scripture.[13]" Along these lines, he asks, "seeing that Christ and all the apostles with all the angels of Heaven, if they were here, could preach no more than is preached of necessity unto our souls: how then should we receive a new article of the faith without Scripture, as profitable unto my soul when I had believed it as smoke for sore eyes."[14] Even Christ could preach no more, since all is already contained in holy writ; this formulation, which approaches a derogation of Christ in favor of determinate text, · exemplifies the idea of Scripture as self-grounding—Christ's preaching is extraneous in this formulation. Despite Tyndale's stress on the need for the Holy Spirit to dwell in the reader before Scripture can come to life as God's Word, dramatic emphasis is nonetheless given to a notion of writing in terms of autonomous, self-sufficient being.

Tyndale often presents the Christian as grateful recipient of divine promises. However, while simultaneously stressing the Bible's accessibility and comprehensibility, his presentation of its absolute singularity is problematic. Given that he was opposing an oftentimes authoritarian hermeneutic control over the Bible, Tyndale was understandably eager to emphasize the clarity and simplicity of holy writ, claiming that the Bible "hath but one simple, literal sense."[15] But Tyndale also emphasizes the Bible primarily as a source of knowledge, rather than as a medium of transforming and mysterious relationship that escapes any determinate content.[16] Despite Tyndale's statements about the sovereignty of God, he indirectly diminishes the Bible insofar as he implies the possibility of its contents being fully available to the reader.[17]

While distinguishing between idolatrous, human understandings of God and the true self-presentation of God in Scripture, Tyndale goes so far as to equate God with his textually-embodied revelations: "God is nothing but his law and his promises, that is to say, that which he biddeth thee do and that which he biddeth thee believe and hope. God is but his word."[18] Tyndale slips here from an emphasis on the absolute sovereignty of God to the reduction of God to something fully knowable by the human. God becomes a part of reality, rather than its ground, a conceptual move which opens the way for secular modes of thought.

For Tyndale, God's promises and statements of positive content are objectified for our acceptance or refusal. Even before the time of Noah, God "wrote His testament" using sacraments and sacrifices: "And in them they read the Word of God as we do in books."[19] The emphasis here is on interchangeability; the media of revelation do not matter, and the relationship at the heart of the gift of revelation is devalued: what matters most is content. Moreover, revelation is atemporal: it always exists, before its inscription or communication. All of God's revelations come to be contained in the Bible, leaving history devoid of revelatory meaning until the Last Judgment: "all things are opened so richly and all fulfilled that before was promised, and [. . .] there is no promise behind of ought to be showed more, save the resurrection."[20]

As Kearney argues, for Tyndale God's Word "must exist as an anterior, material text," either as writing or ritual.[21] The reformer valorizes Scriptural writing, manifest in sacraments and sacrifices as well as text, as the singular source of knowledge about God's revelation. Yet Tyndale also understands Scripture as an ideal archive, as existing beyond time. More is attentive to Tyndale's effacement of material contingency and to the rejection of history as a site of revelatory unfolding, contending that Tyndale "must also put in, that all [the apostles'] writing is kept and reserved safe, and ever shall till the day of doom."[22] Attention to Biblical rhetoric and history, and to the particularity of the various books' contexts, is obliterated by Tyndale; the Bible is effectively dematerialized and dehistoricized. With the modern elevation of the Bible and Shakespeare according to the concept of cultural heritage, we shall see reproduced similar notions of atemporal idealization and autonomous content articulated within an apocalyptic framework. What becomes particularly evident in this latter context is the image of a singular book which is both material object and ideal archive. Whereas Tyndale is writing before the English Bible could take on such iconic cultural status as an object (an iconic status he helped produce), a number of early Protestants would treat the Tyndale New Testament with a bibliolatrous veneration strikingly similar to the uses of material culture characteristic of their Catholic opponents.[23] While Tyndale's imaginary is not marked by a fetishized singular book in exactly this fashion, his appeal to Scriptural writing as equivalent to the Word of God nonetheless represents an incipient form of the ideal archive.

The various features of Tyndale's Bible discussed above coincide with theological shifts in the late Middle Ages and Reformation which tended to replace an ontology of mediation, participation, and the analogy of being with an ontology of univocal being. *Univocal* here refers to the late medieval shift towards considering "being" a term posited equally of God and creation. Entities are conceived as self-grounding rather than, as earlier theologies emphasize, participating in the being of God which, as the ground of creaturely being, is analogous but not identical to the being of creatures. This provides a philosophical underpinning for the notion that entities can be epistemologically grasped according to the conditions of "finite knowability."[24] The reformist doctrine of *sola scriptura*, baldly articulated by Tyndale, involves core features of this shift: as Milbank puts it, *sola scriptura* is characterized by a notion of "the text's finite and self-sufficient denotation" and the individual's "direct" confrontation with it.[25] In early modernity, revelation becomes "distorted into a positive, actual content" rather than being mediated by a divinely given "judgment and right desire."[26] Relationship, analogy, mediation, and participation are replaced by ontological reduction to self-grounding being and by epistemological mastery.

II "ONE BOOK IN THE WORLD"

The logic of the reformist Bible discussed above thus ironically anticipates crucial features of secular thought. As the Bible was called upon to perform new functions with modernity these features would persist, albeit in radically new forms, including in what Jonathan Sheehan calls the "cultural Bible"[27] that emerged in the late eighteenth and nineteenth centuries. Owing to its being threatened on theological grounds, throughout the eighteenth century the Bible became reauthorized on the basis of various modern scholarly disciplines. This separation of the Bible from theology ultimately led to the Bible being constructed as the fountain of Western cultural heritage—a notion still very much with us.[28] One of the shifts associated with the rise of the cultural Bible was that religion became recast as culture and culture as religion, and we find the Bible construed as an archive according to a radically new set of criteria. It becomes constructed as a supreme repository of humankind's highest linguistic achievement and of the most powerful and universal narratives expressive of human experience.

During this era of the cultural Bible we find Shakespeare constructed as an archive in ways which strikingly parallel this newly formulated Bible. Shakespeare is called upon to serve analogous functions to holy writ as a preserver of the crucial foundations of culture against the possibility of future catastrophe, in ways which mirror the Tyndalian logic discussed above.[29] The professor of rhetoric George Saintsbury's 1887 *History of Elizabethan Literature* gives a particularly vivid demonstration of the linkage of Shakespeare and the Bible as ideal archives of western culture:

> The plays of Shakespeare and the English Bible are, and will ever be, the twin monuments not merely of their own period, but of the perfection of English, the complete expressions of the literary capacities of the language, at the time when it had lost none of its pristine vigour, and had put on enough but not too much of the adornments and the limitations of what may be called literary civilisation.[30]

Saintsbury's investment in ideal archives is apparent in his emphasis on the completeness of Shakespeare and the Bible's expression of the English language's powers, and on the everlasting nature of what he calls, in a metaphor expressing determinate and consecrated materiality, these "twin monuments."

Starting in the mid-nineteenth century and extending into the early twentieth, Shakespeare became construed in explicitly religious terms (even being incorporated into Christian worship), powerfully intensifying earlier bardolatrous trends.[31] Many of the period's writers who painstakingly track parallels between Shakespeare's writings and Bible passages were anxious to contrast the divine inspiration of Scripture with the human status of Shakespeare, and to stress that Shakespeare's genius was a gift of God.[32] In a sermon concerning Shakespeare's Biblical influence, Charles Wordsworth presents Shakespeare's writings as a stream which reflects "shining in its depths the starlike truths of the Bible"[33]; the image suggests an understanding of God's relationship to creation as involving reflection, analogy, and a mysterious mixture of connection and distance, rather than revelation as positive, determinate content. At the same time, Wordsworth would go so far as to write that the "secular Bible" of Shakespeare gives "a full and accurate system of religious doctrine"[34]: emphasized here is Shakespeare as total archive, encapsulating what Linda Rozmovits describes as "the complete range of possibilities for human behavior."[35]

The increasing alignment of Shakespeare and religion could be taken in an explicitly anti-Christian direction, albeit in a way which sustained the narrative of the ideal archive imagined as a singular book. Algernon Charles Swinburne begins his book *Shakespeare* with the following:

> There is one book in the world of which it might be affirmed and argued, without fear of derision from any but the supreme and crowning fools among the foolishest of mankind, that it would be better for the world to lose all others and keep this one than to lose this and keep all other treasures bequeathed by human genius to all that we can conceive

of eternity—to all that we can imagine of immortality. That book is best known, and best described for all of us, simply by the simple English name of its author. The word Shakespeare connotes more than any other man's name that was ever written or spoken upon earth.[36]

Charles LaPorte points out that Swinburne is both continuing a tradition of Victorian bardolatry which constructed Shakespeare as the "greatest author ever," while deliberately invoking the idea of the "one book" which civilization cannot afford to lose, only to replace its familiar referent, the Bible, with Shakespeare.[37] Significantly, Swinburne's proclamation that "it would be better for the world to lose all others and keep this one than to lose this and keep all other treasures bequeathed by human genius to all that we can conceive of eternity" echoes the Biblical "For what is a man profited, if he shall gain the whole world, and lose his own soul?"[38] Swinburne invokes eternity and immortality—"all we can conceive of eternity," "all that we can imagine of immortality"—and connects them to imagination rather than theology, drawing on their religious meanings and transferring the value associated with them to Shakespeare. Swinburne's is a deliberately transgressive invocation of bardolatry, taken to an irreligious extreme.[39]

As LaPorte goes on to demonstrate, Swinburne is echoing Thomas Macaulay's praise of the English Bible: "if everything else in our language should perish, [it] would alone suffice to show the whole extent of its beauty and power."[40] When viewed within a long historical perspective, the subversiveness of Swinburne's reworking of Macaulay is significantly defanged, since Macaulay's championing of the Bible in linguistic and cultural terms already undermines the traditional theological criteria according to which the Bible was valued. Moreover, Macaulay and Swinburne are united in that they both reveal another important feature of the mutually involved construction of Shakespeare and the Bible during this time, a construction exemplary of secular textual ontology: the imagining of the ideal archive. Swinburne's claim that "it would be better for the world to lose all others and keep this one than to lose this and keep all other treasures," like Macaulay's "[it] alone would suffice," stresses the absolute singularity of the books of Shakespeare and the Bible; disavowing any sense of culture as a set of relationships, what is stressed here is an absolute, self-sufficient unity.

Macaulay's praise of the English Bible's language is echoed in the early twentieth century by Saintsbury in a book on English prose rhythm, in a way which also emphasizes the image of the so-called Authorized Version of 1611 as an ideal archive. Here, the ideal archive is powerfully depicted as a book which is a singular object. Saintsbury writes,

> So long as a single copy of the version of 1611 survives, so long will there be accessible the best words of the best time of English, in the best order, on the best subjects—so long will the fount be open from which a dozen generations of great English writers, in the most varying times

and fashions, of the most diverse temperaments—libertines and virtuous persons, freethinkers and devout, poets and prosemen, laymen and divines—have drawn inspiration and pattern; by which three centuries of readers and hearers have had kept before them the prowess and the powers of the English tongue.[41]

Despite Saintsbury's passing reference to the "best subject matter," the passage's emphasis is not on the Bible's theological content. Instead, he celebrates the astonishing diversity of those who take their inspiration from Scripture, which constitutes a marked contrast to the transcendent singularity of the Bible, represented as a "single copy," which miraculously preserves the best words, order, and subject matter.

For Macaulay and Saintsbury, the English Bible is explicitly presented as an exhaustive archive, but one defined in very narrow ways. Saintsbury's story about a single surviving copy is based on the notion of the book as physical object, as is Swinburne's invocation of Shakespeare as the "one book" that humanity can least afford to lose. Of course, these images of transcendent yet also particular physical books are also evocative of an idealized archival function: they are shot through with ideas of singularity, preservation, boundedness, unity, and plenitude. These visions suggest that this plenitude is somehow fully contained by the physical object of the book, since the prospective calamity is presented in terms of the loss of the Bible as object.[42]

Moreover, the idea of archival preservation in the face of potential destruction is emphasized by Macaulay, Swinburne, and Saintsbury. All three imagine a scenario of future loss and against this the "one book" whose survival will allow for the preservation of civilization, a precursor to the more genial desert island scenario. They thus replace the Christian vision of history moving towards a full and complete revelation with history moving towards destruction, against which Shakespeare or the Bible stands as the "one book" which will preserve the bases of civilization.

III   "A HIDDEN DEPOSIT"

Those who appeal to encrypted messages in the works of Shakespeare for evidence that the Stratford actor did not write the plays and poems represent a high-water mark in the fetishizing of transparent, stable, self-sufficient meaning; they cast several of the central assumptions about textual ontology and epistemology at the heart of the modern Shakespeare–Bible nexus in sharp relief.[43] The cryptographic analyses of Shakespeare examined here critically depend upon the book as a material object. They not only rely on the spatial arrangement of words and other characters on the page as signs to detect the encrypted meanings, but they are also pervaded with the physical details of imagined repositories of secret messages. They imagine the materiality of the book, and the ontology of the putative cryptic messages hidden within, in terms of self-grounding univocity. These messages are also framed by narratives of revelation and impending catastrophe resembling those traditionally associated with religion. Anti-Stratfordian cryptographers mirror the hopes, fantasies, and ontological assumptions that we have seen are crucial to the history of the Bible.[44]

Ignatius Donnelly's cryptographic analyses of Shakespeare's texts are among the most revealing of the secularized apocalyptic impulses of what Shawn James Rosenheim calls the "cryptographic imagination." Donnelly is one of the most passionate, eloquent, and imaginative of the Shakespearean cryptographers, and his narratives of secrecy and discovery are powerful and indicative of the prevalent philosophical and emotional underpinnings of the story of the ideal archive. Donnelly's cryptographic project asks Shakespeare to perform similar functions to the archival Bible discussed above: that is, to serve as an ideal site of preservation in the face of a future dissolution of the world. He is also particularly illuminating of ways the cryptographic treatment of Shakespeare is based in assumptions of direct, unmediated communion with both the past and revelatory experience. These features resemble certain impulses central to religion; here they are shaped by an ontology of self-sufficient entities and an individualized epistemological mastery characteristic of secularity.

The first person to produce a sustained cryptographic analysis of Shakespeare, Donnelly published his monumental, two-volume *The Great Cryptogram* in 1887–8.[45] Donnelly's "evidence" for Francis Bacon's authorship of Shakespeare derives from the particularities of the First Folio's typography, and this volume is presented as one of the great monuments of civilization. Along with Bacon's major works of natural philosophy, *Novum Organum* and *De Augmentis*, the Folio represents the other of Bacon's "great pillars, the one as worthy, as enduring, as world-sustaining as the other."[46] The Folio is a monument, an epitome of stability, upon which the world foundationally depends.

Against the overwhelming evidence which would be amassed in the twentieth century, Donnelly views the First Folio as an exemplar of accurate printing.[47] Typifying the paradoxical logic of those who claim to discover a secret which simultaneously conceals and reveals itself, Donnelly explains that what variation and irregularity the Folio has in pagination indicates, along with the presence of italicized words, a deliberate coded message.[48] Donnelly also constructs the material text as a complete reflection of the author's singular intentions rather than being the result of the collaboration of multiple agents including the author(s), printers, and publisher, and more broadly as an artifact shaped by contemporary social, cultural, and political contexts.

In addition to typographical clues, various scenes in Shakespeare's plays are cited as vehicles for coded messages; Donnelly states that many of these scenes are pure nonsense, present only to signal the cryptic mean-ings behind them.[49] The logic here is exemplary not only of cryptographic treatments of Shakespeare generally but even more broadly of a herme-neutic tendency characteristic of modernity: the sign is dispensable once the signified meaning is extracted, owing to a starkly dualistic under-standing of signification. What is solely important and fetishized here is discovery.[50] Unlike in premodern readings of the world for signs of divine meaning, for Donnelly the signs are ultimately expendable, significant only as indexes for the real meaning. In the premodern allegorical world view which read history and Scriptural accounts in relationship to their eschatological fulfillment, the typological sign is not merely expendable, dualistically and absolutely other to its fulfillment or referent; both sign and referent participate in one another.[51]

Donnelly's secularist hermeneutic is also expressed through imagina-tive reveries centered on physical sites and material objects shrouded in secrecy. His cryptographic imagination is imbued with the etymological and conceptual parallels between secret messages and graves. Indeed, many people have been obsessed with the epitaph on Shakespeare's tomb possibly containing cryptic messages. The word "cryptographic" and "crypt" share the Greek etymological root *kryptos* (secret).[52] Cryptographic analyses of Shakespeare repeatedly incorporate ideas of physically entombed evidence corresponding to the secret textual messages.[53] Commenting on crypto-graphic Baconians who persistently link hidden textual meaning to physi-cal tombs, Rosenheim suggests that the text itself becomes imagined as a crypt to be entered, whose contents are "brought to light."[54]

Donnelly takes the tomb-cryptic meaning linkage to great imaginative heights, articulating the linkage through his fantasy of an ideal archive. For Donnelly, the cryptic messages and the crypt go hand in hand, following a purported logical necessity: since Bacon would have wanted to make sure people find the cipher, "The existence of the cipher presupposes therefore the existence of a hidden deposit."[55] In his follow up to *The Great Cryptogram*, *The Cipher in the Plays and On the Tombstone*, Donnelly's material imagi-nation is unleashed, and he revels in the physical characteristics of his imag-ined archives. The encrypted evidence he claims exists in the Sonnets and on Shakespeare's tombstone imply the existence, "somewhere in England, bur-ied probably in the earth, or in a vault of masonry, a great iron or brass coffer or coffers" containing "books and papers, many of them 'yellowed with their age,'" confirming Bacon's identity as author.[56] Similarly, Donnelly's contem-porary Orville Ward Owen was convinced that Bacon buried evidence about his authorship of Shakespeare in iron boxes.[57] Donnelly's archive is lovingly imagined in its material specificity: alluding to Bacon's *Sylva Sylvarum*, he opines that it is "covered with 'the wax of watch-candles.'"[58] These intensely physical archives embody Donnelly's ontology of the secret message with its dual fetishizing of enclosure and determinacy.

The physical archives imagined here are repositories of miraculous fullness: Donnelly speculates that the hypothetical iron coffer might contain explanations of ciphers; the papers of Nicholas Bacon and Anthony Coke, "giving the secret history of the reigns" of the Tudor monarchs; and other documents which will shed light on Bacon's period. Donnelly also imagines Bacon's "great library" being here.[59] He later suggests that Ben Jonson may have placed in Shakespeare's tomb "a bottle, or water-tight casket" containing evidence of Bacon's authorship, stating the whereabouts of "the original manuscripts of the Plays, and a world of other matters."[60] In an apocalyptic vein, Donnelly urges humanity to dig up Shakespeare's grave; since we do not know how much time civilization has before its destruction, we need to swiftly access this hidden archive.[61]

Bacon's encrypting is imagined as the creation of an archive against impending chaos: "[Bacon] anticipated the great religious and political revolution which soon after his death swept over England. He believed that the world was on the eve of great civil convulsions, growing out of religious fanaticism, in which it was possible civilization might perish, despite the art of printing."[62] Beyond fears about impending revolution, Bacon's archiving of his messages is framed by the Apocalypse: the messages are designed "to be read when the tempest that was about to assail civilization had passed away,—the Plays surviving, for they were, he tells us, to live when 'marble and the gilded monuments of princes' had perished—even to the general judgment."[63] Drawing out this eschatological trope, Donnelly writes that when the hidden story was finally discovered, Bacon would be resurrected: "he would, through the cipher narrative, rise anew from the grave."[64] The plays would also undergo a figurative resurrection: the secret messages are "[a] great light bursting from a tomb, and covering with its royal effulgence the very cradle of English Literature."[65] The plays are both cradle and grave, the image recalling Christ's resurrection and the empty tomb. In a less religious vein, Donnelly's apocalypticism also includes a vision of cultural universality:

> once the human family grasps the entirety of [Bacon's] inconceivable work, it will be drowned in an ocean of wonder. The Plays may lose their charm; the English language may perish; but tens of thousands of years from now, if the world and civilization endure, mankind will be talking about this extraordinary welding together of fact and fiction; this tale within a tale; this sublime and supreme triumph of the human intellect. Besides it the *Iliad* will be but as the rude song of wandering barbarians, and *Paradise Lost* a temporary offshoot of Judaism.[66]

The cryptic messages for Donnelly represent a universality eclipsing what were once seen as the crowning works of western culture, *The Iliad* and *Paradise Lost*, and will be, he claims, revealed to be merely local and particular.

According to Donnelly, Bacon encrypted the true history of his times; Donnelly imagines a future when the cryptic process he discovered would be refined, and therefore yield more of the "cipher narrative": "And what a volume of historical truths will roll out of the text of this great volume! The inner life of kings and queens, [. . .] the struggles of factions in the courts; [. . .] the Spanish Armada," religious history—"in short, the inner story of the most important era in human history, told by the keenest observer and the most powerful writer that has ever lived."[67]

This is a striking image of revelation and the unveiling of a plenitude of meaning long obscured. Yet Donnelly's rhetoric is most intense not when it touches on the *contents* of the encrypted messages, which tend to be vague and general, but when he proclaims the *presence* of the cipher, and the event of the cipher's discovery. It is less clear that new insights into Elizabethan and Jacobean history would transfix humanity until the end of time than that the existence and revelation of secret messages in the works of Shakespeare would be a source of wonder. A similar sense is evoked in *The Cipher in the Play and on the Tombstone*. Analysis of the Sonnets uncovers the "tremendous record of his life and work, and the history of his time," which would effectively resurrect Bacon: "it would take a new life [. . .] and remain forever;—concentrating upon itself the attention of mankind, till the 'ending doom.'"[68] Humanity will be eternally fixated on the messages Bacon encoded. But again, what rings out the loudest here is the wonder at the presence of the messages: the great revelation will be that Bacon "was the greatest intellect of all time; that by a splendid self-abnegation he has allowed his honors to rest for centuries upon the heads of others."[69] This self-abnegation is temporary—present, like Prince Hal's dissolution, only to set off his eventual glory all the more. Ultimately, Bacon will come to possess the world eternally: when the "cheveril glove" of Shakespeare is turned inside out to reveal its hidden truth,[70] then Bacon will, following the language of Sonnet 55, "'pace forth,' 'gainst death and all oblivious enmity,' and take possession of the world and hold it as long as the earth endures."[71]

Donnelly, like cryptologist readers of Shakespeare in general, in many ways sidelines aesthetic and other cultural matters in favor of a scientific analysis of text as data. But he constructs Shakespeare's texts as an archive exhibiting ideal features we have also seen associated with the Bible, and presents them within an apocalyptic framework. No interpretation is required of the encrypted messages. The event of discovery is an idealized moment of communion between present and past which transcends historical difference and to which the material particularities of textual transmission are inconsequential. The extent to which the dynamic of secrecy and revelation is emphasized in this discourse works in tandem with the construction of the hidden messages; both the process of discovery and status of the text discovered share an ontology characterized by completeness, finality, and closure.

Donnelly's fantasy of discovery is clearly self-serving, but it also bespeaks a sinister fantasy of mastery closely linked to his hermeneutic assumptions and textual ontology. This is particularly apparent in the following imagined scene:

> One can fancy Francis Bacon sitting at the play—in the background— with his hat over his eyes—watching Elizabeth and Cecil, seated, as was the custom, on the stage, enjoying and laughing over some merry comedy, little dreaming that the internal fabric of the play told, in immortal words, all the darkest passages of their own dark lives—embalmed in the midst of wit and rollicking laughter, for the entertainment of all future ages. And so the long-suffering and much-abused genius enjoyed his revenge, even under the very nose of power.[72]

The self is elevated here through a derogation of aesthetic response in favor of a hidden, rational message. Moreover, the self is apotheosized through a narcissistic fetishizing of secrecy. Walt Whitman's poem "Shakespeare— Bacon's Cipher" has been read as expressing the anti-Stratfordians' desire for meaning, and particularly Donnelly's obsession with ciphers.[73] While Whitman shared the views of many anti-Stratfordians, the mystical vision Whitman evokes in his poem, characterized by envisioning "every object, mountain, tree, and star" as containing "[a] mystic cipher,"[74] resembles much more the premodern world of correspondences and participation than Donnelly's world. Donnelly expresses with particular potency the individualistic core of the fantasy of encrypted meanings and their discovery. Meaning is self-contained, existing in an unmediated relationship to the rest of the world, its determinate nature allowing it to be mastered, and in turn giving the discoverer increased prestige and autonomy.

As many have commented, cryptographic theories like Donnelly's are so bizarre because they seem to devalue the plays of Shakespeare, preferring instead banal "messages" ascribed to Bacon or some other putatively authentic author.[75] This is particularly evident in Donnelly, who imagines a time when "[t]he Plays may lose their charm," and, by contrast, the encrypted messages will remain as a universally valued testament to the human intellect. Of course, any value such mundane messages would have is primarily owing to their putative encryption in some of the most valued cultural artifacts of human history. Theories like Donnelly's are disingenuous in the extreme, since they strive to devalue that which gives them meaning: no one would care much about encrypted meanings in texts not possessing the cultural authority and value of Shakespeare's plays. For Donnelly the act and experience of revelation largely trumps the content of that which is revealed, and certainly devalues the vehicle through which the encrypted message is communicated. Donnelly's fantasies of deferred, apocalyptic plenitude represent an apotheosis of the fetish for discovery. For all of Donnelly's avowals of modern liberalism and skepticism about religious zeal, his writing is fraught with religious imagery and irrational belief in a future revelation; however, these instances of "religiosity" are marked by a very modern logic. Inadvertently yet powerfully testifying to Shakespeare's cultural power, and attempting to transmute and subsume that power, Donnelly and other cryptographic interpreters of Shakespeare illuminate a fetish for discovery of a particularly modern cast.

The Bible's refashioning in the Reformation was tied up with religious belief and a massive and deadly political struggle, and of course the cultural apotheosis of Shakespeare as secular Scripture and the cryptographic fetish of apocalyptic discovery represent drastically different cultural and historical moments. Nonetheless, the reformist Bible and the cultural and cryptographic Shakespeare have been called upon to serve a number of homologous functions as ideal archives, and these eminently modern textual ontologies have significant ethical significance. The ethics of construing the Bible as an ideal archive, and its concomitant individualist hermeneutic of discovery, are powerfully articulated by John Milbank, who writes,

> Protestantism had later to develop a science of "hermeneutics" to bring methodically under control the reading of a text which was now problematically self-interpreting, at a distance from and over-against the church community [. . .] the Medieval Bible was itself a more "open" text, whose ethical and anagogical (eschatological) senses *included* the reader himself within an unfolding textual development. Here the reader did *not* stand over against the text as an interpreter, looking for its "essential" sense—for it was assumed, however erroneously, that the "literal" meaning could be fairly readily obtained—but stood in judgement under the text, ready to draw from it new meanings in word and deed under the reinscribing power of the Spirit.[76]

The cryptographic Shakespeare is an extreme case, but an especially illuminating one for that, of a modern, secular construction of textuality. The material book is imagined as a container of an inert, finite, circumscribed meaning, and the book's own materiality becomes closed to social process and collaboration. The fetishizing of the discovery of masterable, univocal meaning ultimately works to affirm the self-grounding individualism of the interpreter. Some of the most intense instances of the construction of Shakespeare according to Biblical paradigms are thus particularly and ironically indicative of the philosophical underpinnings of secular modernity.

NOTES

1. Charles Taylor, *A Secular Age*, Cambridge, MA: Harvard University Press, 2007.
2. See John Milbank, *Theology and Social Theory: Beyond Secular Reason*, 2nd ed., Oxford: Blackwell, 2006; Michael Allen Gillespie, *The Theological Origins of Modernity*, Chicago: University of Chicago Press, 2008.

3. John Drakakis, "Ideology and Institution: Shakespeare and the Roadsweepers," in Graham Holderness (ed.) *The Shakespeare Myth*, Manchester: Manchester University Press, 1988, p. 25.
4. Ibid., pp. 24–6; Paul Franssen, "The Bard, the Bible, and the Desert Island," in Franssen and Ton Hoenselaars (eds) *The Author as Character: Representing Historical Writers in Western Literature*, Cranbury, NJ: Associated University Presses, 1999, p. 110.
5. Stephen Prickett, *Origins of Narrative: The Romantic Appropriation of the Bible*, Cambridge: Cambridge University Press, 1996, p. 3.
6. James Kearney, *The Incarnate Text: Imagining the Book in Reformation England*, Philadelphia: University of Pennsylvania Press, 2009, p. 156.
7. Ibid., p. 269, note 63.
8. John Milbank, Review of *Biblical Hermeneutics in Historical Perspective*, *Journal of Theological Studies*, 1995, vol. 42, 667.
9. Thomas More, *Responsio ad Lutherum*, John Headley (ed.) New Haven, CT: Yale University Press, 1969, pp. 99–101; *A Dialogue Concerning Heresies*, Thomas M.C. Lawler, Germain Marc'hadour, and Richard C. Marius (eds) New Haven CT: Yale University Press, 1981, p. 115; *The Confutation of Tyndale's Answer*, Louis A. Schuster, Richard C. Marius, and James P. Lusardi (eds) New Haven, CT: Yale University Press, 1973, pp. 334–5.
10. Alistair Fox, *Thomas More: History and Providence*, Oxford: Blackwell, 1982, p. 158; Brian Gogan, *The Common Corps of Christendom: Ecclesiological Themes in the Writings of Sir Thomas More*, Leiden: E.J. Brill, 1982, pp. 298–302.
11. Kearney, *Incarnate*, p. 75.
12. William Tyndale, *An Answere vnto Sir Thomas Mores Dialoge*, in Anne M. O'Donnell and Jared Wicks (eds) *The Independent Works of William Tyndale*, vol. 3, Washington DC: The Catholic University of America Press, 2000, p. 24–5. Spelling modernized.
13. William Tyndale, *The Obedience of a Christian Man*, David Daniell (ed.) London: Penguin, 2000, p. 17.
14. Tyndale, *An Answere*, p. 26.
15. David Daniell (ed.), *Tyndale's Old Testament*, New Haven, CT: Yale University Press, 1992, p. 3. By contrast, More places emphasis on the mysterious nature of Scripture (*The Confutation*, p. 337).
16. Tyndale, *The Obedience*, pp. 21–2.
17. For More's affirmation of divine revelation as being beyond our knowledge and the Biblical records, see *The Confutation*, p. 284.
18. Tyndale, *The Obedience*, p. 24.
19. Tyndale, *An Answere*, p. 25.
20. Ibid., p. 26.
21. Kearney, *Incarnate*, p. 82.
22. More, *The Confutation*, p. 335.
23. Brian Cummings, "Iconoclasm and Bibliophobia in the English Reformations, 1521–1558," in Jeremy Dimmick, James Simpson, and Nicolette Zeeman (eds) *Images, Idolatry, and Iconoclasm in Late Medieval England: Textuality and the Visual Image*, Oxford: Oxford University Press 2002, p. 203.
24. John Milbank, *The Word Made Strange: Theology, Language, Culture*, Oxford: Blackwell, 1997, p. 44.
25. Ibid., p. 95.
26. Ibid., p. 49.
27. Jonathan Sheehan, *The Enlightenment Bible: Translation, Scholarship, Culture*, Princeton, NJ: Princeton University Press, 2005, pp. ix–x.

28. Ibid., pp. ix–xi.
29. Linda Rozmovits argues that during this time the increasing secularization of the Bible accompanies the increasing sacralization of culture, especially Shakespeare, following a see-saw movement. (Linda Rozmovits, *Shakespeare and the Politics of Culture in Late Victorian England*, Baltimore, MD: Johns Hopkins University Press, 1998, p. 20.)
30. George Saintsbury, *A History of Elizabethan Literature*, London: Macmillan, 1887, p. 218.
31. Rozmovits, *Shakespeare*, pp. 12–3.
32. Ibid., pp. 16–7, 25.
33. Qtd. in ibid., p. 18.
34. Qtd. in ibid., p. 26.
35. Ibid.
36. Algernon Charles Swinburne, *Shakespeare*, London: Oxford University Press, 1909, pp. 5–6.
37. Charles LaPorte, "The Bard, the Bible, and the Victorian Shakespeare Question," *English Literary History*, 2007, vol. 74, no. 3, 609–28, p. 612.
38. Matthew 16:26, KJV.
39. LaPorte, "Bard," p. 613.
40. Thomas B. Macaulay, "John Dryden," in *The Miscellaneous Writings of Lord Macaulay*, T.F. Ellis (ed.), London: Longman, 1865, p. 94.
41. Qtd. in David Norton, *A History of the Bible as Literature*, vol. 2, Cambridge: Cambridge University Press, 1993, p. 323. Shakespeare is in the background of this praise of the Authorized Version, since Saintsbury directly attributes that version's greatness to the literary excellence of the age of Shakespeare and Francis Bacon. Moreover, as David Norton reveals, Saintsbury sarcastically hints at the possibility that Bacon secretly "wrote" the Authorized Version, thereby alluding to the Shakespeare authorship question and Bacon's putative role as author of Shakespeare (ibid., p. 324).
42. As we have seen, Swinburne's evocative phrase "one book" has marked Biblical associations: the Bible's "unique status [. . .] for the West is reflected by the fact that its title is the same as the generic word for 'book' [. . .] the Bible has appropriated the concept of a book" (Prickett, *Origins*, p. 102). Swinburne's phrase channels the notion of the Bible as object containing a miraculous ideal plenitude.
43. For overviews of the Shakespeare authorship question, see Warren Hope and Kim Holstun, *The Shakespeare Controversy: An Analysis of the Authorship Theories*, 2nd ed., Jefferson, NC: McFarland, 2009; James Shapiro, *Contested Will: Who Wrote Shakespeare?* New York: Simon and Schuster, 2010.
44. Shawn James Rosenheim asserts that "cryptographic fantasies" exemplify a "secularized [. . .] desire to make of Shakespeare the book of books through which a culture can project its fantasies of meaning and history"; despite his suggestive reference to secularization and the "book of books," he does not explicitly connect such cryptographic fantasies to the history of the Bible. (Shawn James Rosenheim, *The Cryptographic Imagination: Secret Writing from Edgar Poe to the Internet*, Baltimore, MD: Johns Hopkins University Press, 1997, p. 153.)
45. For Donnelly's biography, see David Kahn, *The Codebreakers: The Comprehensive History of Secret Communication from Ancient Times to the Internet*, 2nd ed., New York: Simon and Schuster, 1996, p. 874.
46. Ignatius Donnelly, *The Great Cryptogram: Francis Bacon's Cipher in the So-Called Shakespeare Plays*, vol. 2, London: Sampson Low, 1888, p. 564.
47. William F. and Elizabeth S. Friedman draw on evidence about the material conditions of early modern printing to critique cryptographic analyses of

Shakespeare like Donnelly's. (William F. and Elizabeth S. Friedman, *The Shakespearean Ciphers Examined*, Cambridge: Cambridge University Press, 1957, pp. 216–29.)

48. Donnelly, *The Great Cryptogram* vol. 2, pp. 551–5.
49. Ibid, 519, 875.
50. For a discussion of modern hermeneutics fetishizing secrecy and elevating discovery as the de facto route to knowledge, see James Dougal Fleming, *Milton's Secrecy and Philosophical Hermeneutics*, Aldershot: Ashgate, 2008, pp. 1–3.
51. Erich Auerbach, *Scenes from the Drama of European Literature: Six Essays*, Gloucester, MA: Peter Smith, 1973, pp. 71–3; Henri de Lubac, *Medieval Exegesis*, 1959–63, vol. 2, trans. E.M. Macierowski, Grand Rapids, MI: Eerdmans, 2000, pp. 26, 102.
52. Rosenheim, *Cryptographic*, p. 46. Rosenheim also notes that another word associated with secret writing, "hieroglyph," is the "etymological equivalent" to "holy grave" (ibid., p. 45).
53. Ibid., pp. 46–7; Marjorie Garber, *Shakespeare's Ghost Writers: Literature as Uncanny Causality*, London: Routledge, 1987, p. 6.
54. Rosenheim, *Cryptographic*, p. 47.
55. Ignatius Donnelly, *The Cipher in the Plays and On the Tombstone*, Minneapolis: Verulam Publishing Co., 1899, p. 118.
56. Ibid, p. 115.
57. Rosenheim, *Cryptographic*, p. 46.
58. Donnelly, *The Cipher*, p. 115.
59. Ibid.
60. Ibid., p. 363.
61. Ibid., p. 365.
62. Donnelly, *The Great Cryptogram*, vol. 2, p. 514.
63. Ibid., p. 515.
64. Ibid.
65. Ibid., p. 894.
66. Ibid., p. 893.
67. Ibid., pp. 893–4.
68. Donnelly, *The Cipher*, p. 120.
69. Ibid., p. 121.
70. Like the many cryptographers' fascination with the encoded message "M.O.A.I." in *Twelfth Night*, this "cheveril glove" allusion to the same play is unintentionally ironic. Just as "M.O.A.I." is a fake code designed to gull Malvolio, Feste's reference to a "cheveril glove" is part of his discussion of language as fluid and indeterminate, a perspective inimical to that of the cryptographers'.
71. Donnelly, *The Cipher*, p. 121.
72. Donnelly, *The Great Cryptogram*, vol. 2, pp. 563–4.
73. Zachary Lesser, "Mystic Ciphers: Shakespeare and Intelligent Design," *American Literary History*, 2007, vol. 19, no. 2, 350–6, p. 353; Shapiro, *Contested Will*, p. 122.
74. Qtd. in Lesser, "Mystic," p. 353.
75. Rosenheim, *Cryptographic*, p. 152; Kahn, *Codebreakers*, p. 887.
76. Milbank, Review, pp. 667–8.

11 Disintegrating the Rock
Ian Paisley, British Shakespeare, and Ulster Protestantism

David Coleman

I A PAISLEYITE HERMENEUTIC

In 1982, Ian Paisley, moderator of Northern Ireland's Free Presbyterian Church, perceived his religious and cultural identity to be under threat by the visit of Pope John Paul II to the United Kingdom. In a pamphlet published in protest to the planned visit, Paisley suggested a way of maintaining Ulster Protestant identity:

> Do we want to preserve our heritage? The remedy is in our hands. Let us all diligently, in private, read this Book and hide its precious words in our hearts as its words are the great preservatives from sin.[1]

"This Book" is, of course, the Bible. Although Paisley represents an extreme evangelical strain of late modern Ulster Protestantism, his reverence for "the Book," a reverence typologically represented by the upper-case initial letter granted in Paisley's text, is of a piece with the wider textual interests of Northern Irish Protestantism. In terms of the materiality of textual transmission, the Bible is still conventionally imagined in this culture in the form of a printed codex; but Biblical commentary and interpretation—equally central to the culture's sense of its own identity—are often expounded in more apparently ephemeral forms of text, including the sermon, the pamphlet (as here), and a variety of electronic media. These particular ways of encountering and disseminating Biblical texts and images are shaped by particular contexts and by particular media; a similar claim, this essay will argue, can be made for Ulster Protestantism's engagement with the Shakespearean text.

In some ways, then, this essay should be seen as an attempt to refine the ongoing critical exploration of the conjunction "Shakespeare and Ireland." This pairing has undoubtedly given rise to a rich yet politically complex cultural heritage. From a literary-critical perspective, one of the most significant results of the study of Shakespearean reception and appropriation in post-partition Ireland has been the illumination of specific sites of resistance to the Britishness which the Shakespearean legacy is often taken to embody in such post-imperial contexts.[2] This finding is particularly prevalent in the study of writers born in the post-1921 jurisdiction of Northern Ireland, but associated with the Catholic minority population of that statelet; for example, Rebecca Steinberger has argued that Brian Friel's appropriation of the Henriad functions as a rewriting of the British colonial project, whereas a number of critics have drawn attention to the complex "Shakespeare" imagined in the poems of Seamus Heaney, a Northern Irish poet famously resistant to the claims of "British" identity which "Shakespeare" may embody.[3] Surprisingly little attention, however, has been paid to "the other side" of the cultural divide in Northern Ireland; that is, the community of Ulster Protestants, and the ways in which the very specific sense of British identity found in that particular community may be inflected in Shakespearean ways. Conversely, scholarship has been well aware of the significance of Scripture for Ulster Protestantism, particularly (as is the case with Paisley) in its more fundamentalist aspects. In Ulster Protestantism, as has often been the case in Anglophone cultures, Scripture and Shakespeare have occasionally been yoked together to propound a rhetorically forceful political perspective.

A large body of critical work exists on Ulster Protestantism and, although this work rarely addresses the Shakespearean appropriations undertaken by Ulster Protestant writers, it does offer useful ways of conceptualizing the textual hermeneutic of Ulster Protestantism. That hermeneutic is directly related to what David Hempton has identified as the specific "cultural values" of Ulster Protestantism: "belief in a personal God, commitment to a particular land, unwavering hostilities to perceived enemies, obedience to a divinely sanctioned legal code, adherence to a prophetical interpretation of human destiny and the employment of Biblical language and thought forms to interpret the wider world."[4] While all of these are distinctive features of Paisley's writing, it is the last—employment of Biblical language and thought forms—which is of particular interest, as it demonstrates both how verbatim quotation and contextualization are not necessarily important to Paisley's conception of the Bible, and how any other text—Shakespeare included—must of necessity come a distant second to the influence of the Bible.

This essay will argue that there is a distinctive hermeneutic apparent in the Shakespearean and Scriptural appropriations by Paisley, but that such a hermeneutic is always shaped by the material qualities of the artifacts which Paisley uses to propound his message. In Paisley's characteristic form of Scriptural fundamentalism, key phrases are repeated at politically and rhetorically opportune moments, frequently divorced both from their original textual formulations, and from the complex history of textual transmission which brings them to Paisley's attention; by and large, this is also true of the way in which he reads Shakespeare. In what follows, I will examine four distinctive means by which Paisley combines a Scriptural and Shakespearean hermeneutic: the sermon; the political speech; the political pamphlet; and electronic text. I want to suggest that the "disintegrative" aspect of the Paisleyite hermeneutic thrives when the codex form itself becomes disintegrated; thus, although Paisley rhetorically lays claim to the traditions of early modernity, and although his political opponents may caricature his position as "pre-modern," the correlation of the nature of his hermeneutic strategies with the material forms through which that hermeneutic is pursued suggests that his is a particularly late-modern form of Scriptural fundamentalism. I will begin by pursuing an extended investigation of the political and cultural significance of one particular instance of Paisley's Shakespearean appropriation; I will then conclude by examining the prevalence of this Paisleyite hermeneutic across a variety of material textual artifacts.

II POLITICAL MISAPPROPRIATION: *LOCRINE* AND THE LEGITIMIZATION OF BRITISH ULSTER

Paisley's Shakespearean reading, like his Scriptural, is characteristically directed towards an engagement in contemporary political affairs. Paisley was the leader for over thirty years of Northern Ireland's Democratic Unionist Party (DUP), a political party dedicated to maintaining Northern Ireland's membership in the United Kingdom, closely associated with a populist appeal to disaffected working-class Unionists, and evangelical Protestants (including members of Paisley's own Free Presbyterian Church). In the first decade of the twenty-first century, Paisley's DUP overtook the traditionalist Ulster Unionist Party to become the largest political party in Northern Ireland in terms of electoral support; as a result, Paisley became Northern Ireland's First Minister in 2007.

In February 2006, when the political tide in Northern Ireland was clearly turning in Paisley's direction, he addressed the DUP's annual conference, and made one of his occasional references to Shakespeare (given the populism of the DUP's political strategy, and the association of Shakespeare with a "high" realm of culture far removed from Paisley's core vote, direct reference to Shakespeare in a public context has been an occasional, rather than a frequent, feature of Paisley's political career). Looking back over the party's 35 years of existence, Paisley claimed to be "reminded of some lines of Shakespeare," and promised to "make them my own."[5] He then delivered his "Shakespearean" quotation:

> Let come what will, I mean to bear it out,
> And either live with glorious victory
> Or die with fame, renown'd in chivalry.
> He is not worthy of the honeycomb
> That shuns the hive because the bees have stings.[6]

What followed was an analysis of the text, not in literary-critical terms, but in something more akin to a typological reading, as Paisley attempted to demonstrate how the (unnamed) speaker's situation was comparable to that of himself and his political colleagues: "We have been stung on many occasions by journalistic bees, by broadcasting bees, by political bees, by ecclesiastical bees, by government bees and swarms of others, yet we have survived to enjoy the honey."[7] The political work that Paisley's quotation and analysis performs is apparent: the DUP were at this point enjoying an unprecedented level of electoral popularity, and Paisley's self-construction as an embattled, but principled, potential martyr for his cause is supported by the appeal to the authority of a Shakespearean progenitor.

Yet if the immediate political impact of the analysis is clear enough, the more substantial significance of this moment might be the way in which Shakespeare is here used to forge a sense of Ulster Protestant identity. Strategic appropriations of a Shakespearean legacy, of course, have been used in the north of Ireland as elsewhere to promote particular social and political agendas; in that sense, there is nothing strange about Paisley's choice of quotation. What is strange is that the quotation is not, in fact, from a play which any twenty-first century scholars or editors ascribe to Shakespeare. The lines are from the anonymous Elizabethan tragedy *Locrine*, printed by Thomas Creede in 1595 and, according to the title page, "Newly set foorth, ouerseene and corrected,/ By *VV. S.*"[8] *Locrine* was not included in the First Folio of 1623, but was part of the so-called Shakespeare apocrypha which enlarged the second impression (1664) of the Third Folio of 1663 (suggesting that Paisley's Shakespearean canon may be more catholic than his Biblical one). Paisley's analysis, of course, shows little attention to the formal qualities of the text which he appropriates, and if he is not a literary critic, the untraceable provenance of his "Shakespearean" quotation suggests that neither is he a historian of the book. Paisley, presumably, does not realize that these lines are *not* Shakespearean; neither, presumably, does his audience. The quotation is employed for two reasons: to lend intellectual weight to the speech, through an allusion to a "Great British" writer, and to provide a pithy moral exemplum about resistance in the face of adversity.

Thus far, one might argue, this is conventional. One rarely looks to a politician, particularly a demagogue such as Paisley, for close attention to the complexities of textual transmission and authorial attribution. But Paisley, as I have suggested, is not just a politician; as the leader of the Free Presbyterian Church, he also has been one of the most visible religious figures in Northern Ireland, famous (among other things) for his apocalyptic interpretations of the Bible (including, infamously, reviving early modern modes of thought by denouncing John Paul II as the Antichrist of Revelation in the European Parliament in 1988).[9] Paisley's Scriptural hermeneutic is in some ways similar to his Shakespearean hermeneutic. Later in the 2006 speech, he performs the trick again of yoking a quotation entirely out of context, this time from 1 Corinthians: "If ever the eternal truth was vindicated, it was vindicated in the past few hours. *The hidden things of darkness were brought to light.* Evil cannot be covered."[10] This is, as I have suggested, a characteristic feature of Paisley's particular brand of Scriptural fundamentalism. He goes on to tell his audience that:

> There will be no inclusive executive with Sinn Fein as long as the IRA is in business and engaged in criminality. The day for the inclusive executive on such a basis is over for ever. It is buried in a Sadducee's grave from which there is no resurrection. The foundation of the Agreement stinks in the grave, dug with the spade of truth.[11]

This is not quotation, but paraphrase (one may recall Hempton's stress on the importance of Biblical forms of thought for Ulster Protestantism) or even another instance of typology: the Sadducee's grave as a precursor to the Belfast assembly. It is a remarkable way of thinking and of reading, in tune perhaps with some of the apocalyptic currents of early modern thought. But it is recognizably post-early modern to the extent that it treats "Shakespeare" as an authority, albeit a lesser authority than Scripture; the typological approach, one will recall, presents the unnamed speaker of the "lines from Shakespeare" as a precursor of Paisley and his political colleagues. Thus Shakespeare and Scripture are here yoked together to support Paisley's version of British Protestantism, an intensely context-specific manifestation of late modern ethno-religious identity.

The great irony of all this is that, had Paisley ever read *Locrine*, he may well have been less enthusiastic about drawing attention to the text in this way, since the tragedy can be read as challenging some of the historical legitimacy which Paisley may have intended the "lines from Shakespeare" to lend to his political project. (The play is also open to a much more relativist conception of religious practice than is Paisley's fundamentalist faith).[12] The full title of the 1595 edition of *Locrine* draws attention to some of its preoccupations: *The Lamentable Tragedie of Locrine, the eldest sonne of King Brutus, discoursing the warres of the Britaines, and Hunnes, with their discomfiture: The Britaines victorie with their Accidents, and the death of Albanact. No lesse pleasant than profitable.* As this makes clear, *Locrine* is a tragedy derived from the *Brut* narrative, that collection of legendary material popular throughout the late medieval and early modern periods as a myth of origins for the British people. The *Brut* narrative gained added legitimacy, of course, when James VI of Scotland ascended the English throne in 1603 (Anthony Munday's *Triumphs of Reunited Britannia*, which also retells the *Brut* legend, is just one of many texts to explicitly characterize James as a second Brut: "Welcome *King Iames*, our second *Brute* and King"), but the succession crisis of the 1590s also popularized explorations of the British past.[13] *Locrine*'s Britain, imagined before the seventeenth-century Plantation of Ulster by English and Scottish Protestants, is emphatically not Paisley's Britain. In the play, Britain is divided by the Humber and the Severn, not by the Irish Sea. Britain is a contiguous landmass, not an archipelago. There is no mention of Ireland, and certainly not of Ulster. Of all the early modern texts which Paisley could have chosen to support his vision of Britain, then, *Locrine* is hardly the most obvious.

In details as in overall preoccupations, in fact, the specter of *Locrine* threatens to haunt Paisley's speech, undermining its confident rhetoric by drawing attention to Paisley's lack of engagement with early modern texts. An example can be found in Paisley's employment of the discourse of terror and terrorism. In an opportunistic apostrophe to the then-current British Prime Minister and American President, Paisley sought to ally his vision of a resurgent Ulster Protestantism with the values espoused by the global War on Terror: "All around the world today the United States and the United Kingdom are busy spreading the message of democratic values [. . .] But I say to Mr Blair and Mr Bush that Northern Ireland will not settle for second best [. . .] You cannot be anti-terrorist in the whole world with the exception of Northern Ireland."[14] Paisley's rhetorical trump card in his opposition to Sinn Fein, Northern Ireland's largest Irish Republican party, is to draw attention to IRA terrorism, the very word signifying the strategic anathema of twenty-first century Western political discourse. Straightforward in its own terms, the strategy is nevertheless undermined by Paisley's careless reading of *Locrine*, which presents Brutus, founder of Britain, as the epitome of "terror" in the style of Marlowe's Tamburlaine. Ate, as chorus, refers to "valiant *Brute* the terror of the world,/ Whose only looks did scarre his enemies;" Brutus himself refers to his "heart [. . .] That was a terror to the bordring lands;" Locrine refers to "*Brutus* that was a terror to his foes [. . .] a terror to his enemies" (A3v, A4r, B3v-B4r). Assarachus, voicing a conception of British identity under siege which might normally appeal to Paisley's sense of self, nevertheless identifies "terror" as one of the components needed for successful political resistance: "Now who is left to helplesse *Albion*,/ That as a piller might vphold our state,/ That might strike terror to our daring foes?" (I1r). "Terror" in the play is clearly understood as a legitimate military and political technique, a stance which works against the anti-"terror" rhetoric employed by Paisley. Reinstating the terrorism of *Locrine* also implicitly undermines the fragmentary strategy of interpretation pursued by Paisley: in other words, by isolating fragments of text, Paisley aims to give them a meaning which they do not possess in their original contexts.

Sixteenth-century "terror," one might reasonably object, is not twenty-first-century "terror," and in that sense (one could argue) Paisley's sense of historical difference might be more sophisticated than this reading allows. However, following Terry Eagleton's recent exploration of the "metaphysics" of terror, one can argue that the kind of "terror" which *Locrine* enjoins—the terror necessary for the foundation of a state—is in fact linked to contemporary political terror in an almost umbilical fashion. For Eagleton, the state is founded on an act of terroristic violence; the most obvious example of this in modern Europe is the French Revolution. But the violence of the revolution is, hypothetically, the same manner of violence which instates any political order. Thus, "the truly terrible sublime [. . .] is the lawless revolt which established the political order in the first place."[15] Terror and violence are at the core of the state: "established political order sublimates the terror which originally went into its making."[16] In one way, then, *Locrine* can be seen as a text which demystifies the violence inherent in the construction of statehood, thus posing a problem to Paisley's opposition of democracy and terrorism. If *Locrine* revisits the foundation of Britain just a few decades before the Plantation of Ulster was to initiate a conception of British Ulster, then the violence which it portrays can be seen as proleptic of the seventeenth-century attempts to create a new Britain. On this reading, Eagleton's view of Northern Ireland—that it is among the "states which find it hard to live down their tumultuous beginnings because they are too raw and recent"—is in some sympathy with *Locrine*.[17]

However, Eagleton may well be thinking of the creation of Northern Ireland in the twentieth century, rather than its potential conception in the Plantation of Ulster; what both Eagleton and *Locrine* demonstrate is how the passage of time grants political legitimacy to revolutionary violence. *Locrine* can also, then, be read as a text which naturalizes particular types of violent conquest; as such, there are ways in which the text could be used to support Paisley's political project. Brutus is not a native of Albion and has to dispel an indigenous rebellion to gain mastery over the land; in this, perhaps a parallel could be traced between Brutus and the seventeenth-century "undertakers" of the Ulster Plantation. Brutus, addressing his followers, outlines clearly his and their status as settlers: "From thence vpon the strons of *Albion*/ To *Corus* hauen happily we came,/ And queld the giants [. . .] And in that Ile at length I placed you" (B1v). If Paisley did read *Locrine*, then, he chose not to draw parallels between the mythical settling of Albion by Brutus and the seventeenth-century settling of Ulster by Anglo-Scottish Protestants; but these seventeenth-century settlers could have found in texts like *Locrine* a potential justification for their actions.

If the play is proleptic of Paisley in a number of ways—its interest in the political construction of Britain, its yoking of militaristic and religious imagery—nevertheless it does contain moments which challenge Paisley's interpretive hermeneutic. For instance, the only character to use the term "scripture" (referring to writing in general, rather than specifically divinely inspired writing) is the clown, Strumbo (D4v). And it is Strumbo, in conjunction with his beloved Dorothy, who outlines the point which Paisley, so many years later, wants to resist: that interpretation is a difficult process, that meaning is rarely apparent. It is a telling moment:

Dorothy: Truly M. *Strumbo*, you speake too learnedly for mee to vnder-
stand the drift of your mind, and therfore tell your tale in plaine
terms, and leaue off your darke riddles.
Strumbo: Alasse mistresse *Dorothie* this is my lucke, that when I most would, I
cannot be vnderstood: sothat my great learning is an inconuenience

vnto me. But to speake in plaine termes, I loue you mistresse *Doro-thie*, if you like to accept me into your familiaritie (C1v).

The context here is that Strumbo has attempted to woo Dorothy through the medium of verse; Dorothy rejects verse as "dark riddles," and both speakers characterize the turn to prose as a turn towards "plaine termes." It is a point which is not without Scriptural significance; the proclaimed literalism of a radical Protestant viewpoint might be expected also to stress "plaine terms" over "darke riddles," and of course the contrast recalls the Pauline conception of human knowledge as "through a glass, darkly." But of course no text, as Strumbo is aware, is a "plaine term" in the sense that it unproblematically yields up its meaning to the reader. The fact that Paisley reads both Scripture and "Shakespeare" strategically suggests that he too, despite protestations to the contrary, is aware of this fact. Thus Strumbo's negotiation between registers, when read in conjunction with Paisley's mis-attributed quotation from *Locrine*, can call attention to the specific ways in which Paisley too constructs meaning from potentially opaque texts.

This becomes important when looking at the specific passage from which Paisley quotes in his address to his party. In the 1595 Quarto it appears as follows:

Let come what wil, I meane to bear it out,
And either liue with glorious victorie.
Or die with fame renowmed for chiualrie,
He is not worthie of the honie combe
That shuns the hiues because the bees haue stings,
That likes me best that is not got with ease,
Which thousand daungers do accompany,
For nothing can dismay our regall minde,
Which aimes at nothing but a golden crowne,
The only vpshot of mine enterprises,
Were they inchanted in grimme *Plutos* court,
And kept for treasure mongst his hellish crue,
I would either quell the triple *Cerberus*
And all the armie of his hatefull hags,
Or toll the stone with wretched *Sisiphon* (F1v).

In the 1595 text of *Locrine*, then, the speech serves not so much as a marker of determination in the face of oppression as a signifier of a single-minded pursuit of earthly glory and ambition, recalling the conquering feats of Marlowe's Tamburlaine. The speaker, Hubba son of Humber, is no Tamburlaine, defeated as he is in battle by the British. But he is a Scythian, and he does share the characteristic (in this play) Scythian tendency to draw on a classically inspired bank of imagery. When Paisley appropriates this speech in Belfast in 2006, then, he ventriloquizes the voice of a Scythian

invader of Britain, a challenger to the island-wide system of devolved government installed by Brutus. Paisley borrows the voice of a violent invader,
who seeks to overthrow a form of political rule which the play works to
naturalize. This is surely not Paisley's intention, and reinstalling *Locrine* in
the discussion highlights one of the glaring deficiencies of Paisley's hermeneutic, namely, that in removing historical and material contexts, it aims to
give utterances a meaning dependent only on the present circumstances in
which they are enunciated. Calling attention to the textual history of those
utterances, by contrast, complicates and destabilizes Paisley's meaning.

III   EARLY MODERNITY IN AN AGE
OF MEDIA PLURALIZATION

It is more than a little ironic, perhaps, that if Paisley adopts an anti-contextual approach to the reading of early modern texts, this is nevertheless
largely because he is following in the footsteps of a characteristically early
modern method of reading the Bible. Paisley disintegrates texts, separating
them into short units of meaning; as I shall argue in this section, he also
reintegrates these units into a variety of different textual forms, expounded
through a series of different material media. But such disintegration of the
Bible was common—and commonly criticized—in early modernity too,
and can be traced to the features specific to the Bible when encountered
as a printed codex. As Paul Saenger has shown, the processes of printing
the Biblical text in the early modern period can be seen to be the catalyst
for "the introduction and eventual perfection of graphic techniques for the
designation of specific verses within Biblical chapters."[18] In other words, it
is the development of the Bible as a *printed* book that is responsible for "the
modern system of numbered verses."[19]

   This change in the visual appearance of Scripture had implications
for early modern reading practices and hermeneutic strategies. Patrick
Collinson has argued that the English (printed) Bible was read in a variety
of ways in early modern England.[20] Primarily, it was read as a narrative
whole, "quite literally from end to end."[21] Yet the practice of dividing Scripture into verses also meant that other types of reading were possible: "Biblical knowledge was commonly encapsulated in weighty and apparently
conclusive gobbets and (as we say) sound-bites of authoritative scriptural
doctrine."[22] As I have suggested above, this is Paisley's characteristic way of
reading, for both Scriptural and non-Scriptural texts. There was some early
modern opposition to this way of reading (including significant opposition from John Locke); and Collinson's characterization of the interpretive
limits fostered by this mode of reading—itself, of course, encouraged by a
radical change in the manner of material engagement with the Bible—is as
accurate a description of Paisley's hermeneutic as it is of that of his early
modern forebears:

For the Reformation, it was either not the case or not a matter of importance that St Paul was a human agent, limited by the contingencies of the time and the space that be [sic] inhabited [...] The motive of protestant expositors and readers, at whatever level, was professedly anti-historicist, making of "Scripture" a text which was not only harmonious but of timeless validity.[23]

Thus Paisley and Hubba, the Sadducee's Grave and the Belfast Assembly, God and Ulster, stand outside time, outside history. Peter Stallybrass's contention that Collinson overstates the frequency of the practice of continuous reading in early modern England—that "the book [...] not only allows for discontinuous reading; it encourages it"—lends even greater weight to the claim that Paisley's engagement with early modernity repeats the ahistoricity of the early modern engagement with the Biblical text.[24]

Paisley, then, works self-consciously to construct a particular vision of early modernity, a version which is ahistorical in its emphasis upon a timeless anti-Catholicism, as if sixteenth-century anti-Romanism and twentieth-century anti-Romanism were the same thing. Paisley works with a canon of early modern radical Protestant and/or anti-Catholic authorities, from which Shakespeare—by virtue of his confessional indeterminacy—is of necessity normally excluded. Paisley's occasional willingness, then, to employ Shakespeare as an authority is telling, revealing as it does the force of the modern conjunction of "Shakespeare" and "Britain" and the lingering imperial taint of Shakespearean appropriation.

Paisley's more frequent, non-Shakespearean, identification with early modernity can be seen, for example, in an address (a political sermon, of sorts) delivered at Belfast's Martyrs Memorial Free Presbyterian Church in February 1972 (in the midst of one of the most intense periods of violence in the "Troubles") and published later the same year in pamphlet form as *United Ireland—Never!*[25] In this text, Paisley urges his congregation to imagine the ongoing violence in the north of Ireland as analogous to the atrocities of the seventeenth century (and one may here recall Paisley's penchant for typological, anti-contextual readings of history): "Let's remember 1641 when Ulster had her dark Saint Bartholomew's a parallel to the massacre of the Huguenots of France, when every river in this Province was dyed red with the blood of the Protestants."[26] The sermon and the pamphlet go on to praise other early modern figures associated with a hostility to the Catholic church: "that great and mighty puritan Oliver Cromwell [...] the Church of Rome tirade against him until this day;" "William, Prince of Orange of Glorious Memory;" and "Old John Knox [...] He knocked popery one great blow that she has never recovered in Scotland to this day."[27] Paisley is not, at this point, interested in the writings of these figures; rather, he is caricaturing them in order to pursue the ahistorical analogy. The Paisleyite manner of reading history is typological in the manner of the Paisleyite Scriptural hermeneutic: Ulster Protestants, like the ancient Israelites, are an oppressed people, but will be delivered through the intervention of a divinely inspired agent (the implication, of course, being that Paisley too is such a prophetic figure).

Paisley's engagements with early modernity, then, are not disinterested but are instead often addressed to specific political pressures (which is not to deny the foundational significance of early modernity for Paisley's sense of national and religious identity). Shakespeare, it may by now be apparent, is always a potentially problematic figure in Paisley's view of early modernity, as his posthumous position as a representative of Britishness is not reinforced by an easily identifiable anti-Catholicism (this is one reason why Paisley is more likely to quote Milton than Shakespeare). Paisley's pamphlet *No Pope Here* (which was briefly mentioned at the start of this essay) champions a number of Protestant writers of the sixteenth and seventeenth centuries. It praises "the great Protestant reformer, John Knox," Milton's view that "Popery is a double thing to deal with," "all the English reformers, including Tyndale, Latimer, Cranmer, Bradford, and Jewell," Ridley's declaration that "the See of Rome is the seat of Satan," Luther's vision of the Pope as "the Anti-Christ of the Scriptures," Melancthon's "convictions that Rome is the Babylon of the Apocalypse," Calvin and Tyndale's association of the Pope with Anti-Christ, and the 1611 King James Version translators' identification of the Pope with the "Man of Sin" (8, 13, 32–4). Many more instances of early modern anti-Catholicism are aggregated in Paisley's pamphlet. But the only Shakespearean reference is, unusually, an allusion by Paisley himself which, in contrast to the 2006 misappropriation of *Locrine*, neglects to identify Shakespeare as its source:

> To me, a Bible-instructed Protestant, Rome may paint her face and attire her hair like Jezebel of old, but I still recognise the murderous wrinkles on the brow of the old scarlet-robed hag. She may clothe herself in her finest attire but underneath the gorgeous robes I see the leprous garments of her whoredoms [. . .] Rome may extend her gloved hand (well may it be gloved, for upon it is "that damned spot" the innocent blood from which she shall never be cleansed) but I will never take it (88).

Lady Macbeth and the Whore of Babylon are here conflated in an image which works to enlist Shakespeare (while significantly refusing to mention him by name) into the service of the misogynistic anti-Catholicism which Paisley aims to promote. The indelibility of the damned spot is a significant image for Paisley perhaps because it stresses the ineradicability of sin; as I have argued elsewhere, the spots of *Macbeth* can be read as proclaiming the failure of the Catholic system of forgiveness from sin.[28] Paisley's appropriation of *Macbeth* as an anti-Catholic text thus constructs it as a part of the tradition of early modern Protestantism encapsulated by the pamphlet's long verbatim quotations from Foxe's *Actes and Monuments* (48–9, 56, 65).

If this pamphlet offers an image of the typological relationship between early and late modernity, it also offers another glimpse of Paisley's way of reading the Bible. Throughout *No Pope Here*, Paisley reiterates the familiar Protestant claim that Catholicism is anti-Scriptural; the text goes further than this, however, by claiming that almost all contemporary Protestants have also become anti-Biblical: "Jesuits cleverly trained and cleverly planted have succeeded in overthrowing belief in the Bible in the training institutes of the larger Protestant denominations" (39). Paisley's self-construction as a neo-prophetic figure, speaking uncomfortable truths to power, is in evidence throughout the pamphlet. Allied to this is a confident sense— shared by the early modern Bible readers whom Collinson discusses—that the Bible contains a singular message ("let it be said with great plainness and straightforwardness of speech that true Protestantism is Bible Christianity, the Christianity of the Bible" [79]) and—also like early modern evangelicals—a corresponding fetishization of the Bible as material and metaphorical codex:

> Rome has burned this book but it has stood the test of fire. Like the three Hebrew children there is not even the smell of fire upon it. It is God's unburnable book. Rome has overwhelmed this book in a flood of false doctrine, but it has stood the flood test. It could not be drowned. It rose above the billows of apostasy and heresy, God's unsubmersible Word. Rome has buried this book in a heap of legend and babylonianism but it refused to be buried and rose triumphant from what Rome thought was a Sadducee's grave. It has stood the grave's test. It is God'sunconcealable [sic] Law. No potency can disintegrate this rock. It is God's impregnable, imperishable Word. Read it; believe it; obey it; treasure it (82).

This is obviously not a strategy of Biblical interpretation as conventionally understood, but rather a rhetorical celebration of the Bible, the orator's delight clearly audible even in print (one may recall Paisley's praise of Hugh Latimer's "pulpit style and power" [67]). Catholicism is thus not just non-Scriptural, it is determinedly *anti*-Biblical: "Rome [. . .] fears the Word of God hence her determined efforts to destroy its circulation and discredit its eternal truths" (82).

As this essay has sought to suggest, Paisley's manner of quotation—a fragmentary and disassociative one—threatens to give the lie to his claim that "No potency can disintegrate this rock," for Paisley's method of reading and interpreting, like that of many early modern readers of the Bible, is fundamentally disintegrative, isolating verses, lines, and passages from the textual situation in which he finds them and reconstituting them to serve new functions. This is true not just of his Scriptural allusions (as in the variety of uses to which Paisley puts the figure of the Sadducee's grave) but also of his approach to Shakespeare and of his approach to his own writings.

David Jasper has recently argued that "the nature of Biblical authority in an increasingly post-ecclesial age continues to change" and that, accordingly, "the interpretation of the Bible must also respond to the growing range and availability of interpretive media."[29] On one level, of course, Paisley's *interpretation* of the Bible and of Shakespeare has remained consistent over the past half-century; but, on another level, he has engaged with the "range and availability of interpretive media" to which Jasper refers. In the 1970s and 1980s, the pamphlet form—as in *No Pope Here* and *United Ireland—Never!*—suited Paisley's needs: short, relatively cheap to produce, easily disseminated among tight-knit communities, the pamphlet was Paisley's preferred form of distributing written communication. Since the 1990s, the Internet has increasingly come to be a more efficient means of undertaking this kind of communication, and Paisley has embraced electronic media, as witnessed by his (potentially misleadingly titled) website, *The European Institute of Protestant Studies*.[30] The material printed in the earlier pamphlets often appears on this website, recycled as lectures for specific occasions or as general "information" about the relationship between Catholicism and Protestantism. In the "Sword—Biblical Teachings" section of the website, one can find—verbatim—the amalgamation of the damned spot and the gloved hand, of Lady Macbeth and the Whore of Babylon—that one finds in *No Pope Here*. The lecture was posted on the *EIPS* website in 1998, with a note stating that it is an adaptation of a sermon preached in 1963; *No Pope Here* was published as a specific act of political intervention in 1982, with no indication that any of the text was previously available in another form; the 1998 electronic version remains freely accessible in 2010. Thus Paisley's attempt to enlist Shakespeare to an anti-Catholic British identity uses the same textual example over almost five decades, but enlists it in radically different political and material—oral, printed, and electronic—contexts at different points in time. On one level, of course, the fact that the text stays the same is indicative of the faith which Scriptural fundamentalism places in textual stability; but the changes in the transmission of that text, and the way in which the text can so easily be implanted into a new context, suggests that Paisley's Shakespeare, like his Scripture, is a rock which has in fact been disintegrated into a number of fragments, each resisting further diminution perhaps, but nevertheless rather forlorn in their isolation.

NOTES

1. Ian Paisley, *No Pope Here*, Belfast: Martyrs Memorial Publications, 1982, p. 89. Further page references are given in the text.
2. Mark Thornton Burnett and Ramona Wray (eds) *Shakespeare and Ireland: History, Politics, Culture*, Basingstoke: Macmillan, 1997.
3. Rebecca Steinberger, *Shakespeare and Twentieth-Century Irish Drama: Conceptualizing Identity and Staging Boundaries*, Aldershot: Ashgate, 2008; Jennifer Wallace, "'We Can't Make More Dirt': Tragedy and the Excavated

Body," *Cambridge Quarterly*, 2003, vol. 32, no. 2, 103–11; Neil Rhodes, "Bridegrooms to the Goddess: Hughes, Heaney, and the Elizabethans," in Burnett and Wray (eds) *Shakespeare and Ireland*, pp. 159–72.

4. David Hempton, *Religion and Political Culture in Britain and Ireland: From the Glorious Revolution to the End of Empire*, Cambridge: Cambridge University Press, 1996, p. 100.
5. Ian Paisley, "Text of Speech by Ian Paisley, then Leader of the Democratic Unionist Party (DUP), to the DUP's Annual Conference in Belfast (Saturday 4 February 2006)," *CAIN Web Service (Conflict Archive on the Internet)*. Available at http://cain.ulst.ac.uk/issues/politics/docs/dup/ip040206.htm (accessed 18 September 2008).
6. Ibid.
7. Ibid.
8. Anon., *The Lamentable Tragedie of Locrine*, London: Thomas Creede, 1595, sig. A2r. Further references appear as parentheses in the text.
9. Anon., "Headliners: Papal Audience," *The New York Times*, 16 October 1988. Available at http://www.nytimes.com/1988/10/16/weekinreview/headliners-papal-audience.html (accessed 11 May 2010).
10. Paisley, "Text of Speech."
11. Ibid.
12. Williard Farnham, "John Higgins' *Mirror* and *Locrine*," *Modern Philology*, vol. 23, no. 3, 1926, 307–13.
13. Anthony Munday, *The Trivmphes of Re-Vnited Britannia*, London: 1605, sig. B4v.
14. Paisley, "Text of Speech."
15. Terry Eagleton, *Holy Terror*, Oxford: Oxford University Press, 2005, p. 52.
16. Ibid., p. 53.
17. Ibid., p. 57.
18. Paul Saenger, "The Impact of the Early Printed Page on the Reading of the Bible," in Saenger and Kimberley van Kampen (eds) *The Bible as Book: The First Printed Editions*, London: The British Library, 1999, p. 39.
19. Ibid., p. 39.
20. Patrick Collinson, "The Coherence of the Text: How it Hangeth Together: The Bible in Reformation England," in W. P. Stephens (ed.) *The Bible, The Reformation and the Church*, Sheffield: Sheffield Academic Press, 1995, pp. 84–108.
21. Ibid., p. 91.
22. Ibid., p. 92.
23. Ibid., pp. 95–6.
24. Peter Stallybrass, "Books and Scrolls: Navigating the Bible," in Jennifer Andersen and Elizabeth Sauer (eds) *Books and Readers in Early Modern England*, Philadelphia: University of Pennsylvania Press, 2002, p. 46.
25. Ian R.K. Paisley, *United Ireland —Never! An Address by Ian R. K. Paisley*, Belfast: Puritan Printing Company, 1972.
26. Ibid., p. 7.
27. Ibid., pp. 7, 8, 10.
28. David Coleman, *Drama and the Sacraments in Sixteenth-Century England: Indelible Characters*, Basingstoke: Palgrave Macmillan, 2007, pp. 111–30.
29. David Jasper, "Biblical Hermeneutics and Literary Theory," in Rebecca Lemon, Emma Mason, Jonathan Roberts, and Christopher Rowland (eds) *The Blackwell Companion to the Bible in English Literature*, Chichester: Wiley-Blackwell, 2009, p. 33.
30. *The European Institute of Protestant Studies*, available at http://www.ian-paisley.org (accessed 26 July 2010).

Contributors

David Coleman is a Senior Lecturer in English (Early Modern Literature) at Nottingham Trent University, UK. He is the author of *Drama and the Sacraments in Sixteenth-Century England: Indelible Characters* and *John Webster, Renaissance Dramatist*.

Travis DeCook is an Associate Professor of English at Carleton University, Ottawa. He researches Reformation Biblical debate and the cultural and intellectual implications of millenarianism in early modern England. He has published on early modern utopian literature, the Reformation Bible, and the history of the book.

Alan Galey is an Assistant Professor in the Faculty of Information at the University of Toronto, where he also contributes to the graduate program in Book History and Print Culture. He is the author of articles appearing in *Shakespeare Quarterly*, *Literary and Linguistic Computing*, *College Literature*, and the Palgrave Macmillan *History of Reading* (forthcoming).

Charles LaPorte is an Associate Professor at the University of Washington. He is the author of *Victorian Poets and the Changing Bible* (University of Virginia Press, 2011) and a number of articles on nineteenth-century literature and culture.

Randall Martin is Professor of English at the University of New Brunswick. He has edited *Henry VI Part Three* for the Oxford Shakespeare (2001) and *Every Man Out of His Humour* for the forthcoming *Cambridge Works of Ben Jonson*. He published *Women, Murder, and Equity in Early Modern England* in 2007 and is currently writing a book on Shakespeare and Paul.

Barbara A. Mowat is Director of Research emerita at the Folger Shakespeare Library. She is co-editor (with Paul Werstine) of the Folger Library Shakespeare editions and consulting editor for *Shakespeare Quarterly*.

She publishes primarily on Shakespeare's dramatic romances and on the history of the editing of his texts.

Andrew Murphy is Professor of English at the University of St Andrews, Scotland. His authored books include *Shakespeare for the People: Working-class Readers, 1800–1900* (Cambridge University Press, 2008) and *Shakespeare in Print: A History and Chronology of Shakespeare Publishing* (Cambridge University Press, 2003).

Edward Pechter has taught at universities in Canada, the United States, and England, and is Distinguished Professor Emeritus at Concordia (Montréal), and Adjunct Professor of English at Victoria (British Columbia). His most recent book is *Shakespeare Studies Today: Romanticism Lost* (Palgrave Macmillan, 2011).

Scott Schofield is a course Instructor in the Department of English at the University of Toronto and a Fellow at the Centre for Reformation and Renaissance Studies. He has written on various topics in early modern literature, including work on religious politics and antiquarianism. His current research is in the history of the book, and particularly on reading practices in early modern England.

Paul Werstine is Professor of English at King's University College at the University of Western Ontario. He is editor (with Barbara A. Mowat) of the Folger Library Shakespeare, and general editor (with Richard Knowles) of the New Variorum Shakespeare.

Index